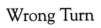

Wrong Turn

Also by Gian Gentile

*How Effective Is Strategic Bombing? Lessons Learned from World War II to Kosovo*

# Wrong Turn

*America's Deadly Embrace*
*of Counterinsurgency*

COLONEL GIAN GENTILE

**THE NEW PRESS**

NEW YORK
LONDON

355.0218
G 338

Requests for permission to reproduce selections from this book
should be mailed to: Permissions Department,
The New Press, 38 Greene Street, New York, NY 10013.

Published in the United States by The New Press, New York, 2013
Distributed by Perseus Distribution

LIBRARY OF CONGRESS CATALOGING-IN-PUBLICATION DATA

Gentile, Gian P.
  Wrong turn : America's deadly embrace of counterinsurgency /
Colonel Gian Gentile.
     pages cm
  Includes bibliographical references and index.
  ISBN 978-1-59558-874-6 (hardback)—ISBN 978-1-59558-896-8
(e-book) 1. Counterinsurgency—Government policy—United States.
2. Counterinsurgency—Case studies.   3. Counterinsurgency—
Malaya—History—20th century.   4. Counterinsurgency—Vietnam—
History—20th century.   5. Counterinsurgency—Iraq—History—
21st century.   6. Counterinsurgency—Afghanistan—History—
21st century.   I. Title.
  U241.G46 2013
  355.02'180973—dc23

                                              2012049114

The New Press publishes books that promote and enrich public discussion and understanding of the issues vital to our democracy and to a more equitable world. These books are made possible by the enthusiasm of our readers; the support of a committed group of donors, large and small; the collaboration of our many partners in the independent media and the not-for-profit sector; booksellers, who often hand-sell New Press books; librarians; and above all by our authors.

www.thenewpress.com

*Composition by Westchester Book Composition*
*This book was set in Goudy*

Printed in the United States of America

2   4   6   8   10   9   7   5   3   1

*For Gee Won*

# CONTENTS

*Acknowledgments*                                                              *ix*

*Preface: A Personal Note—the Hell of Baghdad*                                 *xiii*


Introduction: The Conceit of American
Counterinsurgency                                                              1

1. The Construction of the Counterinsurgency Narrative   11

2. Malaya: The Foundation of the Counterinsurgency
   Narrative                                                                   35

3. Vietnam: The First Better War That Wasn't                                   59

4. Iraq: A Better War, Version 2                                               85

5. Afghanistan: Another Better War That Wasn't                                 113

Afterword: Truth as a Casualty of COIN                                         137


*A Note on Sources*                                                            *142*

*Notes*                                                                        *145*

*Index*                                                                        *181*

# ACKNOWLEDGMENTS

This book represents an intellectual journey by me to understand the recent American war in Iraq and the ongoing American war in Afghanistan. In many ways this book is dedicated to the men and women of Eighth Squadron, Tenth Cavalry, and that very hard and bloody year we spent doing counterinsurgency operations in western Baghdad in 2006. This book is also a historian's journey into the past via primary evidence to understand how history has been used and abused to explain these current wars.

I am indebted to the West Point history department senior leadership, namely Colonels Lance Betros and Matthew Moten, for the support, advice, and thoughtful criticism that they have given me. Other colleagues at West Point have been instrumental in the writing of this book. Colonel (retired) Kevin Farrell, a former combat battalion commander in Iraq, was a key source of intellectual inspiration and encouragement for the book. In addition to providing a most useful critique of my Vietnam chapter, Colonel Gregory Daddis has been a constant sounding board for ideas; the warp and woof of the book has been shaped by our many discussions. Robert Citino read an earlier version of the book and gave it a needed spark when the embers were starting to cool; he has also been a good friend and intellectual mentor. So too has Roger Spiller from the days when I was his student at the School of Advanced Military Studies (SAMS) up to the present. Other West Point faculty members, past and current, have influenced my thinking greatly: Steve Barry, Wynne Beers, Paul Belmont, JP Clark, Chip Dawson, Casey Doss, Robert Doughty, Jonathan Due, Greg Fontenot, Joe Glatthaar, Ben Greene, Matthew Hardman, George Herring, Jennie Kiesling, Dwight

Mears, Paul Miles, Dave Musick, William Nance, Clifford Rogers, Pilar Ryan, Seanegan Sculley, Ty Seidule, John Stapleton, William Taylor, Greg Tomlin, Steve Waddell, Keith Walters, Jason Warren, Sam Watson, Jackie Whitt, and Gail Yoshitani.

Douglas Macgregor, Carl Prine, and Celeste Ward-Gventer have had a huge influence on my thinking. This book would have never come about without their ideas, encouragement, and friendship.

I deeply appreciate the people who took the time to read either the entire manuscript or individual chapters. Michael Few and Robert Mihara read the entire manuscript, provided thoughtful comments, and have helped me think through problems of American strategy. Lawrence Kaplan read an earlier version of the book and helped me recast certain parts of it for the better. Celeste Ward-Gventer read my personal note and introduction and gave me some helpful suggestions to refine and tighten both portions. Karl Hack took a needed wire brush to my Malaya chapter, and Huw Bennett also gave me some important ideas for improvement on it. Joe Glatthaar, George Herring, Brian Linn, Peter Maslowski, and Roger Spiller read earlier versions of the Vietnam chapter. Kelly Peyton Howard and Austin Long read the Iraq chapter and provided some very important suggestions and additions. The Afghanistan chapter received some very helpful and critical readings by Lloyd Gardner, Peter Maslowski, and Paul Miles. Any mistakes or flaws in the book are of course my own.

When I first began writing the book in the fall of 2010, Eric Lupfer of the William Morris Agency provided some key guidance on how to frame and structure the book and worked on it with me during the early stages.

The benefit of being a history teacher is students. I am especially indebted to my history major students at West Point who have helped me to refine my thinking and arguments: Julian Allison,

Josh Clevenger, Leo Fischer, Baker Flagg, Nate Martel, Stephan Murphy, Nate Peterson, Charlie Phelps, and Joseph Putnam.

I am grateful to the faculty and students at the Command and General Staff College at Fort Belvoir, Virginia, for allowing me to speak each quarter for the past four years on counterinsurgency and strategy. I also owe a lot to Dave Dilegge and the participants of the *Small Wars Journal* blog. Many of the ideas and arguments of this book have been forged in the fire of discussions and debate in these two forums. Douglas Porch has been a kindred spirit; his historical writings and arguments on imperial military history have been a guidepost for me. The work of Andrew Bacevich has influenced my thinking greatly. Brian Linn and Conrad Crane have provided important advice and guidance to me over the years.

I am indebted to West Point's Dean of the Academic Board and the Bradley Foundation for grants that helped pay for research trips. I also appreciate the administrative assistance of Melissa Mills of the history department.

I owe a special debt of gratitude to Stephen Biddle for introducing me to the Council on Foreign Relations and to James Lindsay and Richard Haass for giving me the opportunity to spend a year at the council. That year I learned a great deal from colleagues at the council: Amy Baker, Dan Barker, Les Gelb, Randy George, Jason Mangone, Seth Meyer, Amity Shlaes, Dan Yoo, and Micah Zenko.

Thanks to Daniel Weggeland and James Russell for providing me with numerous documents from their own research on Afghanistan and Iraq.

Other individuals over the past five years have helped me think through problems of history and strategy, two themes that underpin this book: Kevin Benson, Robert Brigham, Paula Broadwell, Caleb Cage, Phillip Carter, George W. Casey, Sandy Cochran, Michael Cohen, Danny Davis, Andrew Exum, Joshua Foust, Lloyd Gardner, David Johnson, Lawrence Kaplan, Austin Long, Anne

Marlowe, Peter Munson, Kelly Peyton Howard, Bing West, James Willbanks, Don Vandergriff, and Marilyn Young.

Although he did not read or work with me on this book, Barton Bernstein, my former dissertation adviser at Stanford University, has had a huge influence on me as a historian. When I had my first book published twelve years ago, I said I owed him a lot then; I still do now.

Many thanks to Marc Favreau and the staff at The New Press for finding something of value in this book in its early stages and for helping me see it through to completion.

My wife, Gee Won, and our children, Michael and Elizabeth, give my life meaning—without them nothing else would matter to me.

# PREFACE
# A PERSONAL NOTE—THE HELL OF
# BAGHDAD

*"Spate of Bombs in Baghdad Kills 46 Iraqis"*
—Sabrina Tavernise, *New York Times*, October 30, 2006

*The soldiers and marines told us they feel that they now have a superb
commander in Gen. David Petraeus; they are confident in his strategy, they see real results, and they feel now they have the numbers
needed to make a real difference.*
—Michael O'Hanlon and Kenneth Pollack,
*New York Times*, July 30, 2007

One evening in late October 2006, I sat down in my small office
in my tactical command post at a forward operating base in western Baghdad to check e-mails and do some paperwork. It was a
typical early evening after a long and bloody day on the streets of
Baghdad in that most hellish year of Iraq's sectarian Civil War.
The cavalry squadron that I commanded was caught in the middle of it. As I worked through the e-mails in my inbox, one in
particular caught my eye. It was from my division commander,
then Major General James D. Thurman. General Thurman had
sent to all of his brigade and battalion commanders a draft of the
army's revised doctrine for countering insurgencies. He told us
that the army's writing team for the doctrine was soliciting comments from the field army and would be interested to hear our
thoughts. Over the next week at various times I tried to read
through the draft of the new doctrine, but there were too many

other things going on that demanded my attention, which kept me from reading carefully this "new" doctrine.

My squadron had taken over an area of western Baghdad almost nine months before, in early January 2006. It had proven to be a long, hard, and deadly year. We had five men killed in action and many more seriously wounded, including those suffering the unseen trauma of witnessing what happens to a society during a civil war. Over the course of that year, my squadron had been hit by over 350 improvised explosive device (IED) attacks, averaging close to one a day. Some of them proved to be quite deadly. Numerous other forms of attack plagued us, such as sniper fire, small arms fire, mortar fire, rocket-propelled grenade attacks, and suicide car bombings. For the first month and a half of operations in western Baghdad, we were primarily focused on working with the Iraqi security forces to improve their fighting qualities, with the idea that soon we would transition security responsibilities to them. We also held to a theoretical principle of counterinsurgency (COIN) that the population must be protected, since this had been a primary element of our predeployment training.

The al Qaeda bombing of the revered Shia al-Askari shrine in the Iraqi city of Samarra on February 26, 2006, changed everything for us (and for the Iraqis too). The bombing set off a wave of reprisal attacks by Shia militias—often assisted either directly or indirectly by Iraqi police—against local Sunni population centers in Baghdad. We spent the next three weeks in a constant process of movement, positioning, some fighting, and protecting Sunnis and their mosques from Shia attacks. It also became very clear to me, during those weeks after the al-Askari bombing, we were not dealing just with a simple problem of insurgency, but instead were in the middle of a complex Iraqi sectarian civil war. The brutality of that war became more and more apparent as the months of 2006 wore on.

The saddest and most tragic indicator of the civil war was the numbers of dead bodies being dumped daily on the streets of Baghdad where we patrolled, operated, and fought. We saw so many of them—victims of both sides, Shia and Sunni—that one's joy for life would never be the same. One squadron patrol in late October just north of the district of Kadra in northwestern Baghdad came across a bundled group of six dead men, tied together by a rope as if sitting in a circle with their backs facing inward. Their heads had all been cut off and thrown into a ditch along the side of the road where they were placed. We could never determine which side they were on, Shia or Sunni. It was often so very hard to tell. On a different occasion, my own patrol came upon a sobbing Shia woman in Amriya, clutching her dead infant, shot in the head with a pistol. Her Sunni husband lay dead on the street, killed by Sunni insurgents who didn't like the idea of a Shia woman living in Amriya and married to a Sunni man. That sad scene is seared into my memory.

That night as I sat alone in my office thinking about that poor woman and what would become of her, I thought that, in a twisted way, it would have been better if my men had killed her husband and child, even if by accident and unintentionally. At least then we would have been able to take care of her by giving her a substantial amount of money for her loss. For her, I imagined, would it really have mattered which side of that multifaceted civil war had done the killing? A few weeks later, one of my squadron patrols, which had been operating along the airport road, came across a taxicab off to the side of the road with a bloodied, middle-aged woman sitting in the back. The taxi driver, who was drunk, told my men that he had gotten too close to a private security truck with armed men in it, they fired a few bursts at his car to warn it off, and one round hit the woman in the back as she tried to turn away from the fire. The security contractors didn't stop and drove on to wherever they were headed. My men took her to a local Iraqi hospital and got her contact information. I requested a compensation fund from my higher headquarters for her but was denied because, as I was told, there was no provision in the money regulations to compensate Iraqi civilians who were victims of U.S. private contractors. I should have lied and said we had done it. Why couldn't we compensate this poor woman? In the end, it was American taxpayers who were paying these security contractors anyway. I had no answer for that question, only the thought of that poor woman and what would become of her. I still wonder.[1]

By February 2007, we had been home back at Fort Hood, Texas, for almost three months, and I had at last been able to read the final publication of the army's counterinsurgency doctrine, Field Manual 3-24 (FM 3-24), Counterinsurgency, which had been issued the previous December. While reading the doctrine I remembered the violent and complex Iraq Civil War that I had been part of in 2006. Yet this new army doctrinal manual presented a simplistic set of actions to counter an insurgency that distorted what I had witnessed in 2006. The manual told me that if I followed its theory, precepts, principles, and programs, then I could have been successful in Baghdad in 2006.

Because I was trained as a historian, the field manual read to me as an attempt to refight the Vietnam War—but this time in Iraq and with allegedly better tactical doctrine to counter an insurgency. The section in the beginning of the manual called "Paradoxes of Counterinsurgency Operations" was a jumble of dreamy statements that bordered on some mixture of philosophy, theory, and military operational history. The writer of the paradoxes said things like "some of the best weapons for Counterinsurgents do not shoot," that "tactical success guarantees nothing," and that sometimes in COIN "the more you protect your force, the less secure you may be."[2] These paradoxes were clearly an interpretive stance on why the United States lost the Vietnam War, and how, as the paradoxes implied, it could have been won.

But the most fantastic part of this new doctrine on COIN was its description of a population that was caught up in an insurgency. I read the doctrine as a professional soldier. And doctrine to a professional soldier should make sense, it should be authoritative, and it should hold the promise of success if applied correctly. This new doctrine on counterinsurgency told me that in "any situation, whatever the cause, there will be" a population that has a small minority that is on the side of the counterinsurgent force, a small minority that is strongly against it, but in the middle there would be the rest of the population, who were uncommitted to either side. These fence sitters were just waiting to be won over by the counterinsurgent force, as long as it followed the doctrine correctly. Such an explanation did not match at all, not in any way, the complexity of the civil war, the insurgency, and the Iraqi population that I confronted in western Baghdad in 2006. There were few fence sitters in this civil war—only fences, and a red line drawn right through the population—Shia versus Sunni.

As the early months of 2007 passed into the spring and I continued to study the manual, I deepened my conviction that the new doctrine bore little resemblance to what I'd experienced in 2006. So I started to write articles in general-interest and military publications to point out that sense of incongruity and the serious problems I began to see in the doctrine.[3] At this very time, the surge of troops into Iraq led by the vaunted General David Petraeus was at its height, and when the violence in Iraq began to drop precipitously, the makings of the "surge triumph narrative" took shape, with pundits proclaiming that the U.S. Army under Petraeus had finally figured out how to "do" occupations of foreign lands. Army officers and civilian advisers who were part of the surge also played a significant role in the construction of the narrative. One of General Petraeus's senior advisers during the surge, Australian COIN expert David Kilcullen, wrote that the U.S. Army under Petraeus was "finally coming out of its defensive

crouch with which we used to approach the environment," implying that American troops prior to the surge were hunkered down
on large bases and not applying the principles of counterinsurgency correctly.[4]

Having departed Fort Hood and squadron command for West
Point in July to assume teaching duties in the Department of History, I continued to track reports from COIN experts like Fred
Kagan, who were proclaiming the success of the surge and juxta-
posing it to what they viewed as the failed strategy that came before Petraeus arrived. Most outrageously, after a two-week visit to
Iraq in July 2007, Michael O'Hanlon and Kenneth Pollack argued
in a widely read *New York Times* opinion article that Petraeus and
the surge had turned things around in Iraq and had very possibly
put the United States on a path to winning the war.[5]

In the months and years that followed, against a troubling backdrop of U.S. withdrawal from Iraq and the haunting questions
of what the United States had gained from it all, as well as our
broken strategy in Afghanistan, where we refuse to give up on the
promise of counterinsurgency, I continued to examine the historical underpinnings of the COIN narrative and the problems with
American strategy. I have done this from the vantage point of a
historian who is struggling to come to terms with the nation's history of foreign interventions in places like Vietnam, Iraq, and
Afghanistan, hoping that a clear view of that history can help us
understand the problems of the present. I have also examined the
narrative from the vantage point of a soldier who has seen firsthand
the effects of an American foreign intervention at gunpoint. I have
written this book in the hope that these two perspectives can shed
light on the truth of American counterinsurgency warfare and
expose the myth of the counterinsurgency narrative. The wrong
turn America has taken with counterinsurgency is to accept the
notion that these wars were made better simply by enlightened
generals and improved tactics. The reality is quite different.

# INTRODUCTION:
# THE CONCEIT OF AMERICAN
# COUNTERINSURGENCY

*The maverick savior of Iraq, Gen. David Petraeus . . .*
—Victor Davis Hanson, 2011[1]

*After the Baghdad surge, America's military leaders embraced COIN with the fervor of the converted. It became their defining ideology.*
—Rajiv Chandrasekaran, 2012[2]

In 2010, two U.S. Marine Corps captains returned from Afghanistan and reported that after almost nine years of fumbling at counterinsurgency the U.S. military, with newly minted and savvy generals in charge, was finally implementing counterinsurgency "by the book" and making significant progress in defeating the Taliban. Success will come, according to these marine captains, so long as the U.S. military continues with more of the same.[3]

After General David Petraeus assumed command of American forces in Afghanistan in June 2010, he proclaimed that after nearly nine years of war in Afghanistan the United States had finally gotten its "inputs right."[4] The implication here is that prior to his arrival and that of his immediate predecessor, General Stanley McChrystal, the "right inputs" were nowhere to be found. With the right inputs—a few more brigades of troops, correct methods, and, most important, better generals—the promise of success in Afghanistan may finally become a reality.

Petraeus's "inputs" express what has become the most discussed, lauded, and influential military doctrine in generations: counter-insurgency, or COIN. Its canon, FM 3-24, has become an essential and foundational document. A typical American reader strolling through the aisles of a Barnes & Noble bookstore can sip a latte while perusing army doctrine. Within the first month after its release in December 2006, it was downloaded from the Internet 1.5 million times. The University of Chicago Press published it with a foreword written by COIN expert and think tank president Lieutenant Colonel (retired) John Nagl. Samantha Power, special adviser to President Obama, wrote a *New York Times* review of FM 3-24 in 2007, wherein she characterized the manual as a "21st Century strategy."[5] In a jacket cover endorsement to the Chicago Press edition, General Petraeus remarked that the manual is surely "on the bedside table of the President, Vice President, and the Secretary of Defense" and, according to the general, "deserves" a place on the bedside table of every American too.[6]

Although the general public has only just become aware of the counterinsurgency doctrine since the 2007 surge in Iraq, the story of modern American counterinsurgency follows a narrative arc anchored on four modern wars. These include the British campaign against Communist insurgents in Malaya from 1948 to 1960, the American war in South Vietnam from 1965 to 1973, the recently concluded American war in Iraq from 2003 to 2011, and the ongoing American war in Afghanistan, which began in late 2001.

In the popular telling, counterinsurgency aims to win the hearts and minds of local populations by providing security along with economic assistance, bridges, schools, roads, and other elements of infrastructure, and finally good governance. As this is accomplished, the population will ally itself with the government and the counterinsurgent force, thereby forcing the insurgents to fight in the open, where they will be hunted down and killed or captured.[7] A wildly popular COIN refrain within the ranks of the

American military and defense experts is that in counterinsurgency an army "can't kill its way to victory." Only if the population is won over to the counterinsurgent side, so the thinking goes, can the enemy then be tracked down and either killed or captured.

As this book will show, however, the idea that counterinsurgency works is wrong—and history supports this assertion. Moreover, if the goal of American counterinsurgency has been to win the hearts and minds of local populations in places like Iraq and Afghanistan, that simply has not happened. Nor, if history be the judge, will it work in the future.

This is not the first time that the U.S. Army has taken a deadly wrong turn with its doctrine. In the early years of the United States' participation in World War II, the army came up with a doctrine that completely misunderstood the importance of the tank as the consummate weapon of offensive, maneuver warfare—something the Germans had already figured out with their blitzkrieg operations into Poland and France. Instead the American army relied on lightly skinned tank destroyers that proved to be a disaster in practice in North Africa and later in Europe because they were not suited for offensive operations against German tanks. As the eminent military historian Robert Citino has argued, the American army's emphasis on the tank destroyer proved to be "one of the great doctrinal wrong turns of the century."[8] The doctrine of counterinsurgency that emerged in 2007 surely must be the second great wrong turn after the tank destroyer.

One of the architects of the Iraq surge, retired army general Jack Keane, said after the Vietnam War that the American army had failed at counterinsurgency under Westmoreland, but in the middle of 1968 General Abrams had changed "to a counterinsurgency strategy . . . designed to protect the population." Abrams's new strategy, Keane argued, turned the war around. Criticism of Westmoreland and praise of Abrams exemplify one of two recurrent themes in today's COIN narrative. The first theme is of armies starting off in the wrong boot, fumbling and failing. A second theme, extending the first, depicts an army that learns and adapts—from its lower ranks, surely, but mostly because a better general is put in command. The tide of a war is turned, hearts and minds are won, and victory is achieved. And the narrative would play itself out in Iraq and Afghanistan in the same way. Popular historian Victor Davis Hanson rejoiced that "the maverick savior of Iraq, Gen. David Petraeus," had arrived on horseback to save those wars and make them better too.[9]

Another way to view the rise of COIN is as a reinvention or overhaul of the status quo. President George Bush's claim that once Petraeus took command in Iraq in early 2007 there was a "reverse" of "existing strategy" neatly summarizes this reinvention.[10] Other necessary and arguably more important conditions became secondary or forgotten altogether. General Petraeus's "right inputs" embody the reinvention of the U.S. Army and, in the case of Afghanistan, all but ensure victory, it was said. Thus counterinsurgency, at least since the surge of troops in Iraq in 2007, has become a model for American warfare in the future. Premised on the lessons of Malaya and Vietnam and armed with the methods of success from Iraq that are finally being applied in Afghanistan, counterinsurgency promises to succeed where competing strategies have been tested and found wanting.

The rise of military leaders from the counterinsurgency school has been meteoric and may continue even after their careers. For example, General Stanley McChrystal, after his relief from command in June 2010 for his staff's disparaging remarks about their political masters, teaches leadership classes at Yale University. McChrystal has such star power that he is allowed to teach accredited courses on an "off-the-record basis," meaning that students cannot discuss what was said during the class outside of it.[11]

The counterinsurgency narrative still resonates within the highest levels of the American military. The chairman of the

Joint Chiefs of Staff, General Martin Dempsey, released a report in June 2012 assessing what the American military had "learned" from the past eleven years of war since the al Qaeda attack on 9/11. The report is striking in its underlying acceptance of the prime pillars of the counterinsurgency narrative: that the American military was largely fraught with mistakes and fumbles during "the first half of the decade" as it fought its counterinsurgency wars in Iraq and Afghanistan. But then, adhering to the arc of the counterinsurgency narrative, in the "second half of the decade," the American military, and implicitly the army, began to learn, adapt, and get better at fighting the wars in Iraq and Afghanistan and other minor operations around the world. Although the report never mentions specific savior generals, like Petraeus in Iraq or McChrystal in Afghanistan, the examples it cites of improvements in tactics and operational methods generally occurred during their tenures in command.[12] The recurring theme throughout the report is of a military fumbling and failing during the "first half of the decade," then finally starting to get it in the second half.

As the model for American warfare in the future, counterinsurgency threatens to transform the American army and other parts of the defense establishment into a force organized for nation building, exporting stability to the troubled and obdurate precincts of the globe. Accordingly, the U.S. Army already has shifted its organizational structure toward light infantry in place of mechanized armor forces. Two thirds of the active army combat brigades today consist of light infantry, the shock troops of COIN, the remainder being heavy brigades of tanks and Bradley fighting vehicles—the latter increasingly being viewed as unwanted stepchildren and embarrassments from an earlier age of warfare.[13]

There are, however, numerous irreparable defects in this counterinsurgency narrative. To begin with, it finds little support in the historical record. What the historical record does show is that there were no tectonic shifts between a fumbling army that was reinvented by a savior general into a better counterinsurgency army. In Malaya, Vietnam, Iraq, and Afghanistan, there was more continuity than not between commanders and their operational methods of countering insurgencies. In Malaya, the British won because they crushed the Communist insurgents militarily. In Vietnam, there was only an unwinnable war prolonged by a dysfunctional grand strategy. In Iraq, violence diminished in 2007 not because the U.S. Army saw the light under General Petraeus, but because conditions such as the Anbar Awakening and the Shia militias' decision to stand down combined to reduce violence. And in Afghanistan the comments of American soldiers to investigative journalist Douglas A. Wissing that "counterinsurgency isn't working" reflect the reality of that ongoing struggle and the fact that it has not been made better by enlightened COIN generals.[14]

Still, the idea that COIN works as long as the right general is put in charge will not go away. Elites and opinion makers have come to believe in the promise of counterinsurgency as though it were a religion, complete with its very own Bible, high priests, Messiah, and rebirth. As with most religions, evidence of its truth may be gleaned in the most unlikely places. Recently, a magazine writer was traveling on a rural road outside of Kabul, Afghanistan, with former American chairman of the Joint Chiefs of Staff Admiral Michael Mullen when a bevy of young children pelted the admiral's vehicle with stones in anger over American presence in the country. When the writer asked why this was happening, the admiral's press officer, sitting in the front of the vehicle, remarked that it "shows the children have confidence in the security situation that they feel they can throw stones."[15]

More worrisome than the delusion of an individual American military press officer, general, or think-tank pundit is the monopoly that counterinsurgency has over thinking about strategy and policy. In 2010, President Barack Obama sought from his military leaders an alternative to nation building in Afghanistan.[16] His senior military leaders, transfixed by the promise that counterinsurgency can work in Afghanistan and supercharged by the myth that it worked in Iraq, could offer no alternative to long-term American counterinsurgency, i.e., nation building at the barrel of a gun. Vice President Joseph Biden told President Obama—after listening to General Stanley McChrystal's recommendations for a comprehensive counterinsurgency campaign—that he did not see "how anyone who took part in our discussion could emerge without profound questions about the viability of counterinsurgency." For the vice president, it would have required a leap of faith to believe that counterinsurgency in Afghanistan the way McChrystal proposed to do it could work.[17] But Biden's is the minority perspective. The cult of counterinsurgency responds to multiple needs, unrelated to national security as such. Advocates of American intervention in the world's trouble spots tend to be quite fond of counterinsurgency. After all, a focus on the mechanics of intervention and state building—counterinsurgency operations— means that the underlying motives and ideologies of American intervention will seldom be called into question. Instead the focus remains on the procedures and tactics and logistics of interventions rather than on the causes, ideologies, and motives that bring them into being.

Above all, the cult of counterinsurgency lulls people into thinking that war is about soft power, that American soldiers sent overseas to tame a civil war or stop an insurgency will do so in a less harmful way. Yet my year in western Baghdad showed me and my study of history has reaffirmed that war at its most basic level is about death and destruction. Counterinsurgency warfare is no different, and its results on the ground can be as destructive as conventional warfare. At the height of the American counterinsurgency surge in Iraq, where Petraeus supposedly armed his army with a more enlightened, more humane doctrine of counterinsurgency warfare, Iraqi deaths caused by American firepower tripled as compared to previous years.[18]

Should American foreign policy and the strategy to carry it out be determined by the tactics and concepts of counterinsurgency? Should the American military, especially the army, be transformed into an all-purpose constabulary force tailored for nation building at the expense of an army that can conduct sustained combat at the higher end of the conflict spectrum?[19] Counterinsurgency theorists have a ready and affirmative answer to all of these questions, but to America's peril. Some have argued that counterinsurgency has lost its luster within American policy circles, that it is no longer in vogue since the likelihood of another American counterinsurgency campaign along the lines of Iraq and Afghanistan in the years ahead is dubious at best.[20] COIN, however, is already morphing into a new form: responsibility to protect, or R2P, whose proponents seek to intervene militarily in the affairs of states that are committing acts of violence against civilian populations. These R2P advocates speak the same language of American counterinsurgency, and they share with the COIN advocates the same hyperconfidence in American military power. Already there are calls for intervention in Syria's ongoing civil war by using military power in a "precise" way to protect Syrians from acts of violence by their government. Like counterinsurgency, R2P is expeditionary; like counterinsurgency, R2P fails to understand that when military force is applied to "protect" local populations, it more often ends up killing innocent people and destroying things in the process.[21]

In this book I hope to drive a stake through the heart of the notion that counterinsurgency has worked in the past and will therefore work in the future in whatever form it morphs into. Yet this is not a call for isolationism. If the United States' civilian leaders decide to use the American military to intervene in trouble spots of the world, it will follow the orders of its civilian masters. But policy experts and the American people should use it with a realistic sense of what a successful intervention will require. It won't be cheap. It won't be easy. And it will take a very long time. And most important, any military intervention should be undertaken with a clear understanding of the reality of war, which inevitably involves death, destruction, and human suffering.

# 1

## THE CONSTRUCTION OF THE COUNTERINSURGENCY NARRATIVE

*Her [Kim Kagan's] account details the ways in which the American military developed and applied counterinsurgency principles in Iraq, at a time when many said the war was unwinnable or even lost. This is an indispensable guide to those who wish to understand how the U.S. military adapted to Iraq's political landscape and how it began turning failures into successes.*

—Senator John McCain, 2009[1]

In his endorsement of Kimberly Kagan's 2009 book *The Surge: A Military History*, Senator John McCain noted that it offered a view into how an army transformed itself from failing at counterinsurgency to succeeding at it. The senator's endorsement repeated the basic outline of the counterinsurgency narrative: of armies fumbling at COIN and losing a war but then being transformed into an army that goes on to win. Knowingly or not, Senator McCain had come to recite the stock narrative of counterinsurgency.

That narrative has an important history of its own. Institutions, governments, and even armies spend a great deal of time and energy trying to influence and shape perceptions,[2] as in America's recent war in Iraq. Just weeks into the fighting in 2003, President George Bush told the American people that it had been a roaring success, complete with a MISSION ACCOMPLISHED banner on board a U.S. Navy aircraft carrier where he was speaking. A few years later, by 2005–2006, that initial triumphant narrative had given way to a new one. Among those in the know, Iraq had now become a quagmire, a disastrously failed war that directly paralleled the unhappy experience of Vietnam. A few years later, the narrative morphed again: now a wise general had ridden out to the theater of war, reset a failed army that had gone off the rails, and rescued victory from the jaws of defeat.

There are many reasons why the story of the Iraq surge and General Petraeus's application of COIN simply doesn't hold up to scrutiny. The story depends heavily on historical precedent, on other stories of other wars in different and distant places. The COIN argument is a blend of some history, a lot of myth, and suppositions about roads not taken, as analysts today imagine what might have been if different strategic decisions had been made in the past. COIN depends on a narrow and selective view of histories that are messy and complicated. Revisiting those histories, in all their messiness, is essential for understanding why COIN has failed and will continue to fail as an American way of war. Until we do so, the explanation of these wars will be dominated by writers who conform their stories uncritically to the narrative.[3] The historical bedrock on which the narrative developed was a very different war, involving very different antagonists: the British war against Malayan insurgents. From Malaya, the story traveled to Vietnam. A British colonial officer during the Malayan Emergency, Sir Robert Thompson, thought that the British model for defeating Communist insurgents in Malaya in the 1950s could be applied directly to fighting the Viet Cong insurgents in the jungles of South Vietnam in the early 1960s, and he told the South Vietnamese president Ngo Dinh Diem as much. Thompson saw no significant differences between Malaya and Vietnam: the "enemy," he noted, was "exactly the same."[4]

Senior American military advisers on the ground in Vietnam at that time saw Thompson's proposals as unrealistic, a naive attempt to transfer the Malayan experience to a location in which the existing military conditions, society, culture, and politics were very different.[5]

After America lost the war in Vietnam, explanations began to emerge. Many, looking back with Thompson's recommendations on their minds, concluded that the war *could* have been won *if* the U.S. Army had used different tactics. One school of thought among "if-only" historians argued that the war could have been won if the U.S. Army under Westmoreland had done counterinsurgency correctly, by focusing on winning hearts and minds, as Thompson had earlier suggested. The counterinsurgency narrative as it would later emerge in Iraq and Afghanistan was born with the if-only histories of the Vietnam War. Arguments of the hearts-and-minds, if-only school resonated deeply in the ranks of some American army officers after Vietnam and would come to fruition in the writing of FM 3-24.[6]

The term *counterinsurgency* came into use by the American military in the late 1950s because of the American army's discomfort with the label used in the French and British armies: *counter-revolutionary warfare*. In the Cold War context, and given America's own revolutionary heritage, it became a matter of political and social sensitivity to reframe these kinds of military operations as counterinsurgency.[7]

Modern counterinsurgency is age-old antiguerrilla warfare in new clothes. As he cut a swath through the Middle East in the fourth century B.C., Alexander the Great countered rebellious indigenous peoples while at the same time fighting opposing armies that were similar to his own. King Henry V of England had to worry about angry French peasants sniping at the rear of his army as he moved around northern France in 1415, before and after the battle of Agincourt. Prussian General Helmuth von Moltke faced the prospect of a French people's war against his army as it laid siege to Paris during the Franco-Prussian War in 1871. In the Korean War, from 1950 to 1953, the United States and its allies had to deal with Communist guerrillas attacking their lines of supplies. Rebellion, guerrilla attacks, and insurgency are nothing new to war.[8]

The American war in Vietnam has produced a focus on insurgencies and guerrilla warfare to the point where some policy makers and analysts have convinced themselves that war in the future, as the retired British general Rupert Smith has argued, will be fought primarily, if not only, "amongst the people." Writing in 2005, in the years following the end of the Cold War, General Smith, in his book *The Utility of Force*, argued that "war no longer exists." For Smith, the type of war that no longer existed was what he characterized as "industrial war"—war that ended, as he says, with the two atomic bombings of Japan in 1945. At that point a new kind of war took over, what he calls "wars amongst the people," which he largely puts in a direct line with irregular, small wars and counterinsurgency warfare in the past.[9]

For the American army and many parts of the American defense establishment, Smith's vision has become the model for future war. Since the publication of FM 3-24, counterinsurgency has moved beyond simple doctrine and has become gospel. FM 3-24's effect permeates other army doctrinal manuals, such as FM 3-0, *Operations*, and FM 3-07, *Stability Operations*. Lieutenant General William B. Caldwell IV, who was charged with overseeing the writing of the army's stability operations doctrine, posited that:

> The future is not one of major battles and engagements fought by armies on battlefields devoid of population; instead, the course of conflict will be decided by forces operating among the people of the world. Here, the margin of victory will be measured in far different terms than the wars of our past. The allegiance, trust, and confidence of populations will be the final arbiters of success.[10]

14

The idea of populations as the prize in war, that they are the focus, that the "trust" of local populations is to be won by military forces and then connected to the supported host-nation government—these ideas are drawn directly from the pages of FM 3-24.

The dogmatism of American counterinsurgency has obscured from view the reality of American war, which has primarily been one of improvisation and practicality. Over the course of American history, there have been strategic shifts in terms of the threats and enemies that the United States had faced. With each of these shifts came a different approach to fighting wars or preparing for them in peacetime. For example, in the American Civil War, General Ulysses S. Grant carried out a strategy of exhausting the Southern armies through large-scale combat. A quarter of a century later in the Philippines, the American army improvised and adapted to fight and ultimately defeat an insurgency against the U.S. colonial government. The U.S. military's approach has not been an ideological one of wanting to fight only wars consisting of big battles.[11]

Hearts-and-minds counterinsurgency has become the primary operational instrument in the army's repertoire for dealing with insurgency and instability throughout the world.[12] Since the golden rule of American counterinsurgency is that local populations must be "protected" so that they can be won over to the side of the government and separated from the insurgents, America has been led down a one-way street in its efforts to combat local insurgencies: long-term nation building. The surge in Iraq, led by General Petraeus, seemed to make it all workable, even potentially doable elsewhere. Even in the wake of this disastrous war and the parallel quagmire in Afghanistan, pundits and writers still see a bright future for more counterinsurgency operations in foreign lands.[13]

This theory and practice of American counterinsurgency traces its roots to Western military attempts to counter Communist revolutionary movements in Third World countries after World War II, especially to the fall of China to Mao Tse-tung's Communists in 1949. Indeed, it was the Maoist model of Communist revolutionary movements after World War II that so captivated Western militaries and produced a theory of countering insurgencies. Since Mao proclaimed metaphorically that it was the insurgent fish who swam in the sea of the local population and gained support and protection from them, the counterinsurgency theory that developed had as its basic guiding principle that the population had to be won over to the counterinsurgent side. These were basic principles derived by military officers and analysts from the British experience in Malaya, the French in Indochina and Algeria in the 1950s, and the United States in the early 1960s as it began to look toward an increasing military effort in South Vietnam.[14]

The Malayan Emergency, as it came to be called, was a struggle between the British-led forces against the Malayan Communist Party from 1948 to 1960. The British won. But flawed interpretations like Sir Robert Thompson's as to *how* they won influenced early American actions in Vietnam and, more important, *reactions* in the years following America's loss. Thompson played a substantive role in the formulation of South Vietnamese president Ngo Dinh Diem's Strategic Hamlet Program. As a high-level foreign adviser to Diem, Thompson was sure the Malayan model would work in Vietnam, and he convinced Diem to apply it, almost blindly. In Vietnam, though, resettling hundreds of thousands of rural folk with long-standing ties to the land proved to be an utter failure.[15] These two wars—their conditions and context—were starkly different, yet the faith in counterinsurgency and its contemporary model of perceived success in Malaya blinded people like Thompson into thinking it would automatically work in Vietnam if only its precepts and rules were adhered to.[16]

As the Vietnam War turned sour for the United States after the Tet Offensive in 1968, there began a sustained criticism that the American army had become too firepower-intensive and had lost sight of the key to victory: winning the hearts and minds of the South Vietnamese people by better methods of counterinsurgency. The notion of the possibility of a "better war" had emerged in circles of American military officers and generals in Vietnam as the United States withdrew its forces between 1969 and 1972. The better-war thesis essentially argued that the war against the South Vietnamese insurgents, or People's Liberation Armed Forces (PLAF), was turned around by General Creighton Abrams after he took command from his predecessor, General Westmoreland. The latter, as the better-war proponents tell it, had fought the war wrongly by trying to win it with conventional military operations and massive usage of American firepower. The right approach would have been pacifying the rural countryside and winning the Vietnamese population over to the government's side. Westmoreland, in the better-war thesis, becomes the failed general who didn't "get it," but Abrams did and turned the tide of the war toward victory in the South by 1972.[17] But alas, the Vietnam War was lost not by the military but by weak politicians back in Washington, D.C., who refused to continue material support to America's South Vietnamese allies. The seeds of the better-war thesis were planted, and they grew into a powerful treelike belief system in the years that followed.[18]

As with the counterinsurgency narrative's explanation of Malaya, the notion of a better war in Vietnam and a savior general there who turned his army around is fiction. The primary historical record does not support the idea of a better war under Abrams, who was more like Westmoreland than not. Both Westmoreland and Abrams relied primarily on massive U.S. firepower to accomplish their missions. Tapes of weekly discussions among Abrams and his key staff and commanders show that he was just not that interested in pacification and winning hearts and minds.[19] And as in Malaya, where there was no tectonic shift of operational method with the British field army, in Vietnam the operational framework for the U.S. Army throughout the war remained a combination of search-and-destroy, pacification, and training the South Vietnamese military forces. A contemporary observer of American combat operations in Vietnam, the military historian Charles B. McDonald, noted as much in a speech he gave at the Army War College in 1976. McDonald told the War College officers that he had heard from soldiers and at least one general officer of the tectonic shifts that Abrams had supposedly brought about, "but that simply was not the case" and the changes that did occur were "evolutionary rather than revolutionary."[20]

The United States did lose the war in Vietnam but not because its army didn't do counterinsurgency tactics earlier in the conflict. The United States lost the war in Vietnam because it failed at strategy and policy; it should have discerned early on that the war was unwinnable at a moral and material price that the American people were willing to pay.[21]

In the years immediately after the fall of Saigon, there was an early attempt at rehabilitating the army's reputation. General Creighton Abrams died of cancer in 1974. Very soon after his death and closely tied with the fall of Saigon, the army began a concerted effort to tell the "Abrams story" through interviews of officers who had served with him in Vietnam. One of the key themes that came out in these hundreds of interviews was the idea that General Abrams had come to command MACV (Military Assistance Command, Vietnam) as the war had been stalemated or lost after Tet, had turned it around, and through his leadership had actually won the war on the ground. In this telling of the war, the army didn't lose it but actually won, only to have it lost on college campuses and in the halls of Congress. The theme of better tactics saving a lost war began to emerge.

Three books stand out as early representations of the possibility that the war could have turned out differently, perhaps even victoriously, if the United States had fought it differently, with better counterinsurgency tactics. Larry Cable's *Conflict of Myths*, Gunther Lewy's *America in Vietnam*, and Andrew Krepinevich's *The Army and Vietnam* all argued similarly that the army never fully comprehended the kind of war it was fighting—a revolutionary people's war—and instead relied on conventional operations and an overly destructive application of massive American firepower. For these three authors, the United States in Vietnam should have directed the majority of its effort toward pacification of the countryside by the winning of support of the rural peasantry. The war might have been won, these authors posited, if the U.S. Army had transformed itself from a firepower-intensive force to one focused on hearts-and-minds counterinsurgency. Malaya, for Krepinevich, Cable, and others, became the model of how to do hearts-and-minds counterinsurgency correctly, while Vietnam became the model for failure. As Sir Robert Thompson did in the early years of the war, these writers in the years following America's defeat furthered the Malaya-Vietnam connection.[22]

As the American army rebuilt itself in the 1980s with an operational and doctrinal focus away from counterinsurgencies and toward fighting the Soviet Union in a major superpower confrontation, some in the army and defense establishment started to worry that the army was not preparing to fight more likely wars in the future—wars of counterinsurgency. This line of thinking argued that the U.S. Army had become overly consumed with conventional war and the heightened use of firepower as in the Vietnam War, to the exclusion of proper hearts-and-minds counterinsurgency tactics, and it was making the same kind of mistakes all over again by the end of the 1980s. To these defense thinkers, it was Vietnam redux.[23]

In 1986 a four-star American army general, John R. Galvin, wrote a widely read and influential article in one of the army's professional journals, *Parameters*, on the intellectual climate within the army. Galvin argued that by the mid-1980s, the army had become too cozy in its "comfortable" zone of conventional operations. What it needed was to break free of the known framework of conventional operations and accept what he believed was the way of war in the future: irregular and counterinsurgency wars fought for the loyalty of populations.[24]

This idea of properly preparing for counterinsurgency would be used by COIN experts during the Second Iraq War to browbeat the American army into thinking that things turned out the way they did because—as in Vietnam—it had not prepared properly for counterinsurgency operations. It's interesting that a few years before the publication of Galvin's *Parameters* article, a young David Petraeus was the general's aide. Petraeus noted later that Galvin "would become [my] most important mentor."[25]

The 1990s saw a number of books published that fell in line with the counterinsurgency narrative. In 1995, H.R. McMaster, an army officer and decorated combat veteran from the Gulf War (first American Iraq War), published *Dereliction of Duty: Lyndon Johnson, Robert McNamara, the Joint Chiefs of Staff, and the Lies That Led to Vietnam*. It was a searing indictment of America's senior political and military leaders. Showing an early inclination toward the counterinsurgency narrative, McMaster argued that the Vietnam War was not lost on the battlefield or by the American media, but instead because of the lies of American leaders that prevented a winning strategy from emerging. There was a better war to be had in Vietnam, implied McMaster, but the lies of Johnson, McNamara, and the Joint Chiefs prevented it from coming about. During America's second war in Iraq, McMaster would become one of the most strident proponents of American counterinsurgency.[26]

Building on McMaster was Lewis Sorley, whose 1999 book, *A Better War: The Unexamined Victories and Final Tragedies of America's Last Years in Vietnam*, argued that Abrams had succeeded in turning the war around in 1968, had reoriented the American army on classic counterinsurgency tactics, and had actually won the war in the South. Abrams had changed the "tactics" of the war "within fifteen minutes" of taking command, Sorley contended.[27]

John Nagl's Oxford University doctoral dissertation, published in 2002 as *Learning to Eat Soup with a Knife: Counterinsurgency Lessons from Malaya and Vietnam*, complemented Sorley's book nicely. Nagl's book was a culmination of two decades of thinking among counterinsurgency experts on Malaya and Vietnam. Nagl argued that the British Army in Malaya was adaptive and innovative, following a model of organizational learning that Nagl set out in his first chapter, and that is why they won the war. In Vietnam, however, argued Nagl, the American army did not learn and adapt toward the correct methods of counterinsurgency because it was too focused on firepower and not enough on winning hearts and minds. Implicit in *Learning to Eat Soup with a Knife* was that if Abrams had gotten the call to lead the American effort at the start of the war, America might very well have won it. Nagl's book has become very influential within the American army and defense establishment. It seemed to explain both wars so perfectly, and it seemed to offer a solution to the war in Iraq.[28]

General Petraeus certainly agreed with Krepinevich and Nagl that to win in Vietnam the army "would have been much better with tactics that fell under the heading of counterinsurgency" rather than "search and destroy." Petraeus's summation of what went wrong in Vietnam encapsulates the fundamental misunderstanding of Vietnam within the counterinsurgency narrative: that the war could have been won if only counterinsurgency methods were used. During the surge in Iraq, Petraeus would come to represent the way Vietnam should have been fought because, as the narrative portrayed, he was finally doing counterinsurgency correctly.[29]

During the first three years of America's second war in Iraq, from 2003 to 2006, when violence grew steadily amid a strident

Sunni insurgency and sectarian civil war, there was brewing within American military and defense circles the idea that a better war could indeed be had if only the army would "learn" counter-insurgency. Suddenly, and in a certain sense to COIN adherents, *finally*, the lessons of Malaya and Vietnam could be applied and the proof of the better-war thesis revealed, in real time in Iraq. Retired Australian army officer David Kilcullen, who would soon experience a meteoric rise as one of the leading counterinsurgency experts in America, wrote a widely read article in the journal *Military Review* titled "28 Principles of Counterinsurgency," in which he laid out the "classic" principles of counterinsurgency as derived from certain historical cases, like Malaya, Algeria, and Vietnam. In 2005 Krepinevich, drawing on his work on the American army in Vietnam, called for a reformulation of American operations in Iraq. Naturally he drew on "history lessons" and argued that "winning hearts and minds" had worked for the British in Malaya but the U.S. Army failed at it in Vietnam—but it could work in Iraq just as in Malaya if only the American army fighting there figured it out. Following on the heels of Krepinevich was a British Army general who had served with the American army in Iraq in 2004 and 2005. Brigadier Nigel Aylwin-Foster thoroughly thrashed the American army, which he blamed for causing many of the problems in Iraq that had developed with the insurgency since 2003. Foster saw the American army making the same "mistakes" as in Vietnam with a hyperfocus on firepower and killing the insurgent enemy. Naturally the solution for Foster was what Abrams had tried to do in Vietnam and of course what the British were able to do in Malaya.[30]

During the end of 2005 and the beginning of 2006, as American soldiers continued to die in Iraq and bloody scenes of chaos and violence filled CNN coverage and the front pages of newspapers, the counterinsurgency narrative hardened. *New York Times* columnist David Brooks wrote in 2005 after two increasingly bloody years of American military efforts in Iraq that a new way was needed. Brooks drew on the counterinsurgency narrative: the British had won hearts and minds in Malaya, and Abrams had turned the American army around in Vietnam and done it there too, so why not now in Iraq? As Brooks surveyed the Iraq War scene, there seemed to be a fumbling American army that was unable to correctly apply proper counterinsurgency methods. For Brooks, another war, much like Vietnam, was about to be lost by bad tactics—unless a better general could come along and save it.[31]

When Brooks's article came out, I was in squadron command at Fort Hood, Texas, in August 2005, deeply engaged in training my squadron for our upcoming deployment to Iraq. I remember coming out of the field and settling into a comfortable weekend at home. I woke up Sunday morning and read Brooks's article, and it rubbed me the wrong way, because in our training for deployment, we were already preparing to do those very tactics that Brooks had recommended the army shift to. So I pushed back and wrote a letter to the editor that the *New York Times* actually published:

David Brooks has been seduced by the myth of pundits like Andrew F. Krepinevich Jr. who write about counterinsurgencies and the Vietnam War: that the war could have been won if the United States had adopted the oil-spot strategy.

This myth is built on certain historical "lessons" or "models," like the British in Malaya. But if you look at the case of Malaya, you will see a context that is radically different from Vietnam and, more important, present-day Iraq.

The example of Malaya is often cited by those who believe that there is a template to follow for "winning" in Iraq. Such reductionist templates are seductive because they offer easy-to-understand solutions for complex problems.

Is the oil-spot template feasible for the United States in Iraq? It sounds nice, but what number of American troops would be required to carry it out?

One can argue, counter to the facts, that Vietnam would have been winnable if the United States had deployed, say, two million to three million troops to carry out the oil-spot strategy. But was this ever politically realistic for the United States in Vietnam? Is such a rise in troop numbers and time commitment realistic today in Iraq?

(Lt. Col.) Gian P. Gentile
Fort Hood, Tex., August 28, 2005[32]

I never heard from Brooks. My squadron deployed to Baghdad in December 2005 prepared to do the tactics that Brooks had figured the army wasn't doing (but we were). This was probably my first exposure to the counterinsurgency narrative and its conflict with my actual experience and thinking.

The year 2006 was pivotal for the rise of counterinsurgency in the American army. A number of critical activities and events occurred that would set the stage for the surge of troops in early 2007. First was the drafting of the counterinsurgency doctrinal manual, FM 3-24, at Fort Leavenworth, Kansas, under the tutelage of General Petraeus. With a savvy nose for the American political scene, Petraeus kicked off the writing effort in February 2006 with a conference at Leavenworth that had as its participants such luminaries as *New Yorker* writer George Packer and Sarah Sewall of Harvard University's Carr Center.[33] The conference was meant to convey the sense that the principles and ideas developed in the field manual were being vetted by the finest minds of the American military and defense establishments, academe, and the media. The backdrop of the yearlong effort to write the COIN manual was the growing violence of the civil war in Iraq, which by late 2006 had reached a bloody and hellish crescendo. In the minds of the conference attendees at Fort Leavenworth was the thought that the doctrine they were writing would be applied in Iraq and might be the solution.

The final version of FM 3-24, published in December 2006, drew heavily on the British experience in Malaya and the U.S. experience in Vietnam. The manual cited Malaya as a model for counterinsurgency in training local police forces and in emphasizing the overall political context and the imperative of establishing a legitimate government. Then the population could be won over to the counterinsurgent side with minimum force, with close cooperation between military and civil authorities under the rule of law, and with tactical flexibility for the counterinsurgent force. Such a perception of the British way of counterinsurgency, as historically blinkered as it surely was, reinforced the idea among many American COIN experts that the British had gotten it right not only in Malaya but in other twentieth-century wars of counterinsurgency.[34]

The writers of FM 3-24 also relied heavily on another European practitioner of counterinsurgency, the French army officer David Galula, and on his experiences in command of an infantry company in Algeria in the 1950s. Galula's book *Counterinsurgency Warfare*, with its tactical methods of "clear, hold, and build" and his descriptions of local populations caught up in an insurgency, became the tactical framework for FM 3-24. FM 3-24 repeated verbatim Galula's iconic assertion that "in any situation, whatever the cause," there will be a small minority for the government and a small minority for the insurgency, the rest of the population sitting in the middle waiting to be won over by either side.[35]

Despite the hype that the manual was grounded in scholarly rigor, it was in fact devoid of contemporary political science scholarship on the nature of civil wars, of which insurgencies are usually a part. Yale political scientist Stathis Kalyvas argued that "the manual breaks little new ground" and "its substance can be found" in the works of Galula and Thompson, along with a few others. Kalyvas also noted that the manual "betrays zero impact by [current] political science research."[36] But because it fit neatly within the counterinsurgency narrative, the manual appeared to be authoritative, supposedly grounded in the "enduring principles" of counterinsurgency and vetted by some of the country's finest minds.

The manual's writers seem to have accepted as proven the conclusions of Thompson and Galula and the arguments about Vietnam that had been put forward by people like Nagl and Krepinevich. Nagl has acknowledged that Galula's book and essays on the French experience in Algeria played a very influential role in the writing of FM 3-24.[37] But recent scholarship has shown that what Galula said worked for him in Algeria actually did not.[38] Moreover, there is the broader question why a group of American army officers, retired and active, along with civilian intellectuals, would use French COIN tactics in Algeria as the basis of army doctrine when the French in the end lost that war.

FM 3-24 rests on a set of basic assumptions: that the British were successful in Malaya because they applied correct hearts-and-minds counterinsurgency methods, that Galula's COIN tactics in Algeria worked, and that the Americans could have won in Vietnam if only they had done counterinsurgency correctly.

Once the manual was published, its story flourished. Experience in Iraq and Afghanistan and a clear view of the historical record showed very early its deep flaws, but the narrative around FM 3-24 proved durable. Many senior generals had their reputations built around it. COIN became difficult to modify and even more difficult to challenge.

Furthermore, the COIN narrative had begun to spread beyond military and policy circles. It was popularized extensively by the mainstream media and by authors such as *Washington Post* writer Thomas Ricks, whose book *Fiasco* dished out special opprobrium to the American army for fumbling, severely, at counterinsurgency between 2003 and 2006. Ricks thought the army was making the same mistakes it made in Vietnam: too much firepower and no proper counterinsurgency. Yet there were some bright spots that Ricks had observed when he visited American combat units in Iraq in 2005 and early 2006. It was "a different war" in western Baghdad, he noted. Ricks had embedded with my cavalry squadron for about a week in early February 2006. In *Fiasco* he used numerous quotes from soldiers in my outfit about our approach to operations. One of my noncommissioned officers told Ricks that our operations were focused on "hearts and minds." One of my subordinate troop commanders, Captain K.K. Robinson, told Ricks that much of his time was spent "engaging the population." In *Fiasco* Ricks took a favorable view of us, a view that would change significantly in his subsequent book, which came out three years later. But the brightest spot that Ricks observed in *Fiasco* was Colonel H.R. McMaster and the operations of his cavalry regiment in the restive northern city of Tall 'Afar. One COIN expert told Ricks that McMaster's year in Tall 'Afar "will serve as a case study in classic counterinsurgency, the way it is supposed to be done." Alas, lamented Ricks at the end of *Fiasco*, the bright spot of McMaster would be "yet another road not taken" by the rest of the army in Iraq.[39]

As 2007 began, better-war thinking was all but begging for deployment, and it found an audience in political and military circles consumed by the idea that if something drastic wasn't done quickly, the war in Iraq would be lost. At a neoconservative think tank, the American Enterprise Institute, Fred Kagan, assisted by retired American army general Jack Keane and others, had written a plan to save Baghdad. In "Choosing Victory: A Plan for Success in Iraq" Kagan argued that "victory was still an option," implying that the war would be lost if something radical was not done. Kagan highlighted the newly published FM 3-24 and boasted that because it was premised on the COIN principle of protection and security of the population, it reflected "the wisdom of generations of counterinsurgency theorists and practitioners."[40] Although he did not come out and say so, in order to make his plan work, he needed a better general. It was the pivotal moment in a pivotal year for the rise of American counterinsurgency.

Enter General Petraeus, the newly published FM 3-24, Kagan's surge plan, and the actual surge of troops that began in February 2007. By late summer 2007, a mere six months after the surge started, violence was dropping precipitously in Iraq. The reasons for the drop in violence were complex: the spread of the Anbar Awakening (a revolt against al Qaeda in Iraq by Sunni tribes in western Iraq) and the co-opting of Sunni insurgents in Baghdad and other parts of Iraq; the decision by Shia militia leaders to halt their deadly campaign of slaughter against Sunni civilians; and the fact that Baghdad had become sectarian, separated into a Shia-dominated city with small enclaves of Sunnis. To be sure, the extra surge brigades played a role in the reduction of violence, but largely in their ability to reduce al Qaeda's numbers and strength through combat action.[41]

The surge triumph story fit squarely in line with the larger narrative arc of counterinsurgency, following in the footsteps of Malaya and Vietnam. In October 2007, as the violence in Iraq began to drop significantly, former *New York Times* reporter Clifford May saw the main cause of the reduction in violence to be an enlightened general named David Petraeus, who outfitted his army in Iraq with new methods for conducting counterinsurgency. May juxtaposed the Petraeus surge army with what came before, and accused the pre-surge army under General George Casey of being hunkered down on large bases, content to lie low while the Iraq Civil War raged around it. But once Petraeus came on board and initiated the surge of troops in February 2007, things changed. The result was a reinvented counterinsurgency army under the command of a better general. The difference in counterinsurgency methods between the pre-surge and surge armies was the primary cause for the reduced violence, May argued.[42]

President George W. Bush saw the reinvention of the U.S. Army during the surge as a complete "reversal" of strategy from what came before. The narrative arc of counterinsurgency thus continued from Malaya to Vietnam and now to America's second war in Iraq. President Bush's embrace of the surge and the large body of writings like May's that proclaimed the surge as a triumph of a reinvented army under a better general perpetuate the ongoing narrative.[43]

As the surge was winding down and things appeared to be getting better in Iraq, Afghanistan's worsening situation called for another savior general to reinvent an army that up to that point had not been doing counterinsurgency correctly. The abrupt relief of General David McKiernan in Afghanistan and his replacement with General Stanley McChrystal in spring 2009 had all of the markings of the counterinsurgency narrative being applied directly to Afghanistan. Since Petraeus had seemingly made it work in Iraq and rescued that war from a failing general, why not do surge version 2 in Afghanistan and replace the fumbling general with a better one?

A November 2009 *Newsweek* article betrayed deep-seated acceptance of the narrative arc of counterinsurgency. "The Surprising Lessons of Vietnam: Unraveling the Mysteries of Vietnam May Prevent Us from Making Its Mistakes" suggested that a failing war in Afghanistan might be turned into a better war like Vietnam under Abrams and Iraq under Petraeus. If only the U.S. Army would realize how it fumbled in Vietnam and Iraq but then recovered, success might come about in Afghanistan too. One senior marine general quoted in the article went so far as to suggest a direct line between the successes of General Abrams in Vietnam to the promise of success in Afghanistan with General McChrystal. Naturally, Petraeus was the implied middle general in this triumvirate. For the *Newsweek* article, the right "inputs" were falling into place in Afghanistan: a better general was on board and a reinvented army was in the making.[44] The promise of tactical success at counterinsurgency was on the horizon in the "graveyard of empires."

Many people seem to have become comfortable with the idea that "reinvented" armies doing counterinsurgency under innovative generals can rescue wars that should not have been fought in the first place or have been fought under a failed strategy and policy. The reinvention of armies is a seductive concept, because it takes the onus of responsibility for war—and ultimately its success and failure—away from elites and policy makers and places it solely in the hands of a field army and its generals. Almost one hundred years ago, Georges Clemenceau warned, "War is too important to be left to the generals." In Stanley Kubrick's *Dr. Strangelove*, General Jack D. Ripper perverted that dictum, saying, "Today war is too important to be left to politicians." The deadly embrace of American counterinsurgency is bringing the mad general's quip to life as policy.

Since counterinsurgency seems to have seduced American policy makers to believe that wars of nation building can be won simply by technique and better generals, we appear to be doomed to repeat the same mistakes for a long, long time. General Petraeus recently reflected on how long the United States would be at war in Afghanistan. He said, "I don't think you win this war. I think you keep fighting. . . . This is the kind of fight we're in for the rest of our lives and probably our kids too." After a lengthy set of discussions in the fall of 2009 over the number of troops to be committed to Afghanistan, President Obama wrote a memorandum for his military leaders on strategy. The president made quite clear that he did not want to do long-term nation building or a comprehensive counterinsurgency campaign in Afghanistan, and he placed specific time limits on his Afghan surge, noting that the first of those surge forces would begin to withdraw in summer 2011. When he received push-back from his senior military leaders, who were advocating something different, he was told by a military aide, Colonel John Tien, that he did not see how the president could "defy [his] military chain here" on their preferred course of action for long-term counterinsurgency in Afghanistan. So to ensure that his senior army officers in Afghanistan understood that he didn't want to pursue long-term nation building, the president issued a memo explicitly stating as much, along with a time limit on operations and reaffirmation of his core political objective, the destruction of al Qaeda. When asked about the apparent contradiction between Petraeus's advocacy of long-term COIN in Afghanistan and the president's more limited plan, an aide to Petraeus said, "We didn't pay much attention to that memo."[45]

In a speech at the American Enterprise Institute in May 2010, Petraeus captured perfectly the main points of the counterinsurgency narrative:

Our effort in Iraq was beginning to struggle. Despite progress in a number of areas, the insurgency was spreading. Levels of violence were escalating. Political progress was at a virtual standstill. And in the wake of the February 2006 bombing of the Samarra Mosque, one of the holiest sites in Shi'a Islam, sectarian violence, in particular, began to grow at an alarming rate. A sense of fear and terror grew through the summer as the violence began to tear apart the very fabric of Iraqi society. And while new operations periodically arrested the downward spiral at various intervals, in their wake the violence grew even more. . . . [Army Chief of

Staff] General Schoomaker wanted even more change, as he, too, was beginning to recognize the urgency of the situation in Iraq. And so, when he sent me to Fort Leavenworth, he gave me some simple, direct guidance. "Shake up the Army, Dave," he told me. I was delighted to salute and help do just that.

In other words, the American army was losing the war and it needed a different general to "shake things up" and bring about a radical transformation of the army. As the general continued his speech, he went on to note that he and a few other military officers, along with some civilian experts, got the "big ideas right" and ensconced them in FM 3-24:

- focusing on security of the population;
- living among the people to do so;
- holding and building in areas that have been cleared;
- promoting reconciliation—while pursuing the irreconcilables relentlessly;
- achieving civil-military unity of effort;
- living our values;
- being first with the truth;
- fostering initiative; and
- learning and adapting.

The American army in Iraq, then proclaimed the general, armed itself with the additional five surge brigades and, more important, with the general's big ideas of counterinsurgency and applied them directly in Iraq in 2007:

Thus, as the first of the surge forces arrived in Baghdad, we focused on securing the population; doing so by living with the people, rather than by commuting to the fight from big bases; fostering reconciliation where possible while relentlessly pursuing al Qaeda and the other irreconcilables; achieving civil-military unity of effort; and so on, all enabled, of course, by the additional forces being deployed as part of the surge. It got harder before it got easier, as you'll recall, and we experienced tough fighting and many difficult days. But ultimately, coalition and Iraqi forces were able to reduce the level of violence by well over 90 percent and to achieve a level of security that, while not without periodic horrific attacks, allowed the repair of infrastructure, revival of the economy, investment by international firms, and the conduct of elections—all of which gave rise to new hope in the Land of the Two Rivers. In large part, this hope was created as a result of the changes our Army, together with the other services, made in the United States in 2006 that enabled the subsequent implementation of our big ideas on counterinsurgency in Iraq in 2007.

Thus, argued General Petraeus, the surge of troops carrying out a very new and different method of counterinsurgency, along with their Iraqi partners, were the primary cause for the lowering of violence in late 2007.[46]

*

The COIN mystique surrounded Stanley McChrystal's entrance into command in Afghanistan in spring 2009, but the story on which the current practice of COIN depends is not supported by evidence. It is a myth. From this flawed narrative, we end up with the simplistic idea that the United States can intervene militarily to rebuild entire societies if the tactics are just right and the right general is put in charge. It is a recipe for perpetual war. A better understanding of the flawed historical narrative of counterinsurgency warfare, one that exposes the fallacy that counterinsurgency and armed state building actually worked in practice in Malaya, Vietnam, and Iraq and is currently working in Afghanistan, might lead to a way out of this nightmare.

# 2

## MALAYA: THE FOUNDATION OF THE COUNTERINSURGENCY NARRATIVE

*Overcoming this organizational resistance to change would require the dramatic intervention of a single man. . . . The Empire Strikes Back. . . . Templer Takes Over. . . . A comparison of British army doctrine and techniques with those it had previously developed at the end of 1951 demonstrates the evolution of a comprehensive doctrine for counterinsurgency . . . victory was achieved.*

—John A. Nagl[1]

*The Malaya insurgency provides lessons applicable to combating any insurgency.*

—Field Manual 3-24[2]

Jotting down observations in his notebook on the conduct of security-force field operations in Malaya in late November 1951, the new director of operations, General Sir Robert Lockhart, noted that his predecessor, Lieutenant General Harold Briggs, had "achieved a good deal of order and method into the campaign." There were indications that the leaders of the Communist rebellion were significantly "worried" about their future prospects, noted Lockhart. The general was quite pleased with the performance of the British field army in Malaya at the time, which he said was quite "well trained." Lockhart noted that the British Army was effective in military operations that had denied food and supplies to insurgents who had become separated from their support base of ethnic Chinese civilians due to relocation into settlement camps. To be sure, work needed to be done to defeat the insurgents, but Lockhart's largest concern was with the Malayan police force, which he said was neither "well trained" nor "properly organized."[3]

Three years later, in 1954, as the Emergency was winding down and it was clear that the Communist insurgents had been broken as a significant threat to the British and Malayan government, the director of operations, Lieutenant General Geoffrey Bourne, stated in a planning directive for 1955 that the "Briggs-Templer 'steady squeeze' plan carried out over the last four years has made real progress."[4] Continuity between commanding generals (Generals Harold Briggs and Gerald Templer) and in the field operations of the British Army during the critical Emergency years from 1948 to 1954 was cited as the key to breaking the back of the insurgency.

Yet the counterinsurgency narrative that developed after the American war in Vietnam held the opposite—that instead of continuity between Briggs and Templer, there was radical discontinuity between the two in terms of their generalship and the way their respective armies fought the war. The same argument was made about the United States in Vietnam. In this narrative, Westmoreland (the failed general) was replaced by Creighton Abrams (the better general), who radically altered the course of the war by getting the American army to do counterinsurgency correctly. Malaya became the model for how the United States could have won the war in Vietnam if only the U.S. Army had followed its methods and put the right general in charge. And years later, viewed from the angle of the American war in Iraq in 2006 and the drafting of FM 3-24, Malaya became a primary historical reference point for counterinsurgency doctrine.

In the years following the end of World War II, the British Empire was crumbling, and the British sought to withdraw from many of their colonial possessions. This was the case in Malaya, but there the British were reluctant to leave it in the hands of a burgeoning Communist movement with political and economic links to China and the Soviet Union. The Malayan Communist Party was almost entirely composed of ethnic Chinese Malayans, who constituted about 40 percent of the overall population. Since the defeat of the Japanese, the Communists had been agitating to establish a Communist-led government in the wake of the British departure. The British-led government forces and other significant parts of Malayan society were willing to fight to stop them. The Malayan Emergency, as it came to be called, lasted from 1948 to 1960, although most of the heavy fighting was complete by 1955. After almost twelve years of struggle against the Malayan Communist insurgents, the British side won.

But *how* the British victory was secured is the key question for the narrative arc of counterinsurgency.[5]

From the start of the Emergency, the British colonial government had many advantages against its Communist enemy. Even though the governing structure of the British was disrupted by the Japanese occupation during World War II, the British quickly reestablished the institutions of state and governance that they had developed along with the Malayans during their eighty years of formal colonial rule. There was a police force in place throughout the country, and in the immediate years following World War II it saw an influx of British police leaders who had had extensive experience in other colonial areas, such as Palestine. There was a system of informal control throughout the country, in the form of British rubber planters and tin mine managers, who acted as little outposts of quasi-governmental authority. In addition, there was a British army of ten combat battalions; it was largely a conscript army but also had some leaders with jungle warfare experience in World War II. The Malayan economy was also relatively strong, especially after the start of the Korean War in 1950, which created huge demand for Malayan rubber and tin. Chin Peng, the Malayan Communist leader, acknowledged that the British held all the cards and that he was likely waging a futile struggle. "I don't think there was an opportunity for our success. Without foreign aid, we could not defeat the British Army," Chin lamented.[6]

The other significant advantage that the British and Malayans had was the simple but critical fact that the ethnic Chinese population of Malaya was the minority in the country, totaling 39 percent of the overall population. It was that Chinese minority that gave active and material support to the insurgents. Ethnic Malays made up 49 percent of the population; the remaining 12 percent were people of mixed ethnicity. By and large, the ethnic Malays opposed a Communist takeover of their country and supported the British colonial effort to resist it.[7] In the end, numbers mattered, and the Malayan majority offered a decisive advantage to the British. It was a war that it would have been very difficult for the British to lose.[8]

Commenting on the strength and capacity of the Viet Cong insurgents in 1963, only a few years before a major American commitment in South Vietnam, French writer and war correspondent Bernard Fall believed them to be a hardened, effective fighting force. By the end of 1963, Fall estimated that there were "5 regiments, 34 independent battalions, 129 independent companies, and 100 independent platoons," totaling with local guerrilla support upwards of 80,000 fighting men. And by the end of 1964, South Vietnam and the United States anticipated the entry of the North Vietnamese army (NVA), of which Fall said its "ability in jungle warfare was clearly demonstrated in the first Indochina conflict" against the French.[9] The Malayan Communist insurgents whom the British faced a decade earlier had not achieved that level of strength. Indeed, although the ethnic Chinese Malayan Communists had some experience of jungle warfare against the Japanese occupation in World War II, they were not a world-class fighting force compared to the Viet Cong and North Vietnamese army. Nor did the Malayan insurgents receive any external material support from China throughout the entire Emergency. Certainly, the Malayan insurgents had the capability to pose a troublesome threat to the British and Malayan governments through acts of violence, but they made serious mistakes of strategy early on by trying to concentrate their fighting forces in order to challenge the British directly, thus exposing them to British firepower. At their peak, the Malayan Communist fighters numbered no more than 7,500.[10] In sum, throughout the course of the Emergency, there was a relatively unsophisticated Communist insurgent enemy who could receive no significant outside support from an external power. Malaya was nothing like Vietnam.

During the course of the Emergency, from its start in mid-1948, through its most violent years from 1949 to 1952, and through the remaining years to its end in 1960, the major concern for the British and Malayan government was how long it would take to end it, because this related directly to the will of the British public to see it through. Prime Minister Churchill himself appreciated the essence of the problem in Malaya at the height of insurgent attacks in the spring of 1951. He noted in a conversation with the minister of defense that there seemed to be "little if any progress" against the insurgents. What was needed, stressed the prime minister, was a "review of the situation" to put in place any "steps that can be taken to speed up matters." A discussion between General Sir Bernard Montgomery and American Allied commander in Europe, General Dwight Eisenhower, highlighted the concern that taking too long to win the war in Malaya would take away British long-term strength from Europe. For both of them, it was "vital that the Malayan mess should be cleaned up as rapidly as possible."[11]

The American counterinsurgency expert Lieutenant Colonel (retired) John A. Nagl has argued that there was a specific time when the British Army became a learning organization, with the arrival in 1952 of General Templer. This "discontinuity" (which became a major part of the COIN narrative) is echoed in the work of another prominent analyst of the Malayan Emergency, Richard Stubbs, who also sees the tide turn when Templer arrives on the scene and pushes his security forces to pursue a proper "hearts and minds" strategy. But the primary historical record of the British Army in Malaya—reports and historical summaries by the combat battalions that fought the insurgency, along with senior British leader observations of them—shows that there was no discontinuity with Templer's arrival. Instead the overall operational framework for the British Army was continuous and remained largely unchanged throughout the war: it was search and destroy. To be sure, there were significant tactical adjustments within the greater operational framework. Initially, the British Army concentrated on large-unit operations to hunt down and kill insurgents. Once Briggs took over, there were tactical shifts that placed emphasis on a tighter linkage between army combat operations to sever the material link between the insurgents and resettled civilians. But the notion that there was a radical shift in operational method when Templer arrived is not supported by the primary evidence. A British historian who fought during the Emergency as an infantry officer in a British regiment and wrote a short history of the insurgency in 1978 observed that the "task of the British Army during the Malay Emergency was to seek out and destroy the armed and uniformed units" of the enemy.[12]

Within a few months in late 1948, shortly after the British colonial government declared an emergency situation in Malaya to deal with the Communist-led insurgency, the commanding officer of the second battalion, Coldstream Guards, noted that after about three months in the Cameron Highlands of central Malaya, all soldiers in the battalion were "well experienced" at jungle operations. The battalion commander, Lieutenant Colonel J.S. Jocks, appreciated the need to deal with the ethnic Chinese squatter villages on the fringes of the jungle, which supplied food, material, and information to the insurgents. Much of the battalion's operations during these first months of the Emergency were designed to sever the physical links between these Chinese squatters and the insurgents by aggressive jungle patrolling and by relocation of the squatters. Thorough reconnaissance of the area and the insurgent enemy, according to the colonel, was also being conducted so that the knowledge gained "will be of great help in future operations."[13]

In the state of Tampin, in southeastern Malaya about a hundred miles south of the Cameron Highlands, another British combat battalion, the legendary Green Howards, was conducting operations very similar to those of the Coldstream Guards a few years earlier. The battalion operations officer of the Green Howards, Major J.B. Oldfield, boasted that April 1951 had been a very "successful month for the Battalion" in that it had racked up five enemy kills for the month, bringing its total up to twenty-four. Oldfield also noted that in addition to its successful combat actions in killing the insurgent enemy, his battalion was also quite effective "in the amount of food found by the patrols, who thus deprived the terrorists of carefully husbanded supplies." The major went on to comment that the "need to deny food to the terrorists was generally accepted as the quickest and surest means, and by some the only means, to end the Emergency."[14]

The Green Howards, the rest of the British field army in Malaya, the police force, and the intelligence services were all part of a very detailed and well-thought-out plan put into place by the British commanding general, Sir Harold Briggs. Briggs was brought into Malaya in April 1950 and appointed senior director of operations as a step toward unified command in Malaya. Very soon after taking over, Briggs put into place what would become known as the Briggs Plan; two of its critical components were the resettlement of many of the Chinese squatters and military operations to cut off the insurgents' food supplies. The result was to regain control of the key space and people, winning their allegiance once control was established and thereby separating them from the insurgents. A combat battalion noted in its historical report written in mid-1951 that "as a result of the Briggs Plan it was possible to put more pressure on the bandits . . . and to begin work on the squatter resettlement." By the end of 1951, as indicated by the success of combat outfits like the Green Howards, the Briggs Plan was having a decisive effect on the Communist insurgents. Only a month before General Gerald Templer's arrival, the commander of British forces in the Far East, Sir Charles F. Keightley, noted that "Gerald will start off on the best possible wicket as the Briggs Plan is showing some valuable results."[15]

Shortly after assuming overall command in Malaya in early 1952, General Templer had his staff put together a doctrinal manual that codified the tactics and methods the British Army had been using in Malaya since 1948. In a letter introducing the manual, Templer reminded the British field army that its prime purpose was to "kill or capture Communist terrorists in Malaya." Of course this purpose was nothing new, as Templer said he had been "impressed by the wealth of jungle fighting experience available" in the British Army "on different levels."[16] That experience had been accumulating since the start of the Emergency and had been improved by the Briggs Plan, which began to develop in 1951 and 1952 ways of conducting British Army combat operations around the resettled areas. When he arrived in early 1952, Templer inherited a developing operational situation. The most that can be said about changes he introduced is that he accelerated learning by codifying practices already in place and disseminating them throughout the force.

One source of operational continuity for the British Army during the Malayan Emergency was the Commonwealth regiments—

men from various British colonies or former colonies, including East Africans and Nepalese Gurkhas. At any given time during the course of the Emergency from 1948 to 1960, a third or more of the British combat regiments fighting in Malaya were from the Commonwealth countries. And they took a significant number of casualties during the war. Of the 470 British regular soldiers who were killed during the Emergency, about 270 were Commonwealth soldiers, men of color not from the British Isles.[17]

The Gurkhas provided a huge source of continuity for the British Army throughout the Emergency. Gurkha battalions were in Malaya fighting insurgents from the start of the war in 1948 until it finished in 1960. In 1953, the second year of Templer's command, the First Battalion of the Sixth Gurkha Rifles Brigade had spent the month of June tracking down an insurgent leader named Teng Meng in the jungle fringes around the regional city of Ipoh. After frustrating days of tracking, a Gurkha patrol from the battalion laid a successful ambush and killed the insurgent leader. Documents were discovered on his body identifying food suppliers for the insurgents. Within days those suppliers were arrested.[18]

In the British Army, the Gurkha battalions hold an extraordinary reputation, and the British officers who commanded these units became devoted to them. These officers were not among the army elite, but by serving nearly continuously with the Gurkhas, they became highly competent combat leaders and officers. The monthly historical reports for the Gurkha battalions from 1950 to 1955, written by their commanding officers or operations officers, are a model of professional performance evaluations and reporting on unit operations. These reports tell the story of an operational framework for the British Army writ large that remained essentially the same throughout the war: use military force to hunt down and capture or kill the insurgents and break their links with the ethnic Chinese civilians from whom they received their supplies.[19] In the monthly reports, there isn't any documentary evidence showing some kind of huge, seismic operational shift when Templer assumed command. The historical reports are instead a remarkable account of effective and continuous operations by Gurkha battalions.

In 1950, during their first six months of deployment, the Gurkhas tried to track down and kill insurgents, ambush them, or when intelligence was available seek out insurgent camps where supplies were kept. In late July of that year, one battalion conducted a joint operation with the Green Howards, both operating in the Cameron Highlands. Operation Crown, as it was called, was based on information from a police informant concerning insurgent movement and base locations. The Gurkhas and the Green Howards deployed their battalions in and around the jungle fringes of the Camerons for about a week. During the first three days of the operation, not much happened. On the fifth day, the Gurkha battalion's D Company came upon an insurgent camp near a Chinese squatter village, about three miles from the main road. The links to the squatter village were evident in that the Gurkhas found multiple tracks leading from it to the insurgent camp. The camp was destroyed. It wasn't much, but these continuous operations by the British security forces were what ultimately broke the back of the insurgency, one small piece at a time.[20]

The operational framework for the British Army throughout the war remained search and destroy. The British Army that fought in Malaya—at its peak, from 1949 to 1953, about forty thousand troops in twenty-one battalions—destroyed the outnumbered rebels with routine operations, operating in small units of usually no more than twenty to thirty men, tracking down the Communists in their jungle hideouts or laying ambushes on jungle trails. British Army units did in fact learn and improve over the course of the war. This learning and adapting, however, occurred in cycles that followed the temporal deployment of British combat battalions. That is to say, a combat battalion would arrive on the scene, go through a few weeks of jungle training, and its first few months in the jungle would be largely trial and error with many mistakes, but by the end of a year-and-a-half deployment, most British outfits had become quite adept at fighting the Communists. This kind of cyclical learning and adapting can be seen throughout the war. It was a cascade of British combat outfits learning and adapting as they arrived on the scene and then departed. There was no tectonic shift between a British Army failing before a certain point and succeeding at counterinsurgency afterward. Instead, each combat battalion learned through trial and error and generally got better through the course of each deployment.[21]

During his tenure of command, from 1952 to 1954, General Sir Gerald Templer had only a modest impact on the day-to-day operations of the British field army in Malaya. In fact Templer's largest concern (and that of his predecessor, General Sir Harold Briggs) was not the performance of the field army in fighting the insurgents, but the Malayan police force. It was the latter that caused the biggest worries among British and Malayan leaders, because it would be the police force that ultimately would bring control and security to the villages where the ethnic Chinese were resettled. By and large, therefore, the performance of the British field army in fighting the Communist insurgents was never really in question. In the first two years of the Emergency, there was concern among British leaders over frustrated soldiers who applied "rough justice" toward civilians and enemy fighters in the jungle, and there was a lingering desire by senior British tactical leaders to do large-unit sweeps through the jungles. But by 1950, two years before the arrival of Templer, the British Army had settled into an operational framework of small-scale patrols focused on severing the material links between the resettled population and the insurgents. After 1950 British military leaders displayed only minimal concern for the performance of the army, which for the most part was doing exactly what needed to be done throughout the entire twelve-year conflict: hunt down and kill Communist insurgents hiding out in the jungles. As General Keightley noted in a July 1951 letter to the chief of the Imperial General Staff, Field Marshal Sir William Slim, that British Army "battalions are fully deployed and fully occupied at the moment, but this will change as the police improve." A few months later, Slim had gotten an assessment from General Briggs in November 1951 that "the army was doing all that was required of them." Slim emphatically agreed and said he had never been "anything but convinced of this."[22]

However, the actual continuity of British Army operations in Malaya was buried by the counterinsurgency narrative, which instead portrayed a radical transformation after the arrival of Templer. The notion of an army's reinventing itself under an enlightened general became a powerful argument for proponents of counterinsurgency during America's second war in Iraq from 2003 to 2011. It was an idea that seemed to offer a solution to the intractable problems that the war in Iraq was presenting to American military and political leaders by 2006. If the British could turn the war around in Malaya by a tectonic operational shift of the British Army being led by a better general, then why couldn't the same thing be done in Iraq to solve its problems? On the surface it was a perfect cipher that would provide the key to success in Iraq. The precedent was completely devoid of historical truth, yet the counterinsurgency narrative that came to inform strategy and policy in Iraq and Afghanistan was built upon it.

Over the years, and especially since America's loss in the Vietnam War, large-unit sweeps by battalions and brigades thrashing through the woods or jungles trying to flush out insurgents and kill them have come to be seen largely as a waste of time.[23] Instead the argument has been made that these forces should disperse into small units among local populations to win their trust. In Malaya, however, in the first years of the war, large sweeps through the jungles by British Army battalions and even brigades actually proved quite effective. Even if they did not result in capturing or killing many insurgents, they disrupted the insurgents' bases and reduced their material support. General Lockhart commented favorably on large-unit operations a good three years into the Emergency, concluding that they gave "confidence" to the local population and that Communist "bandits" were killed as a result. Lockhart never came close to suggesting that they were a waste of time and that the British Army should stop doing them.[24]

Probably the most important effect of the large-unit sweeps, especially the ones conducted during the first year of the Emergency, was to fragment the insurgents into smaller bands. This was no small matter, because Chin Peng's initial strategy during the first two years of the war was to establish secure base areas around the fringes of the jungles, where he could build large, conventionally organized forces like those Mao had assembled in China. Sociologist Lucien Pye, who conducted field research on the Communist insurgents in Malaya from 1952 to 1953, came to similar conclusions. Pye noted that the large-unit sweeps and conventional operations by the British Army in the early years of the war were the main cause of the Malayan Communists' inability to carry through their initial military strategy of establishing large base areas and concentrating their own forces.[25] For all of the derision that large-unit sweeps would incur within the counterinsurgency narrative, in the early years of the war in Malaya they worked. If the British Army had dispersed itself into small outposts throughout the country to live among the population and win their trust and allegiance, they would have been playing perfectly into the Communist strategy and would have paid heavily in blood for such a foolish operational method.

Even though British Army operations prior to 1950 were having a significant effect against the insurgent enemy, they were not tightly linked with police activities or the massive forced resettlement of the Chinese. In early 1950, the British government placed in command General Sir Harold Briggs, who implemented the measures later known as the Briggs Plan: removing up to half a million ethnic Chinese civilians from the jungle fringes, tailoring procedures so as to keep British field units operating around the resettlement villages, and centralizing control of the spy networks.[26]

Briggs's first priority was a countrywide program to physically separate the ethnic Chinese squatters from the Communist insurgents. Land-hungry and poor, the Chinese had eked out a rough living of small-scale farming and livestock herding by clearing plots of land that they did not legally own along the jungle fringes.[27] Briggs, with the encouragement and support of Sir Henry Gurney, the British high commissioner of Malaya, used the police and military security forces to resettle close to five hundred thousand of these people. The scope of this resettlement was striking, especially considering the number of people being relocated and the short time in which it was accomplished—three years. In general, and when compared to other resettlement programs that proved disastrous for the people involved—such as those in the Second Boer and Vietnam wars—it went relatively smoothly. In part, this was due to the fact that the squatters had lived on the land for only a short time, so there was no deep-seated resistance to being moved. The British Army and Malayan police under the leadership of Briggs also put together an efficient process of moving people to camps that were already set up and waiting for them.

Resettlement was only half of the solution. The other half was more efficient use of military force that worked together with the resettlement program to break the physical link between the resettled squatters and the insurgents. The Briggs Plan put in place "framework operations," in which British Army field units were emplaced with Malayan police forces into certain areas for a long time, allowing these units to learn about the people, the terrain, and the enemy while conducting daily operations to hunt down and kill insurgents and patrol the jungle. Framework operations also came to involve more extensive operations against insurgent bases and suppliers exposed by informers.[28]

The third component of the Briggs Plan was the reorganization of certain parts of the British and Malayan command and intelligence structure. One of the early problems in the Emergency was coordination among police, British field army, and intelligence agencies. Briggs put into place committees at the state, province, and district levels that brought the three counterrevolutionary components together. The result was improved cooperation between the police and the field army and improved dissemination of intelligence on Communist activities. Ultimately it would take the appointment of General Templer as a supremo, an appointed dictator of sorts or boss of bosses who had the combined powers of chief military officer and civilian commissioner, to optimize coordination among the various security, intelligence, military, and civilian units, but the refinements that Briggs put into place were an essential step in that direction. By the middle of 1951, over a year after Briggs had initiated his program, the Ministry of Defense was able to report to Churchill that resettlement was "largely complete" and that there was evidence that the operation was "seriously hampering the communists."[29]

We now know that the Briggs Plan played a key role in pushing the insurgency to alter its strategic course, which paved the way for British victory.[30] In October 1951, the Communist Party of Malaya and its leader, Chin Peng, issued what have come to be known as the October Directives. These directives involved a significant shift in strategy and operations. Previously the insurgents had used force to intimidate the Chinese population to support their efforts. They had also aggressively attacked British and Malayan police and military forces along the jungle fringes and even within the populated areas. The directives called for the insurgents to move deeper into the jungles, scale back attacks on military and government facilities, and focus on political consolidation through persuasion of the population rather than intimidation through violence. The result was a significant lessening of violence and insurgent activity. The headquarters of the British Far East Land Forces (FARELF) issued weekly summations of the enemy situation in Malaya. Acknowledging the effect of the shift in enemy strategy, a July 1952 report noted that the lessening insurgent attacks were the result of a change in "bandit policy and not inability."[31] Over the following months and years, there would be many theories and explanations developed as to what brought about the shift in Communist strategy, but from the Communist side and in the view of its leader, Chin Peng, the cause was pretty clear: the Briggs Plan.

In his memoirs, Chin Peng noted that the Briggs Plan became his "Achilles' heel." Toward the end of 1951, Peng had realized that the military approach he and his fellow Communists had put into place had been rendered "utterly inappropriate." This was a "bitter pill to swallow." The framework operations under the Briggs Plan had caused great hardship among his fighters by cutting off their food supplies. Chin Peng remembered that after eating a helping of "reeds and rice," one felt full, but the feeling lasted barely two hours. "You then became extremely hungry again . . . we persisted this way for months. The Briggs Plan was working." In January 1952, one of Peng's subordinate district headquarters in Selangor Province issued additional guidance to its fighters and political cadre about the current situation. The guidance acknowledged the October Directives' call to a less aggressive policy, to one of more "subtle . . . penetration and organization of the masses." The guidance went on to point out that these changes of strategy had come about because the "resettlement policy" had physically altered their ability to have direct contact with the "masses." Templer had not yet arrived in Malaya.[32]

For the British and Malayans, who were not aware of the October Directives, by the end of 1951, the war seemed to be stalemated, and a few thought it might be lost. One event brought these perceptions into sharp relief. On October 6, 1951, as Sir Henry Gurney was traveling to a retreat house for senior British officers, his motorcade was ambushed, and he and two police guards were killed. For the insurgents, it was a lucky strike; they had no idea that Gurney was in the convoy.[33] But to the British and Malayans, it didn't matter because the death at the hands of the insurgent enemy of the highest civilian figure in Malaya signified that things were not on track and the war was not going in favor of the British. One historian would characterize the end of 1951 for the British in Malaya as the "worst of times." Another historian would write that Gurney's death was "symptomatic of a losing cause." Still another wrote that the situation at the end of 1951 for the British in Malaya was extremely serious and one of "gloom and despondency."[34]

The COIN narrative in its current form relies heavily on superficial interpretation of events. So it is with its use of Malaya.

In fact, based on the October decision by the Communists to alter their strategy, the British were well on their way to ending the war in their favor. General Sir Gerald Templer arrived in Malaya on February 7, 1952. His charter was to combine the role of director of operations of security forces with that of high commissioner in charge of the civil government. In effect, he was a supremo. It was a smart move to create this position, as it offered the opportunity to finally unify the disparate civil and military efforts to end the Emergency.[35] The newly created supremo position also allowed Templer to knock heads together and force the police and field army to cooperate by sharing intelligence on the enemy. He proved to be adept at assessing bureaucratic problems by firsthand observation, then implementing solutions to them with vigor. He did give a renewed sense of energy and purpose to the British and Malayan efforts. He was also not afraid to use coercive power to punish the ethnic Chinese civilians who were supporting the Communist insurgents. About six months following Templer's arrival, insurgent attacks dropped drastically, leading many to credit Templer and his changes.[36] Templer himself believed this to be the case, as he said years later, "The main reason for the British victory over the [Communists] was due to the fact that in my time in that country—and for the first time—the efforts of all sections, whether military or civil, were properly coordinated and used as one whole."[37]

But it is clear from the record—both British and Communist—that the rebels adjusted their strategy not due to the reorganization of British programs and services under Templer but in response to the effects of the Briggs Plan and resettlement. That is what broke the back of the insurgency and put it on a path to defeat. Chin Peng also downplays the role of Templer in defeating the insurgency: "For all the kudos given to Templer . . . he was not, in my estimation, the man who determined the [Malayan Communist] defeat on the battlefield." Instead, the primary cause of the Communist defeat, according to Peng, was actually Templer's predecessor, General Briggs, and his massive resettlement of Chinese settlers, which isolated the Communist insurgents.[38]

The basic assumption of hearts-and-minds counterinsurgency is that the way to defeat the insurgents is by winning the trust and allegiance of local populations, thus causing them to turn toward the government side. This did not happen in Malaya. Instead, a level of control was placed over the Chinese civilians, who had been forcibly moved into resettlement camps called New Villages. The New Villages had barbed-wire fences around them, Malayan police forces and governmental outposts in them, and the British field army conducting operations nearby to sever any remaining links between the resettled civilians and the insurgents in the jungle. Loh Kok Wah, who was a close observer of the people living in the New Villages, noted that the new governmental and administrative "structures" that the British put into place did not contribute to "the winning of the hearts and minds of the villagers. But subtle and sustained control over the villagers was certainly achieved."[39]

It was clear to Templer's deputy General Lockhart what had brought about the lowered level of insurgent activity. In October 1952, when it had become strikingly noticeable that things had changed, the general described British operations from April 1950 to September 1951 under the Briggs Plan as the crucial ingredient in breaking the insurgency. Lockhart noted that "as these measures grew in effectiveness the terrorists suffered steadily increasing casualty rates." According to General Lockhart, the tipping point was not the arrival of General Templer in February 1952 but instead the October Directives of 1951, which he said caused the Communists to conduct a "drastic review" of their situation.[40]

By early spring of 1952, the effect of the October Directives began to show. In early April a weekly intelligence summary for Templer noted that there appeared to be a trend developing of lowered insurgent activity, especially in violent attacks against civilian and government forces. Yet the reasons why the attacks were dropping remained unclear to Templer's analysts. There was speculation that it could be due to lowered morale of the Communists, which was apparently producing an increase in surrenders, but it was still hard to figure the reasons behind this trend of lowering violence.[41]

In March 1952, the British acquired from a captured insurgent a copy of the October Directives.[42] Over the next several months into summer, the causal factor for the lowering of violence began to make more and more sense to Templer's intelligence analysts. By July the analysts had concluded that the preceding months of May and June were very "gratifying" for British security forces because the attack levels by the Communists continued to drop and were well below the levels of the same period of the previous year. The analysts cautioned in a July report to Templer that it should be "remembered that the Malayan Communists had turned its main effort away from terrorism toward consolidating" its links with the ethnic Chinese. It was clear to these intelligence analysts that the primary cause for the lowering of violence was the change of strategy. To be sure, British security forces and operational methods played a role too, and the analysts noted that the key ingredient that caused the Communists' ongoing problem in the field was the "government's policy of resettlement and food control," which was having a devastating effect on enemy morale. In another July report, the intelligence analysts also concluded that the lower level of insurgent violence was fundamentally due to the Communist change of strategy, largely resulting from the cumulative effects of the Briggs Plan and resettlement, rather than a change in Communist "capacity" to carry out attacks brought about by British forces under Templer.[43]

By fall of 1952, insurgent-driven violence had dropped off sharply for three primary reasons: first, the resettlement of over half a million ethnic Chinese, which physically separated them from the insurgents; second, military operations by the British Army that started in 1948 and remained largely the same throughout the entire war, successfully attacking and killing insurgents and breaking their links with the resettled populations; and third, because of the first two, the change in strategy by Chin Peng and his Malayan insurgents, which reduced violence. It is not that the improvements in organizational structure, intelligence operations, police effectiveness, and Malayan morale were not important; they were. However, they should be seen as optimization of a strategy that had been put into place before Templer ever rode onto the scene.[44]

Toward the end of 1952, these reasons were being buried by the idea that General Templer, as personification of a "new" approach, defeated the insurgency. A September study by Templer's staff highlighted the drastic reduction in Communist-initiated "incidents," at their lowest level since April 1950. Other indicators were strongly positive as well. There had been an increase over the previous three months in contacts that were initiated by British security forces, meaning that they and not the enemy were on the offensive. There were fewer acts of terrorism against civilians and, equally important, the "terrorists" were having "great difficulty in obtaining sufficient supplies of food." In short, and although the report did not come out and say so, the British were on the path to crushing the insurgency and ending the Emergency.[45]

There were many reasons why things had changed so drastically over the last nine months, argued Templer's staff. In a significant shift from their spring analyses, the staff provided a prioritized list of reasons, including food denial, resettlement, better cooperation between the police and field army units, and better propaganda. But the "most important single factor," according to the staff, was "the appointment of General Templer as the High Commissioner and Director of Operations." According to this report, Templer had "given a tremendous lift to morale . . . and imbued the security forces and administration with a new spirit and the will to win."[46]

Templer himself had a strong hand in building the narrative. On his first trip back to London to report to Parliament on the progress of the war, Templer focused his discussions with government leaders and the media on the statistics that showed lowered levels of violence. At a press conference in the colonial office in London in June 1952, Templer boasted that "the progress made during the last six months gives cause for confidence. . . . In that period the monthly average of terrorists killed or captured has been ninety-three. Security force casualties have been reduced by thirty percent and those of civilian by eighteen percent." Templer concluded the briefing by noting that finally on the ground in

Malaya, he had the right inputs in place, or as he put it, "We have a good team working in Malaya and we are going to restore law and order."[47]

The narrative was catching on in London and beyond. The Australian *Sydney Morning Herald* in August 1952 trumpeted Templer's achievements as a "brightening of the Malayan horizon" and said that after "four years of costly and indecisive guerrilla war, . . . Templer was getting results at last." The London *Daily Telegraph* in December 1952 called Templer's actions in Malaya "decisive" in breaking the insurgency and ascribed to his leadership the positive turn of events since his arrival. The *Daily Mail Reporter* pointed out to its readers that the situation in Malaya today is in "better shape" than in the past two years and quoted the British general in command of its Far Eastern Forces as saying that Templer was "the chief reason for the greatly improved situation." In the United States, Templer was on the cover of *Time* magazine in December 1952 with the cover line, "Templer of Malaya: The jungle has been neutralized."

Toward the end of Templer's command, in late 1953, the *Sunday Express* of London noted that as the supremo in Malaya, Templer "brought the six year jungle war practically to a close." A few months later, in early 1955, the *Northern Echo* of England boasted that "history will record that his . . . victories in the political as well as military fields . . . led to the destruction of many communist terrorist bands." The *Daily Telegraph* again chimed in with the chorus of Templer praise, stating that in Malaya "thanks to General Templer's own direction . . . the antiterrorist campaign has subdued its stubborn enemy."[48]

For the British, the victory of arms in Malaya came at a time when they were still stinging from multiple colonial losses during World War II. Showing progress and eventual victory in Malaya by 1955 allowed Britain to regain a certain stature on the world stage after its humiliating departure from Palestine just a few years earlier and the chaos and huge number of deaths at India's breakup in 1947. Success in Malaya provided apparent proof that a Communist insurgency could be tamed and British decolonization managed effectively. Most important, success in Malaya seemed to represent the efficacy rather than atrophy of British power in the world. The narrative of a triumph of British arms led by General Templer (who was cast in the role of Field Marshal Montgomery from World War II) fit squarely with British sensibilities.[49]

But other writers and observers of the Malaya scene at the time were aware of the primary cause for the improved situation. Allington Kennard, a British writer for the Malaya *Straights Times* who had spent many years in Malaya and had written often about the Emergency, shrilly noted in May 1954 that the perception with the British public that things had gotten better because of General Templer was "an illusion." The improvement in the overall situation had much more to do with the effects of Templer's predecessors and the implementation of the Briggs Plan, argued Kennard. He ended by pointing out that the Malayan Communists should get a large part of the credit, since in October 1951 they "issued a directive" that ordered their fighters to stand down and reduce attacks.[50] Another writer for the *Straights Times*, Alex Jossey, criticized a recent article in the British magazine *The Economist* for giving the credit to Templer for "saving Malaya in 1952." Jossey testily noted:

Unfortunately in this connection the magazine makes no mention whatsoever of the notorious directive sent out by the Malayan communist party just before Sir Henry Gurney's murder. This document is of considerable importance because it was in fact an admission that communist terrorism in Malaya had failed . . . that the Malaya communists had reached this conclusion before General Templer had assumed office in Malaya.[51]

In the post–World War II period, the British campaign in Malaya from 1948 to 1960 is still widely cited as the foremost historical example of how to win a war against insurgents. As FM 3-24 claimed many years later, Malaya's historical lessons were relevant for *any* insurgency the United States might find itself fighting. A recent history published by British historian David French on the way of British counterinsurgency argues that the Americans have come to see "Templer and the Malayan Campaign . . . as the personification of a successful counterinsurgency leader, and the Malayan Campaign as the epitome of how to fight such a campaign." Yet French goes on to point out that the key to success for the British in Malaya was "not winning the hearts and minds of the population but establishing physical control over them."[52]

If the United States had never fought a war in Vietnam from 1965 to 1973, the British counterinsurgency campaign in Malaya would have gathered dust on the trophy shelf of its imperial history. But with America's loss in the Vietnam War, Malaya came to be seen as the classroom of counterinsurgency, filled with useful lessons as to why the United States lost its war in Southeast Asia and how it could have won.

# 3

## VIETNAM: THE FIRST BETTER WAR
## THAT WASN'T

*The tactics changed within fifteen minutes of Abrams taking command.*
—Lewis Sorley, *A Better War*, 1999[1]

*In the first three years of the war we were trying to use conventional tactics against an unconventional enemy. That strategy failed miserably. And it was not until General Abrams came in and took over from General Westmoreland who changed the strategy to a counterinsurgency strategy which was designed to protect the population. We saw significant progress against the insurgency and then, by 1971, three years later, it was essentially defeated.*
—General (retired) Jack Keane, architect
of the Iraq surge, 2011[2]

For nearly two generations, American military analysts—and Americans generally—have struggled to come to terms with the meaning and implications of the United States' defeat in Vietnam. The significance of this protracted debate, which has played out in academic journals, the media, and the American military, cannot be overstated, for it bears directly on how American policy makers and military planners have come to think about the projection of U.S. military power into distant parts of the world. The standard critique of American military involvement in Vietnam, which began to emerge while the war was being fought and came into full force shortly after America's loss, was that the war was unwinnable and American strategy should have discerned this basic truth. The eminent diplomatic historian George Herring summed up this interpretation best when he wrote that the Vietnam War was unwinnable at a "moral or material cost most Americans deemed acceptable."[3] Because the United States was not willing to fight the war without limits—namely by allowing the U.S. ground forces to launch an all-out attack on North Vietnam and neighboring countries, committing millions and millions of troops to do it—the war simply could never have been won. Equally important, the South Vietnamese government never came close to establishing legitimacy with the bulk of the Vietnamese people.

Other interpretations have always competed with this correct view. Their basic premise was that the Vietnam War *could* have been won *if only* the U.S. Army had fought it differently on the ground. This better-war thesis, as it came to be known, argued that the U.S. Army fumbled at the war from 1965 through the middle of 1968 under its commander General William C. Westmoreland. Westmoreland's implementation of a flawed strategy was due to the army's desire to fight a conventional war, using massive amounts of American firepower to destroy the Communist forces in Vietnam instead of focusing on the critical element for success, winning the hearts and minds of the South Vietnamese people. The result was that the United States military squandered the loyalty of the people because of the amount of death and destruction it caused from the excessive fighting and the use of firepower. But then, shortly after the Tet Offensive, in the middle of 1968, a general named Abrams came on board. Schooled in the arts of classic counterinsurgency warfare modeled on the British Army in Malaya, he turned the American army around, reinvented it, and defeated the Communists in the South. The American military didn't lose the war. Hippies and college students, antiwar protesters, weak politicians in Congress, and a lack of American "will" prevented continued support to the South Vietnamese government after the U.S. withdrawal, thus making it vulnerable to a North Vietnamese invasion.[4]

The better-war thesis, however, has much more to do with the present than with the past. It provides a more usable history for those who believe modern wars of occupation can be won simply. It tricks Americans into thinking that the war would have been winnable from the start if only the army had done counterinsurgency correctly. This untruth became a bedrock theme of counterinsurgency doctrine as it emerged during the troop surge of 2007.


In 1974, shortly after returning home to the United States from multiple tours of duty in Vietnam, Lieutenant General Julian J. Ewell, former commander of the Ninth Infantry Division, wrote an extended review and analysis of his division's actions in the Mekong Delta during 1968 and 1969. The operations included pacification programs designed to build schools, bridges, and other elements of rural infrastructure and generally improve the lot of the population through civic action with the goal of separating the people from the National Liberation Front (NLF) fighters (referred to at the time as Viet Cong), connecting them instead to the South Vietnamese government. *Sharpening the Combat Edge*, as the general's after-action review was titled, includes a section on pacification operations, which displays a number of photos of American soldiers trying to help the rural population. One photo has a black American enlisted soldier fording a small muddy stream with a belt of machine-gun ammunition draped around his chest while at the same time toting on his back a young and apparently happy Vietnamese girl. Another photo depicts the Ninth Infantry Division's band, with tubas, clarinets, and French horns, playing songs for a group of Vietnamese in a rural hamlet, with the caption "Breaking the language barrier."[5]

But there was another component to Ninth Infantry Division operations in the Mekong Delta—fighting and killing South

Vietnamese rebel combat units—the People's Liberation Armed Forces (PLAF).[6] According to a rather fantastic report issued days after the division's Operation Speedy Express in the first half of 1969, as many as "10,899 enemy" were killed in action (KIA), yet only around seven hundred weapons were found.[7]

A Viet Cong company commander from the Mekong Delta noted in his diary what he feared most about the Ninth Infantry Division's operations. It was not the pacification programs; it was the search-and-destroy missions. He noted that the division had "much greater firepower" than his PLAF fighters and lamented that American tactics based on the quick application of firepower had been very "effective" against the PLAF forces in his area, to the point where they had been put in "great danger."[8]

But the PLAF and its overarching political structure, the National Liberation Front (NLF), survived, and its core remained strong in the countryside. Senior Communist leaders in the South noted by the end of 1971 that even with its pacification programs and superior firepower, "the enemy has achieved some temporary results, but is steadily failing at implementing his basic schemes . . . they failed to destroy or wipe out the revolutionary infrastructure of our local and guerrilla forces."[9]

Both Westmoreland and Abrams conceived of pacification and combat action against PLAF and North Vietnamese army main forces as "one war." The fact that Ewell's division combined these two types of operations demonstrates that they were both fundamental objectives of army counterinsurgency doctrine. The relative weight given to each would, in the words of historian Andrew Birtle, "remain dynamic throughout the war." Over the seven years of major American military commitment, from 1965 to 1972, there would be debates, discussions, and shifts in emphasis of these approaches. However, the basic framework of military strategy in Vietnam remained continuous.[10]

The better-war thesis, however, posits radical change between the generalships of Westmoreland and Abrams. After Vietnam, when the thesis started to grow in influence, it fit nicely in a narrative starting from the British war in Malaya. Both could be claimed to be wars that were nearly lost by armies fumbling at counterinsurgency until rescued by savior generals. Yet the historical record shows continuity rather than discontinuity between the generals and their tactics.

The wars in Malaya and Vietnam were vastly different in scope, context, and scale. In South Vietnam, Communist forces had elaborate sanctuary bases in Cambodia, Laos, and North Vietnam, which generally could not be attacked by the American military due to political constraints placed on it by the Johnson administration. In Malaya, however, the Malayan insurgents could be isolated, a key tactical advantage for the British. In South Vietnam, the Americans and their South Vietnamese allies not only had to fight insurgents who used guerrilla tactics, but also confronted a major part of the North Vietnamese army and a significant number of South Vietnamese Communists who were organized along conventional military lines. In Malaya, after twelve years of fighting, the British Army had 470 soldiers killed in action. In Vietnam after seven years of war, the United States had more than 58,200 killed. The levels of destruction wrought upon the civilian population also shows the vast differences between these two wars. In Malaya approximately five thousand civilians died; in Vietnam the number was close to 3 million.[11]

The path to American involvement in Vietnam began at the end of World War II. After the war, French attempted to reestablish control over its former Indochinese possessions of Cochin, Annam, and Tonkin, as well as Cambodia and Laos. However, Vietnamese nationalists under Ho Chi Minh resisted recolonization and between 1946 and 1954 fought to expel the French. Because the Vietnamese resistance, the Viet Minh, was largely

Communist, the United States saw in them further proof of a worldwide Communist effort led by the Soviet Union to take over the "free countries of Asia." The logic of the Cold War strategy of containment of Communist expansion demanded American action to oppose what were presumed to be Soviet proxies. Over the course of the eight-year Indochina War, the United States committed vast amounts of resources and supplies—but not manpower—to support the French. Yet at the end of 1953, the French army found itself surrounded at Dien Bien Phu by a Viet Minh army under General Vo Nguyen Giap, and the French urgently asked the United States for firepower support—possibly nuclear weapons—to stave off defeat. President Eisenhower refused the request and recommended that the French sign a treaty with the Viet Minh, which they did at Geneva in 1954. The Geneva Accords split the country in two along the 17th parallel with North Vietnam under the Communists and the South under a noncommunist government allied with the United States. Yet the Geneva Accords only froze in place the fundamental political and social problems dividing the Vietnamese people. The Accords had scheduled unification elections for 1956, but the differences between the North and South—and fear on the part of Eisenhower and the South Vietnamese government that the North would win the election—led them to cancel it. Even the physical separation was untidy, as the partition left a substantial number of Viet Minh Communists in South Vietnam. That core group would produce a homegrown Communist insurgency against the South Vietnamese government in Saigon.[12]

As the United States became involved in Vietnam, there were essentially four warring sides. The Communist North sought to reunify all of Vietnam under its writ and produce a Maoist social revolution in the South. South Vietnam's main political aim was to maintain its existence against that North Vietnamese threat. The Communist insurgents in South Vietnam, collectively coming to be known as the National Liberation Front or Viet Cong, sought to overthrow the Saigon regime, to unify Vietnam under a Communist government, bring Maoist social revolution in the South, and, when the United States entered the war, expel all Americans from Vietnam. The fourth side, the United States, aimed to maintain a viable, effective, and anticommunist South Vietnamese government.[13]

From 1954 and the Geneva Accords to the beginning of substantial American commitment of conventional ground and air forces, the American role in Vietnam was largely of advice and material support to the South Vietnamese government and military although it grew substantially after 1961. From 1956 to 1958 South Vietnamese president Ngo Dinh Diem aggressively pursued the remaining Communists in South Vietnam and nearly defeated them. But by 1959 North Vietnam decided to act and began to send large amounts of material support to the South Vietnamese insurgents. Diem's regime came under increasing pressure from elements in his own country that sought major societal and governmental changes. Those pressures combined with the stepped-up PLAF activity produced a number of serious tactical drubbings for the Army of the Republic of Vietnam (ARVN) at battles like Ap Bac in 1963. As a result, in October 1963, a number of generals (with tacit American approval) launched a coup and in the process killed President Diem. But that coup only produced more government instability over the next four years. In late 1964, North Vietnamese army regiments began to move south along the Ho Chi Minh Trail through Laos and Cambodia and into South Vietnam. The stage was set for a commitment of major amounts of American blood and treasure.[14]

In responding to the growing instability of the South Vietnamese government and more military setbacks for the ARVN, President Lyndon B. Johnson in 1965 approved a recommendation from his senior military leaders and decided to take more forceful and substantial measures. Johnson approved a major escalation of ground and air forces that culminated in mid-1968 with over five hundred thousand troops and a substantial commitment of air-power that for three years included a bombing campaign against North Vietnam.[15]

During those three years of major American escalation, the United States fought two wars on the ground in South Vietnam and a third in the air over North Vietnam. The first war was a war of combat action against the North Vietnamese army units that were in South Vietnam and the PLAF regular military forces. Because political constraints put in place by Johnson prevented Westmoreland from taking the war directly into Cambodia, Laos, and North Vietnam itself, the idea was to use American ground troops to force the North to pull out of its positions in South Vietnam. The other war on the ground attempted to pacify the countryside by eliminating the PLAF insurgents and their infra-structure by improving security, economic conditions, South Vietnamese government–controlled physical infrastructure, and governance. The war in the air over North Vietnam was called Rolling Thunder, and it used the American air force and navy to bomb selected industrial and transportation targets in the North. The United States also conducted bombing campaigns to try to halt the supplies brought down from North Vietnam and into the South through Laos and Cambodia along the Ho Chi Minh Trail.[16]

Westmoreland (as did Abrams) actually saw both of these ground wars as essentially one. Westmoreland referred to this one-war concept by way of a metaphor of a boxer, whose right hand stays close to the body and defends the population through the process of pacification carried out by the South Vietnamese gov-ernment and army (with American assistance). The left hand—in Westmoreland's mind the more powerful one because it jabs and therefore maintains the initiative—strikes continuously at the North Vietnamese army and Viet Cong main force units to keep them at bay, away from South Vietnamese pacification efforts.[17]

During the first months of major American action in Vietnam, Westmoreland reminded his commanders to not become so enamored with battlefield success that they take their eyes off of what was essential to the success of their mission: pacification of the rural areas. He lectured his subordinate commanders about the nature of the war in Vietnam: "The War in Vietnam is a political as well as military war. It is political because the ultimate goal is to regain the loyalty and cooperation of the people." Westmoreland reasoned that it made more sense for the South Vietnamese government and its army to conduct the pacification effort, while the better-trained and better-equipped U.S. military took on the NVA and VC. In March 1966, a special study group initiated by the army chief of staff, General Harold K. Johnson, issued a report titled *A Program for the Pacification and Long-Term Development of South Vietnam*, or PROVN; it approved Westmoreland's strategy. The number-one priority for the U.S. military under Westmoreland's command, argued PROVN, was "the defeat of Peoples' Army of Vietnam [NVA] and Main Force Viet Cong units and the reduction of Viet Cong guerillas." This was necessary, the writers argued, because fighting these main-force units by the U.S. military would provide a shield for South Vietnamese pacification.[18] The early American battles of Ia Drang in November 1965 and search-and-destroy operations such as Cedar Falls in early 1967 were products of Westmoreland's overall military strategy, which sought to balance pacification with combat action. In Westmoreland's thinking, if the NVA and PLAF were not pushed back from pacification efforts, they would easily disrupt such efforts with military strikes and intimidation. He saw the two methods as tightly bound up into one overall military strategy. For one to work, the other had to work too. The trick, of course, for Westmoreland (and later Abrams) was to do just that, make them both work in a country wracked with civil war and in the face of a significant conventional fighting force—the NVA and PLAF—that would react and fight back.[19]

Westmoreland had a background in counterinsurgency warfare. During his years as superintendent at West Point from 1960 to 1963, just before his Vietnam command, Westmoreland worked assiduously to integrate the most cutting-edge ideas on counterinsurgency into the cadet-training programs and curricula. The changes he brought about made clear his commitment to understanding this new counterinsurgency warfare and to ensuring that the future army leaders from West Point would understand it too. Westmoreland also organized counterinsurgency conferences at West Point and brought such speakers as the French counterinsurgency expert David Galula.[20]

In the years leading up to Vietnam, the American army as a whole was also trying to understand counterinsurgency warfare. Army strategists cast their net widely, considering numerous historical cases of counterinsurgency warfare to help them write a new doctrine for a new era. They paid close attention to the British in Malaya, to the Huk rebellion in the Philippines in the 1950s, to Che Guevara's activities in Cuba, to the French in Algeria, and of course to Mao's successful rebellion in China. On the eve of major American escalation in Vietnam, the army issued a new manual on counterinsurgency warfare, FM 31-22 *U.S. Army Counterinsurgency Forces*. The manual noted that counterinsurgency was ultimately a "war for men's minds" in which winning popular support revolved around establishing "civic action" programs that would build the institutions of a modern state. But counterinsurgency warfare also involved the American army killing the insurgent enemy, and FM 31-22 cautioned its readers not to forget that essential task.[21]

After the initial battles fought by the First Cavalry Division at places such as Ia Drang in late 1965, the NVA and PLAF main force units realized that they had to be much more careful with how they confronted superior American firepower. They began to avoid large-scale combat at the level of an Ia Drang whenever possible, aiming instead to hit, cause damage, and then move off. By 1966, after a year of hard fighting, General Westmoreland advised General Earl Wheeler, the chairman of the Joint Chiefs of Staff, that the United States was in for a "long pull" of a war in South Vietnam. He acknowledged that American airpower had caused significant disruption to the Communist supply chain in North Vietnam, on the Ho Chi Minh Trail in Laos, and in western Cambodia but said the United States still confronted a formidable fighting force, which American military operations would continue to repel from pacification areas.

From the outset of the war, then, American forces were compelled to approach the conflict by accepting the political constraints placed upon them and then devising the two-part strategy. Westmoreland knew quite well that search and destroy could succeed only if the people outside the cities, the vast majority, could be forced or persuaded to oppose the revolution.[22]

In March and April 1967, the First Brigade of the 101st Airborne Division conducted Operation Summerall in the Darlac Province of central Vietnam. The brigade's concept of the operation was clear and simple: conduct "search and destroy operations" to track down and kill NVA units that had been operating in the area. Being successful at search and destroy would allow the brigade to shield the pacification efforts by the South Vietnamese army that were occurring in the surrounding areas. The operation lasted from the middle of March through most of April. In the first phase, one of the brigade's infantry battalions conducted an airmobile assault into an area believed to be used by a VC company. The battalion surrounded a hamlet and reported capturing seven VC fighters. The battalion then "extracted 43 civilians" from the hamlet by air and moved them to the nearby government-controlled village of Cung Son. Other actions produced sporadic contact with NVA units and a handful of kills and captures. The brigade also carried out "civic action" programs designed to provide Vietnamese villagers with food, other provisions, and medical assistance. Commenting on tactical actions like these of the 101st Airborne Division in 1967, General Westmoreland noted that in response to his search-and-destroy operations, "the enemy was on the run, fighting defensively" and trying to avoid contact with American ground units and their superior firepower.[23]

In the Central Highlands of South Vietnam, a swath of mountains in the central western part of the country, in April 1967, the First Brigade of the Fourth Infantry Division was part of Operation Sam Houston, designed to "locate and destroy enemy forces" in Pleiku Province. The brigade's operations officer noted that it was especially important to ensure, once "contact was established," that "artillery and airstrikes were employed on the enemy to inflict maximum casualties . . . before he could break contact." For most of the rest of 1967, the brigade and the division took part in another large-scale search-and-destroy operation in the highlands, Operation Francis Marion. It focused on the western edge of the highlands, along the Cambodian border. This area was home to significant numbers of North Vietnamese army troops. In the first phase of Francis Marion, especially bloody contact was made with NVA regulars. On May 18, a rifle company from the first brigade stumbled upon an entire NVA battalion, beginning a battle that eventually involved a battalion's worth of American troops against an entire enemy regiment. Although the result was reportedly 157 enemy killed in action, it was costly for the Americans, who had 45 killed in this short but sharp and bloody search-and-destroy engagement. In conforming to Westmoreland's one-war strategy, the brigade also conducted a number of civic-action programs in villages. In one of them, one of the brigade's infantry battalions distributed "450 kilograms of rice, 250 kilograms of wheat, and 450 bars of soap."[24]

By the beginning of 1968, Westmoreland's strategy of "one war," which combined search and destroy with pacification, was having an effect. The Tet Offensive, which began at the end of January 1968, was intended at least in part to draw American and South Vietnamese (SVN) military power out of countryside by attacking targets in the cities. Tet was also an admission that the Viet Cong's strategy of defeating the ARVN and the U.S. military decisively on the battlefield had failed and that something else needed to be attempted—which caused a transition to what would become its "talk-fight" strategy.[25]

From the middle of 1968 to 1972, under Westmoreland's replacement, General Creighton Abrams, the U.S. military continued its search-and-destroy operations and increased its emphasis on pacification, as well as on Vietnamization—gradually turning the war over to the South Vietnamese. General Abrams formalized the term *one war* in 1969 in a strategic guidance issued to his subordinate commanders.[26] But Abrams's one-war strategy should not be seen as a radical departure from what came before. After the Tet Offensive, which seriously damaged the PLAF, Abrams did increase emphasis on pacification, but again, this shift was one of *degree* and not of *kind*. As historian Graham Cosmas has affirmed, "On most matters, the new MACV commander [Abrams] shared the views of his predecessor."[27]

The change of command from Westmoreland to Abrams looms large in many accounts of the war, allegedly marking a major strategic transition from Westmoreland's traditional approach to Abrams's embrace of counterinsurgency. In Lewis Sorley's 1999 book *A Better War*, he argues that American tactics "changed within fifteen minutes of Abrams taking command." But the history tells a different story: whatever tactical changes Abrams made in Vietnam, they were minimal and still set within the continuity of the one-war military strategy that Westmoreland had started. In fact, the overall operational framework for American ground forces—search and destroy using large doses of American firepower, combined with pacification—changed very little. Shortly after assuming command of MACV in July 1968, Abrams issued a directive to his subordinate field commanders in which he told them he was prepared to give any of them additional firepower to achieve "the decisive battles" against the enemy in the days ahead. "The commanders who find, fix, and engage the enemy will get the priority," he wrote. A few months later, in September 1968, Abrams issued another directive to his commanders, wherein he encouraged them to maintain the methods and techniques that they had developed over the four proceeding years of fighting in South Vietnam. Abrams stressed the importance of finding the enemy and then "piling on" more combat units, artillery, napalm, and bombs. In this sense, the generalship of Abrams was directly in line with Westmoreland's. The following month, in a Saturday discussion with his staff, Abrams quipped that air force B-52 bombers were his mobile reserve, "the theater commander's artillery." The way American ground forces conducted daily, routine combat operations changed very little from what they had been doing since 1965.[28]

This continuity between Westmoreland and Abrams can be seen in the daily journals and monthly after-action reports. One such instance was the Fourth Infantry Division (4ID) and its operations in and around Pleiku in the Central Highlands in 1969. The purpose of these operations, as the division's monthly assessments stated, was to "detect and destroy enemy forces attempting to disrupt government pacification" efforts, pummeling them with additional ground forces and firepower. In one instance in late February, a scouting party from one of the division's infantry battalions noticed a large bevy of elephants "with packs" that were believed to be used for moving enemy supplies. The scouting party reported that the elephants "were taken under fire" which resulted in "15 elephants KIA, and 7–8 WIA." At around the same time, the village of Kon Horing, about fifteen kilometers south of Pleiku, got caught in the middle of a significant engagement between elements of the Fourth Infantry Division and the Twenty-fourth NVA regiment. As a result, the division command post reported that close to 70 civilians were killed, over 250 had been wounded, and "125 houses destroyed by burning [and] 525 families inhabit these houses." The action ended up producing about "3000 refugees." Fortunately, noted the command post's log, "the situation was under control."[29] Such was the ongoing destructive effect of fighting among the civilian population of South Vietnam. And within this environment of intense combat, attempts to pacify the rural populations by winning hearts and minds continued.

The Tet Offensive of 1968 and the extensive fighting that ensued significantly reduced the numbers of PLAF fighters and NLF political cadres in the countryside, producing a vacuum that the pacification campaigns sought to fill. The first of these campaigns was the Accelerated Pacification Campaign (APC), which started in November 1968 and was completed three months later, in January 1969. This was a spasm of pacification energy aimed at establishing territorial security-force presence in as many contested hamlets and villages as possible and at creating village governing bodies connected to the government. At least in terms of an increase in the numbers of territorial security-force men in the villages and in the numbers of village pacifications carried out, it was a success. According to the Hamlet Evaluation System (HES), the APC had significantly increased the number of erstwhile contested hamlets and villages on the government's side. Of the 1,317 contested hamlets that the APC targeted to convert to government control, HES concluded that by the end of the APC only about 15 percent were left under Viet Cong control. General Abrams and William Colby, the newly appointed director of Civil Operations and Revolutionary Development Support (CORDS, the pacification program), were encouraged by the apparent success of the APC and used it to persuade President Thieu of the importance of continuing programs of pacification in the countryside for the next three years.[30]

To be sure, many parts of the countryside had become relatively quiet, and the PLAF had been significantly weakened by the pacification campaigns. Due to the aggressive expansion of territorial-force outposts in thousands of hamlets and villages, PLAF cadres had become cut off from large segments of the rural population. Their military strength too had been decimated by American firepower. They were pushed up against a wall in wretched sanctuaries close to the Laotian and Cambodian borders and in other isolated spots in the interior. But they were not defeated, and a critical core element remained in place and would emerge once again by the end of 1972, after the Easter Offensive and on the eve of American withdrawal.[31]

In the end, neither Westmoreland's nor Abrams's one-war strategy could overcome the greater will of the Vietnamese Communists to win. Writing years after the collapse of the South Vietnamese government, former South Vietnamese army officer Hoang Ngoc Lung perceived the totality of the Communist commitment to victory in the South. According to Hoang, in the long run, it wasn't better and more ingenious tactics and operations on the part of the Communists that won the war for them, but a "coherent, long-term, immutable devotion to a strategy that assumed, without question, that victory would come eventually to their side." It was total war that the Communists fought, noted Hoang, and the South Vietnamese and the Americans "could not match this concept with any theory of war that they were prepared or willing to follow." In 1969, in what was called his "last will and testament," North Vietnamese leader Ho Chi Minh said that "although our people will endure many more hardships . . . our fight will inevitably end in total victory."[32]

Moreover, even though the PLAF and NLF political infrastructure had been seriously weakened, the government of South Vietnam was never able to win the allegiance of large parts of the rural population. A military adviser in Hua Nghia at the time, Major Stuart Herrington, noted that it was true the pacification efforts were "building schools and clinics and the like, but the government still was viewed with basic cynicism." The reason, according to Herrington, was that "corruption at all levels generally had the effect of angering the people." Herrington went on to observe that the only way rural folk could be reasonably assured of safety from military operations and American and South Vietnamese firepower was to move to a "district capital" or other large government-controlled village. Herrington made this observation in 1971 at the purported height of the pacification campaigns.[33]

Although the appearance of successful pacification through efforts such as land redistribution, the establishment of local governing cadres, and the improvement of local economies and infrastructure convinced American military and political leaders that perhaps hearts and minds were finally being won, such a notion was a chimera. What brought about the perception that the countryside had become pacified was the fact that large numbers of civilians were forcibly removed from contested hamlets and villages and resettled in areas controlled by the government.

It was the hard hand of war, of death and destruction brought about by military operations. A firefight here or an ambush there by a PLAF unit would bring about massive American or SVN retaliation, often destroying homes in hamlets and villages in the process. In order to survive, many villagers simply left the war zones, moving closer to government facilities, which would at least provide safety from American air and ground attacks.[34]

What was proving effective in Vietnam was *not* better programs of pacification or the winning of hearts and minds, but instead a "draining of the pond," to use a metaphor of the time. A CORDS history completed in early 1973, looking back on almost ten years of war, noted that over "seven million Vietnamese have been forced to leave their homes due to military activities." The United States Agency for International Development concluded that in the cities of Da Nang, Qui Nhon, and Cam Ran, over 60 percent of the total population were refugees who had entered the city between 1962 and 1972. A Viet Cong fighter from the village of Quang Dien in Hue Province in the north reported to his superiors that in using "sweep and occupy tactics the enemy has attempted to . . . annihilate all our cadres and local guerillas in order to . . . maintain a permanent pressure on the local population so that the people have to move into their area. . . . This intention has been realized successfully. There are no more people left . . . all the people already moved to the enemy area."[35]

Fighting in the Mekong Delta village of Binh Duc had this effect. Many of the village inhabitants left in the years following the Tet Offensive because of military operations by the ARVN against the PLAF. The fighting also brought about a significant reduction in the Communists' guerrilla forces and political cadres. Because a significant portion of the population of the village had left for government-controlled areas due to the fighting, there were mostly only older men, women, and children left. It was difficult, therefore, for the Communists to collect taxes and material support because of the reduction in the size of the population from whom they drew their support. The increased placement of territorial security-force outposts caused further tactical problems for the PLAF, because they were usually sited on trails or roadways and thus physically severed links between the Communists and few remaining people in the village.[36]

After the Vietnam War, some writers and analysts saw one U.S. Marine Corps pacification effort as the operational key to winning the war in the South. The Combined Action Program (CAP) involved dispersal of small groups of marines (usually no more than twenty men) out into villages to work with local security forces in fighting the Viet Cong. In this program, certain analysts saw a more enlightened way of fighting the war. This conception of what Marine Corps CAPS actually did is inaccurate, however. Marine Combined Action Platoons (CAPs) were really nothing more than dispersed combat marines doing search-and-destroy missions at a small-unit level alongside South Vietnamese forces they were training. They fought aggressively, and their presence boosted the fighting performance of the territorial forces and thus reduced the Viet Cong in the area. But they did not do anything of substance beyond killing the enemy. In the northeastern village of My Thuy Phuong, which had a CAP in it, a councilman said that "one night there was a frightful shooting . . . out in the rice fields. . . . When we got up the next day we saw the [Marines] and [Vietnamese] soldiers bringing in the two bodies, carrying them in a raincoat. We knew the dead men, but the soldiers said they were VC." A contemporaneous observer of My Thuy Phuong noted that the CAPs did bring about an improvement in the fighting effectiveness of the local government forces, "but like the large Marine operations, the CAPS also brought disruption and fear to village life."[37]

General Abrams and his military and civilian advisers came to believe their own reporting. They saw the pacification programs as a huge success. Abrams was so sure of the success of pacification that he was willing to "bet a cigar or something that everybody's kind of happy out there in Long An and Hua Nghia [provinces] because there isn't much going on." The American military and civilian leadership in Vietnam became convinced that they had a "better war" on their hands and, more important, that traditional military victory was still in the cards. Even though the United States military was withdrawing from Vietnam and turning the war over to the SVN government in the process of Vietnamization, the perceived successes of pacification allowed General Abrams and his commanders to focus on using firepower to disrupt the movements of the NVA through Laos and Cambodia. The origin of the better-war thesis for Vietnam was General Abrams himself in his routine discussions and briefings with staff, commanders, and visitors, which were recorded on audiotape and transcribed in Lewis Sorley's *Vietnam Chronicles*. It becomes quite clear from the hundreds and hundreds of pages of transcriptions from 1970 to 1972 that Abrams and those around him believed they had won the war in the South and therefore could concentrate on the part of the war they were most comfortable with: fighting the North Vietnamese army with American firepower.[38]

As a campaign to win the hearts and minds of the rural folk and connect them to the South Vietnamese government, pacification had failed.[39] To be sure, the PLAF and its parent revolutionary movement, the NLF, had shrunk significantly due to the effects of military operations.[40] However, their "core was very deep," in the words of historian David Elliot, and with certain conditions in place could rise up again and provide the pivotal link between the rural population, its own infrastructure and military forces, and those of the North Vietnamese army.[41] The American military and its senior leaders in Vietnam had no clear sense of the depth of that core or of what was actually happening in the countryside.

With the perceived victory in the countryside from pacification, the United States continued along its path to end the war. But that path did not involve strategy—the linking of military and national resources to achieve a political end—but instead a policy called Vietnamization, which would turn the war over to the South Vietnamese. In a sense, the final campaign of the Vietnam War for the United States was not really a campaign at all but a process of modernizing the Republic of Vietnam Armed Forces (RVNAF). The true final campaign of the war—pacification of the rural countryside—had already failed. What was left of American power in Vietnam was held together by the application or threat of superior American weaponry.

In explaining Vietnamization, Nixon's newly appointed secretary of defense, Melvin Laird, told the House Armed Services Committee in 1970 that its objective was "the effective assumption by the RVNAF of a larger share of combat operations from American forces," allowing American forces to withdraw. In fact the buildup of the RVNAF had been going on since the United States first committed itself to the defense of South Vietnam at the end of the First Indochina War. With the political and social outcry after the Tet Offensive, Johnson's resultant withdrawal from the presidential race in 1968, and Nixon's election to the presidency, it became a political imperative to withdraw American forces from Vietnam. But for the Americans to withdraw it became equally important to improve the combat capabilities of the RVNAF with advanced weapons like tanks, attack aircraft, and concomitant organizational structures to confront the Viet Cong and the North Vietnamese army without the assistance of American ground forces.[42]

Nixon and Kissinger came to see firepower as the means to force the North Vietnamese into a negotiated settlement at the Paris peace talks and allow for a "decent interval" from the U.S. departure to the potential collapse of South Vietnam.[43] Abrams and his advisers, on the other hand, saw firepower as a way of winning the war. The difference was profound, and it was revealed in a series of major operations over the next two years that pitted the

American and South Vietnamese militaries in conventional operations against the NVA and PLAF. It was Vietnamization's trial by fire.

Never losing sight of the goals of reuniting both Vietnams and ejecting the American military, the North launched a massive, multipronged invasion into South Vietnam on March 31, 1972. By that point in the war, the American military presence, as a result of a series of withdrawals over the previous two years, was down to about seventy thousand troops, most of them support personnel and advisers to the RVNAF. The Easter Offensive, as it came to be called, lasted for about three months. North Vietnam's goal was to split South Vietnam in two through the Central Highlands while also launching major assaults to capture important cities like Hue and Saigon. Although it made significant gains, ultimately the offensive stalled in the face of air attacks coordinated adroitly by the American advisers with RVNAF outfits.[44]

During the Easter Offensive, displeasure with Abrams on the part of President Nixon and National Security Advisor Henry Kissinger coalesced around a disagreement over how best to use the air force's B-52 bombers. Abrams wanted to use most of them to attack North Vietnamese logistical trails in the North and along the Ho Chi Minh Trail, as well as to provide close air support to the ARVN in its fight against NVA units. Nixon and Kissinger believed the best use of B-52 strikes was to directly attack cities and infrastructure in the North, like Hanoi and Haiphong Harbor, with the aim of getting better concessions at the negotiating table. Kissinger described Abrams's handling of the Easter Offensive as evidence of a senior military officer being stuck in the "routine" of conventional warfare. Nixon was especially critical, calling the military in Vietnam and its approach to using firepower during the Easter Offensive "timid." At the time, both Nixon and Kissinger seriously considered relieving Abrams from command. Nixon wanted a bold stroke by the military, wanted his generals to get off their "backside and give [him] some recommendations as to how" to accomplish his "goal" of ending the war through negotiated settlement with the Vietnamese. Frustrated with Abrams's delays in launching B-52 strikes against the North, Nixon wondered if the general was actively avoiding using American firepower in the way the president wished. Abrams had "shown no imagination," lamented an angered Nixon during the Easter Offensive. Kissinger strongly recommended to Nixon that he "consider relieving Abrams."[45] Nixon and Kissinger wanted the war to end through negotiations to allow the Americans to withdraw; Abrams still saw victory in Vietnam as a possibility, as long as the United States continued to buttress the South Vietnamese military with large doses of American ordnance.

Firepower halted the Easter Offensive, producing a stalemate that persuaded the Americans and the North Vietnamese to sign the long-sought peace treaty that would "end" the war and allow complete American withdrawal, as well as the return of American prisoners of war. For the North Vietnamese, the peace treaty allowed for more than a hundred thousand soldiers to remain in the South. It also recognized the National Liberation Front as a legitimate political entity in South Vietnam. For Thieu and his South Vietnamese government, the treaty produced nothing but frustration and a feeling that they were being abandoned by the United States. In compliance with the Paris Peace Accords, the last American troops departed South Vietnam in February 1973. The war in Vietnam was over for the United States of America.[46]

In a fundamental way, nothing had changed since the end of the Tet Offensive in the summer of 1968. In February 1973, there were still huge numbers of North Vietnamese regular army units in the South, the Viet Cong insurgents were still there, and the South Vietnamese government and its military were still corrupt.

What had changed was the mounting death toll: close to twenty thousand more Americans killed along with many times more of their enemy, and hundreds of thousands of Vietnamese civilians. The United States maintained the hope that even after it departed, the South Vietnamese government would remain in existence, which of course was the overall political aim for the United States all along. But that hope was underwritten by the promise of continuing South Vietnamese access to superior American firepower. In the absence of that firepower, the war would soon come to an end for the Vietnamese people as well.

When the final North Vietnamese offensive began in April 1975, the collapse of the SVN government and military came stunningly quickly. The link between the assaulting NVA army units and the Viet Cong main forces and militia became quite apparent. In Thua Thien Province near the village of Ap Hoa Binh, a short distance from Hue, a company of Viet Cong fighters attacked government strongpoints in and around the village. This Viet Cong attack was done in cooperation with attacking North Vietnamese army forces. South of Hue, other Viet Cong combat units entered the villages of Thuy Thanh and Thuy Phu to attack other government positions. The Viet Cong and NVA leadership was apparently planning the coordinated attacks to test the strength of the SVN government and military positions. The idea that pacification had succeeded and the Viet Cong had been defeated withers under the fact that all three entities cooperated effectively to initially harass SVN government and security forces and then finally overthrow them in decisive coordinated thrusts. The offensive began in March and was over in late April 1975. The iconic image of American and South Vietnamese people being lifted off the U.S. embassy roof by helicopters in Saigon attests to the fragility of the SVN government and military without American firepower to prop them up.[47]

The American political scene at the time had become such that it was politically impossible for Nixon's successor in the presidency, Gerald Ford, to come to the sustained aid of the South Vietnamese government. Congress had passed numerous pieces of legislation during the preceding two years that prevented the president, even if he wanted to, from assisting the South. Observing in South Vietnam during the last three months of the Communist offensive, Army Chief of Staff General Frederick C. Weyand advised that the only hope of halting the attack lay in massive unrestrained application of U.S. firepower. Richard Nixon watched Saigon fall from his home in San Clemente, California, retiring there after his resignation of the presidency due to the Watergate scandal. In his memoirs, written only three years after Saigon's fall, Nixon lashed out at the American Congress and blamed it for the fall of Saigon for refusing to "fulfill our obligations." The essence of the "obligation" was firepower.[48]

But unless the United States was willing to stay in Vietnam for generations to do armed nation building, the collapse of South Vietnam was inevitable.[49] In the end, firepower could not break the will of the North Vietnamese, the NLF, or the PLAF; nor could it correct the endemic problems of corruption within the South Vietnamese government and military. Moreover, it could not connect in a moral and long-lasting way the people of South Vietnam to the government. The United States and South Vietnam lost the war on all fronts. The proof was clear enough with NVA tanks rolling down the streets of Saigon in late April 1975.

For the United States, the essential lesson from Vietnam is that the crucial elements in war are not smarter counterinsurgency tactics, better generals, or more malleable popular support, but clear-headed thinking about policy and strategy that aligns ways, means, and ends relative to national interests and the potential of our enemies. In Vietnam the United States failed at that test.

Unfortunately, in the years that followed, a false lesson was learned from Vietnam—that better counterinsurgency tactics under an enlightened general who reinvented his field army had saved America's failed strategy only to have the war lost on college campuses and in Congress. That idea grew in the years that followed, eventually providing the historical grist for what was to become America's most costly and sustained military engagement since Vietnam, the second war in Iraq.

# 4

# IRAQ: A BETTER WAR, VERSION 2

*Odierno would buck his superiors and push the U.S. military in radi-cally new directions. . . . Odierno would launch a guerrilla cam-paign for a change of direction in Iraq . . . that eventually reversed almost every tenet of U.S. strategy. . . . [Odierno's] growing belief, as he prepared to redeploy to Iraq, [was] that the United States was heading toward defeat.*

—Thomas E. Ricks, 2009

*After overseeing training of the Iraqi Security Forces, General Pe-traeus was assigned to Fort Leavenworth, Kansas to rewrite the Ar-my's counterinsurgency manual. The premise of counterinsurgency is that basic security is required before political gains can follow. That was the reverse of our existing strategy.*

—George W. Bush, 2010

Shortly after the release of his second book on Iraq, *The Gamble*, author Thomas Ricks stated that senior American generals Ray-mond Odierno and David Petraeus had turned the army around during the 2007 surge. Ricks argued that these two generals put into action a very different doctrine in counterinsurgency warfare, changing the preexisting strategy of former commanding general George Casey toward a "radically new direction."[1] General David Petraeus, as his speech two years after the surge at the American Enterprise Institute indicated, naturally agreed. Another writer of popular histories of war, Mark Bowden, crowned Petraeus as the "professor of war," the general who "revolutionized the way America fights its wars." President George W. Bush saw the reinvention of the U.S. Army during the surge as so radical that he said it was a complete "reversal" of strategy from what came before.[2]

The first seven months of the surge, from February to August 2007, were hell. American combat casualties rose to some of their highest levels since the start of the war, and the numbers of civilian casualties from the ongoing sectarian civil war were at brutal levels. So when the numbers of American military and Iraqi civilian casualties started to drop precipitously by September 2007, only eight months after the surge of troops began, many people—in the American army, in policy circles, and in the media—began to ask what might have brought the numbers down. And the answer very quickly coalesced around the idea that the violence dropped because the American army did something different from what came before. This was a powerful moral proposition to the soldiers and marines who had seen so many thousands of casualties during the surge. Claiming responsibility for the lowering of violence justified and helped explain their losses. One soldier remembered those tough days of the surge as a time when his battalion initially got off on the wrong foot, but then started to "get back to the COIN basics that we had read about. Once we began to apply these lessons, things changed in our favor, and never turned back."[3] The idea that the surge turned the tide of the war through a significant shift in operational method provided comfort and would act as a guidepost for the future.

Lieutenant Colonel David Fivecoat, an army officer who believed in the efficacy of counterinsurgency and in the purported transformative leadership of Petraeus, reflected on the surge years later in 2010, when he was a battalion commander in Afghanistan. Fivecoat believed that the surge in Iraq had worked, but in

Afghanistan in 2010, after his battalion had three men killed and hundreds seriously wounded, Petraeus's counterinsurgency methods did not seem to be as effective. In Afghanistan the losses his battalion took became a very difficult moral "burden" for him.[4]

As the Iraq surge triumph narrative started to take shape in summer 2007, many writers, chroniclers, experts, and reporters took up the cause of furthering it. And this same narrative was airlifted almost effortlessly to the simmering conflict in Afghanistan, from which the United States has yet to extract itself. As in Malaya and Vietnam, the triumph narrative crumbles under close historical investigation, but as a guide to the way successive administrations have come to think about the best hope for America's wars against distant insurgencies, the myth of COIN has proved to be remarkably durable.

The surge of troops led by General Petraeus was not the primary cause for the lowering of violence that began in the early fall of 2007. Instead, we must assign that responsibility to a combination of critical factors. First and arguably most important of these factors was what became known as the Awakening of Sunni tribes in Anbar Province, which had been developing for at least two years before the surge began. By the end of 2006, many Sunni tribes in western Iraq had become fed up with the slaughter of Iraqi civilians at the hands of al Qaeda in Iraq. The tribespeople had also grown tired of al Qaeda's attempts to dominate them by dictating the marriages of Sunni women to al Qaeda members and controlling illicit Sunni tribal trade. The American military from as early as 2004 had some important successes in parts of Anbar in working with the Sunni tribes against al Qaeda. These more limited successes combined with the building frustration of other Anbar tribes came to a head in the middle of 2006 and pushed a large number of Sunni groups to cut a deal with the American military in Iraq to join them in fighting al Qaeda. Of course, to sweeten the deal, the United States paid the Sunni tribes large sums of American taxpayer dollars. Very quickly the idea of the Anbar Awakening—Sunni resistance to the extremes of al Qaeda—spread to other Sunni areas in Baghdad and other parts of Iraq and produced similar movements.[5]

These Sunni groups had figured out that they were losing the civil war with the Shia-dominated government led by Nouri al-Maliki. Caught in a closing vise between al Qaeda on the one side and the Shia government and militias on the other, the Sunni groups determined that their best course of action was to ally with the American military. The Sunnis looked to the American military to give them legitimacy through a formal alliance and, at least in public view, credibility with the Iraqi government. It was a way for the Sunni insurgents to live to fight another day.[6]

The significance of the Anbar Awakening and similar Sunni movements in Baghdad and elsewhere to the lowering of violence in Iraq cannot be overstated. It meant, first of all, that Sunni insurgent attacks against the American military ceased, thus lowering American casualties. Then the increased number of American combat brigades arrived just as information provided by former Sunni insurgents now allied with the Americans provided exact identities and locations of al Qaeda fighters for American tactical firepower to target and destroy. With the reduction of al Qaeda came a drastic lowering in the number of al Qaeda–directed bombing attacks against Iraqi civilians, mostly Shia.[7] It was in this way that the surge of troops had its most substantial effect—the reduction of al Qaeda through firepower—rather than a reinvented army and its better general winning the trust and allegiance of the local population.

The Sunni Awakening also coincided with a cessation of acts of violence by various Shia militia groups. Like the Sunnis, many Shia in Iraq had grown weary of the slaughter of Iraqi civilians by its militias. Frustration with various militia groups came to a head in August 2007 when the Shia militia leader Moqtada al Sadr's forces attacked an Iraqi police brigade in the southern city of Karbala. Afterward, Sadr froze his militia's attacks against rival Shia militias, Sunni fighters, and Sunni civilians. Thus widespread intra-Shia fighting—for example, between the Sadr militia and the Badr militia, which was well established in the Iraqi Security Forces—came to a head in August 2007 and ended in a cease-fire. The Shia cease-fire occurred at the same time that the effects of the Sunni Awakening were starting to be felt, further reducing the violence.[8]

The third critical factor that worked to lower violence was the separation of Baghdad into discrete sectarian districts, either Shia or Sunni, as a result of the civil war fought between the two groups in 2005 and 2006. Most of Baghdad had become dominated by Shia, with a few small enclaves of Sunnis. Other parts of Iraq, such as the Sunni Triangle north and west of Baghdad, experienced this same kind of sectarian separation. The American military's use, starting in early 2006, of large concrete walls to physically separate sectarian districts in Baghdad reinforced the separation of sects brought about by the civil war.[9]

Recent new sources of primary data on the levels of violence in Iraq during the years 2005 through 2007 show that by December 2006 civilian deaths produced by sectarian violence had peaked at 3,500 civilians killed that month. From December on, the violence began to drop precipitously, and by the time Petraeus took command in February the overall levels of sectarian violence had decreased by at least one third.[10]

When asked to reflect on eight years of American occupation and what it had meant to them, many Iraqis do not mention the surge of troops as a turning point in the war. *Time* magazine war correspondent Mark Kukis compiled close to seventy interviews of Iraqis about their experiences during the occupation. The interviewees include people of various ages, men and women, insurgents, government officials, security force members, and civilians.

They speak of loss, death, destruction, fear, confusion, anger, frustration, sadness, and much more. But none of the Iraqis interviewed mentioned the surge and the so-called positive effects that it had. There is no sense from them that some sort of tectonic shift occurred in 2007 that made the war better. In fact it was during the months of the surge in 2007 that Iraqis experienced the highest levels of deaths brought about by American firepower. For example, in 2006, the year before the surge, Americans killed 254 civilians, but in 2007, the year of the surge, they killed 681, almost three times as many as during the previous year.[11]

In contrast to the Iraqis, many members of the American military, especially the army, began to convince themselves that the surge was the decisive event that turned the tide. And it was not just the additional brigades of the surge but the notion that what those brigades were doing along with the rest of the American military in Iraq was very different from what came before. Only two months into the surge, General Petraeus told his troops that the reason for the drop in sectarian violence was because of "their hard work." Yet the levels of sectarian violence started to drop in December 2006, two months before the arrival of Petraeus and his purported change in strategy. Writing from Baghdad in January 2008 and looking back on the surge, Major Chris Rogers claimed that his unit in the Sunni district of Amriya had focused on the local "population" and applied the proper techniques of counterinsurgency as prescribed in the new army counterinsurgency manual FM 3-24, thus helping to lower violence in the district. For Rogers, his unit and the rest of the surge army had "learned from their successes and failures" how to apply counterinsurgency doctrine correctly.[12]

The American mainstream press largely fell in line and promoted the surge success story. Linda Robinson, in an account of Petraeus's role in the surge, bluntly states that her book was the story of how Petraeus and the surge "turned the war around." In

*The Fourth Star,* *Washington Post* reporter Greg Jaffe and former *New York Times* correspondent David Cloud compared the "hidebound" pre-surge army that didn't understand counterinsurgency to the successful "Army that Petraeus had forged in Iraq" during the surge. In *The Good Soldiers,* journalist David Finkel of the *Washington Post* cited a combat battalion commander who reflected on his past fifteen months as part of the surge. The battalion commander believed that, along with the other surge forces, his battalion "had won. He was sure of it. They were the difference."[13]

The military-expert class also tacked perfectly with the surge triumph narrative. General Petraeus's adviser David Kilcullen noted in his book *The Accidental Guerrilla* that the surge "turned around a war that many believed had already been lost, through a strategy" of correct counterinsurgency methods. Counterinsurgency expert Janine Davidson argued in *Lifting the Fog of Peace* that the American army went through a fundamental transformation as a result of the new methods and strategy that Petraeus put into effect during the surge. Another counterinsurgency expert, David Ucko, asserted in *The New Counterinsurgency Era* that there was a fundamental shift in operational and tactical methods during the surge that had much to do with the overall reduction of violence, which he says began in late summer and early fall of 2007. In a recent biography of Petraeus, Paula Broadwell claims that he put into place significant operational changes during the surge.[14]

Yet just as in Vietnam, where the army's operational framework remained the same throughout the war, so too in the Iraq War there was more continuity than discontinuity between the pre-surge and surge armies. There was no radical shift in operational method during the surge toward better counterinsurgency practices. Instead the surge army operated largely within the same operational framework that had preceded it. The additional surge brigades did provide more firepower to kill al Qaeda fighters, but otherwise the army operated largely in the same way that it had from the start of the war in Iraq in spring of 2003. For those looking to the idea of a radically transformed army under Petraeus that improved conditions in Iraq, there is little evidence to support such an assertion.

Events in Iraq from 2003 until the end of the American occupation in December 2011 therefore turned not on purported tactical shifts of the American army but on matters of high strategy and policy. The operational framework for the army and marines in Iraq from the start of the war until its conclusion was armed nation building. The fundamental idea that drove operations through nearly nine years of occupation and war was that if the occupiers built a new Iraqi government that was representative of its people, the people would turn away from the insurgents and toward this new and legitimate government. There were shifts and adjustments throughout the eight years of war, with regard to placements of troops, varying methods to confront the insurgency, and areas of priority for American forces. But those differences were more of *degree* than *kind*, and they occurred within a continuous operational framework of armed nation building. The army's new field manual on counterinsurgency contributed to the myth of the surge in 2007, but underneath the facade of radical change was a continuity of operational method and generalship.

Two authoritative histories of army operations in Iraq show convincingly that ground units were adaptive and innovative from the start of the war. Historians Donald Wright and Timothy Reese argue that from as early as spring 2003 through the first two years of the war the army across the board had adapted effectively to counterinsurgency operations. Another study by military analyst James Russell on military innovation from 2005 to 2007 shows that five different combat battalions, from widely different areas in Iraq prior to the surge, were able to learn and adapt to the demands of counterinsurgency.[15] Of course, it makes no sense to argue that there was no change or improvement in the American army from 2003 to 2006 or that from the beginning it was tactically perfect at counterinsurgency. As with the British in Malaya, American combat outfits would deploy and make mistakes, then learn from them, then improve as their combat tours progressed.

In 2003, in Tikrit—the epicenter of the Sunni insurgency in north central Iraq—the brigade that I was executive officer for arrived in the middle of April, shortly after the Hussein regime fell. One of the first briefings that the brigade staff gave the commander was how to go about setting up local governance in the province of Salah Din. Other early activities of the leadership included moving the brigade's combat companies and platoons off the larger bases and out into the population centers, thereby establishing presence and contact with the local population. Rebuilding infrastructure, like roads, businesses, and schools, was also part of our efforts from the start. We also fully realized the need for local security forces and began immediately putting together a police force for Tikrit and the surrounding area. Of course, as the Sunni insurgency began to grow, the brigade also conducted combat operations to fight it, but those combat operations were subsumed within the broader framework of American counterinsurgency.[16]

From the start, my brigade focused on building local governance and security forces, infrastructure and the economy, and combating the Sunni insurgency. Later, in FM 3-24, these things came to be called the "logical lines of operations" in counterinsurgency. In published articles and books, other army officers have testified to this continuity in recalling the actions of their own outfits. Reflecting on his year in Baghdad in command of a combat brigade in 2003 to 2004, Colonel Ralph O. Baker realized from his first days on the ground an important principle of counterinsurgency operations: accurate intelligence on insurgent activities is essential. Colonel Baker figured out very early on that without specific information on insurgents, his brigade would be floundering around in the dark. He therefore quickly put into place processes that developed the kind of intelligence he needed to hunt down and capture or kill insurgents. Another commander in Baghdad in 2004, Colonel Peter Mansoor, noted that even though his brigade had been trained for "high intensity combat," it had quickly made the transition to effective counterinsurgency operations in Baghdad. He observed that his brigade's efforts had improved infrastructure and that the local population supported what they were doing. Operating in the south of Baghdad in 2005, a year after Mansoor had left, Lieutenant Colonel Douglas Ollivant's combat battalion adjusted quickly to the demands of armed nation building. Upon return in late 2005, Ollivant and other officers from his battalion picked up a copy of a 1964 book on counterinsurgency by the French officer David Galula, and they realized that much of what they did in 2005 mirrored his work in Algeria in 1956. Another army major who operated in northern Iraq in the city of Mosul in 2005 noted tactical units practicing counterinsurgency by "living and working with the population." In preparing himself and his armored cavalry squadron for operations in Iraq in 2005 and 2006, Lieutenant Colonel Ross Brown noted that he had read many "historical descriptions of counterinsurgency operations" and affirmed what he saw as the "universally" accepted tenets about them, and the necessary combination of

> military, paramilitary, economic, psychological, and civic actions taken by a government to defeat an insurgency. In such a fight, the host country's population is the strategic and operational center of gravity; thus, winning the people's confidence and support is the centerpiece for operations at those levels. Although there aren't any centers of gravity at the tactical level, gaining the local population's confidence and support is just as important as in the higher echelons of operations.[17]

Colonel Brown did not have FM 3-24 by his side when he fought in Iraq in 2005 and 2006.

Even with American ground units in Iraq doing counterinsurgency, violence continued to climb. With ongoing insurgent attacks against U.S. forces and heightened levels of sectarian violence, U.S. efforts in Iraq seemed on the verge of defeat or stalemate. In September 2006, a senior marine intelligence officer, Colonel Peter Devlin, wrote a damning assessment of the political-military situation in Anbar Province that was leaked to the press. The report concluded that American military efforts had failed to defeat the insurgency in the west and failed to produce a stable Iraqi government and economy in which the people could have confidence. The report was immediately picked up by commentators who used it as proof of American strategic failure in Iraq. The report also seemed to imply that the counterinsurgency efforts by the army and marines had not worked and represented an institutional failure in their inability to halt the violence and pacify the country.[18]

Devlin's report became the pivot from the bad war to the better war that Iraq soon would become. In Malaya the pivot was the assassination of Henry Gurney, which represented the low point of that conflict. In Vietnam it was Tet. Now in Iraq it was the Devlin report, which seemed to describe a military fumbling at counterinsurgency and waiting to be rescued by the savior general.[19]

But the army and marines throughout Iraq were doing the tactics of counterinsurgency correctly. For example, in western Anbar Province in 2004, Marine Colonel Michael M. Walker led a civil affairs group that aimed its efforts at winning the trust of the local Sunni tribes. One of the things Walker's team did was work at reinvigorating the local economy. At the end of his tour, Walker noted that as a result of the marines' effort, the Sunni tribes had come to realize that they offered them "security, governance, and an improved economy," while al Qaeda was offering them a trip "back to the dark ages." A year later, in 2005, in the restive north-eastern city of Tall 'Afar, a longtime hub for Sunni insurgents, who used the city as a base of operations to carry out attacks all over Iraq, the Third Armored Cavalry Regiment under Colonel H.R. McMaster carried out a classic campaign of counterinsurgency. Mc-Master, like Baker and Mansoor before him, anticipated the counterinsurgency tactics called for in FM 3-24. McMaster's use of these tactics proved to be successful, at least temporarily, in Tall 'Afar.[20]

There was a growing realization by army and marine units in Anbar Province that the Sunni insurgent groups were beginning to grow tired of al Qaeda, raising the very real possibility of an alliance between them and the U.S. military. An army brigade from the First Armored Division moved into Ramadi in Anbar Province in late summer 2006 and latched on to the growing un-ease of the Sunni tribes and their willingness to ally with the Americans. Commanded by Colonel Sean MacFarland, the First Brigade First Armored Division quickly assessed the potential of an alliance with the Sunni tribes and developed tactical methods to capitalize on it. The brigade dispersed small units of about thirty men into outposts throughout Ramadi to provide protection and firepower support to the Sunni groups that decided to fight against al Qaeda. By early 2007, after about six months of hard fighting, al Qaeda had been put on the path to defeat in Ramadi, and levels of violence began to drop precipitously. Reflecting on his bri-gade's accomplishment, McFarland noted that his outfit's meth-ods were the same as those of other units that came into Iraq after he left. MacFarland noted that the key factor in reducing violence in Ramadi was the turning of the Sunni tribes away from al Qaeda. If they "had remained allied with al-Qaeda against us, we would not have been able to achieve anything last-ing or of strategic significance," said MacFarland.[21] Without that key condition of the Sunni tribes flipping, violence would have remained at high levels.

The triumph narrative pushes the notion that before the surge the American army had hunkered down on large bases, content to let the violence outside of the wire to soar. But then Petraeus arrives, and lectures his troops that we "can't commute to the fight."[22] However, the narrative wrongly sensationalizes a purported change in operational method from being hunkered down on large bases to living among the population. The Baghdad Sunni district of Amriya highlights this point. According to the battalion commander there during the surge, Lieutenant Colonel Dale Kuehl, he established his first combat outpost (COP) in the district on May 19. In the surge triumph narrative, the emplacement of COPs throughout Baghdad represents what General Petraeus meant when he said the surge troops were no longer "commuting" to the fight but rather living among the population. Yet Kuehl acknowledged that just a few days after the establishment of a COP on the outskirts of the district, he was able to cut a deal with the Sunnis there to ally with his battalion to fight al Qaeda. Like MacFarland in Anbar Province, Kuehl admitted that if the Amriya Sunnis had not "come forward, we would have never been able to secure the population. They were essential in giving us the vital information we needed to effectively target AQI." Thus it was the agreement cut with Sunni fighters, not the establishment of a relatively insignificant combat outpost, that led to the lowering of violence in Amriya. A Sunni woman from the district agreed. She said that there had been security improvements in Amriya, but it was not due to anything different that the Americans were doing. Instead "it happened by the Awakening's effort."[23]

The problems in Iraq had much less to do with the methods of armed nation building that the U.S. Army and Marine Corps were applying on the ground than with key decisions of policy and strategy made at the start of the war. Once the United States decided to invade Iraq, break the regime, then stay as an occupying power to reconstruct it in a way that provided equal representation for Shia, Sunni, and Kurd, the country was very likely set on a path to insurgency and ultimately civil war. By altering the fundamental relationship between Arab and Kurd that had defined Iraq prior to the invasion—toward an American-emplaced "democracy" that structured its new government based on proportional representation of the country's sectarian mix, resulting in a government dominated by Shia—the country was set on a trajectory of civil war.[24] It reached its height at the end of 2006.

The triumphalist surge narrative aligns much too cleanly with the narrative arc of counterinsurgency that we have inherited from Vietnam and Malaya. Under the influence of this story, we've been presented with another reinvented army under a better general, with improved counterinsurgency tactics resulting in new successes on the ground. But the operational record and a clear understanding of the effects of the other, more important conditions—including the Anbar Awakening, the Shia militia stand-down, and the sectarian separation of Baghdad—help put the surge in proper perspective. In fact, the real story in Iraq is one of continuity between the commanding generals and the policies they put in place. This continuity suggests that effective counterinsurgency tactics practiced throughout the war and commanding generals whose generalship was largely the same are not enough to save a war that was fought under a botched strategy and policy. Unfortunately, this same scenario governed American actions in Afghanistan as it started to wind down its war in Iraq.

In 2009, two years after the completion of the surge, General Odierno argued that changed strategy was the prime causative factor for the lowering violence in Iraq that began in late fall 2007. "We changed our tactics, techniques, and procedures to protect the Iraqi population," argued Odierno. This change in operations, the general claimed, then led the various Sunni groups to come over to the American side, because U.S. troops provided security to the Iraqi people. Odierno boasted that "the truth is that the improvement in security and stability is the result of a number of factors, and what Coalition forces did throughout 2007 ranks as the most significant."[25]

Overlooking the fact that as a brigade commander in 2004 in Baghdad he did essentially the same things that the surge army did in 2007, Colonel Peter Mansoor made the point quite bluntly:

> Of greater importance was the change in the way U.S. forces were employed starting in February 2007, when Gen. David Petraeus ordered them to position themselves with Iraqi forces out in neighborhoods. This repositioning was based on newly published counterinsurgency doctrine that emphasized the protection of the population and recognized that the only way to secure people is to live among them. . . . As sectarian violence spiraled out of control, it became increasingly evident that Iraqi forces were unable to prevent its spread. By the fall of 2006, it was clear that our strategy was failing.[26]

For Mansoor, Petraeus brought a new strategy into Iraq in early 2007 that employed the "newly published" counterinsurgency doctrine.

If Mansoor and Odierno were right, then their explanation should be supported by Iraqi people who witnessed the surge and the years that came before. However, the Sunnis in Anbar Province in particular, where the Sunni Awakening began, did not view the surge as a game-changing event. Sterling Jensen was an interpreter for senior American officers in Anbar between 2006 and 2008, and during his time in Iraq he interviewed hundreds of Iraqis about the Awakening and the surge. According to Jensen, the surge was not the critical factor in bringing about their decision to side with the Americans. The decisive element was al Qaeda's infringement of the tribes' control of lucrative smuggling into and out of Syria combined with the increasing levels of al

Qaeda brutality. One of these Iraqis conveyed to Jensen the idea that if al Qaeda had not acted in such brutish ways, there would have "never been an Anbar or Sunni Awakening no matter what COIN tactics the US used. The surge would not have been successful." One of the most important tribal leaders in the Awakening, Abu Risha al-Sattar, didn't want more American battalions and in fact wanted them to simply "stay on their bases." What he needed was American dollars and an agreement whereby American combat forces would no longer be attacking his tribal fighters. In return, Sattar and the Awakening would stop attacking the Americans and instead focus on al Qaeda.

Even al Qaeda members acknowledged the unimportance of the surge in Anbar. A former al Qaeda cleric, Mullah Nadim al-Juburi, who turned against al Qaeda in 2007 and sided with the Americans as part of the Awakening, told Jensen that "had AQ not gone against the different Iraqi national resistance groups, the U.S. would have never convinced a significant enough part of the resistance to turn against AQ in 2006 and AQI/Sunni resistance today would have been similar to the Taliban in Afghanistan but with more clear regional support."[27]

At best, the surge gave Baghdad Sunnis a psychological boost, convincing them that the American military would stay in force in Iraq. This was not an insignificant factor after the December 2006 congressional elections, in which the Democrats won control of both houses and started to talk about bringing an end to the U.S. commitment in Iraq. But the psychological effect of a boost in Sunni morale is different from General Odierno's claimed change in operational framework being the most important factor. Even before the announcement of the surge in December 2006, the November elections and the perception of a quick American withdrawal caused Sunni insurgent leaders outside of Anbar to begin siding with the Americans to fight al Qaeda.

There was a complex mix of other factors that fueled the growth of the Sunni Awakening and helped dampen the violence by the end of September 2007. One was the effect that the second battle of Fallujah in western Iraq in November 2004 had on Sunni insurgent groups and tribes. The battle pitted U.S. Army and Marine units in a large urban clearing operation to remove various Sunni insurgent groups (including al Qaeda) from the city. The result was that al Qaeda was dispersed into other western-province areas, bringing them into conflict with Sunni tribal traders and leaders with whom they vied for political power and control over lucrative tribal trading networks. The other effect of Fallujah was to demonstrate early in 2004 American resolve and a bloody-mindedness that showed Iraqi Sunnis that the Americans were willing to fight hard and spill blood to achieve their goals. Another important causative factor that helped the Sunni Awakening along, never mentioned in the surge triumph narrative, was the role of the Central Intelligence Agency (CIA). Its early work in 2004, establishing relationships with Sunni leaders, came to fruition in 2007. A third often overlooked causative factor in the lessening of violence was the killing power of American and allied special operations forces against al Qaeda. These special operators had developed sophisticated intelligence gathering and quick-response strike capabilities in 2005 and 2006 and were well in place and working before the surge even started.[28]

Nor was there a significant shift in generalship between Casey and Petraeus. A former senior planner for the First Cavalry Division during the surge in Baghdad, Lieutenant Colonel (retired) Douglas Ollivant, credited General George Casey, Petraeus's predecessor, for putting in place many methods that continued into the surge. Casey tends to be seen as a failure in the surge triumph narrative, but Ollivant makes a persuasive case that he was not

... the man who told me to build security stations in Baghdad. .... The man who decided that we would create the Baghdad Operational Command to give the Iraqis control of their Army and National Police units was George Casey. The man who kept us on track with a population security model and kept others from simply turning this into another Baghdad offensive was George Casey.[29]

Yet General Casey undeservedly became the fall guy. President Bush in January 2007 characterized Casey's strategy as "maybe a slow failure." Piling on, Senator John McCain a month later lambasted Casey in the halls of Congress, comparing him to Westmoreland, whom McCain believed failed. McCain asked why the president was promoting Casey to be chief of staff of the army, since he was a general who "pursued a failed" strategy in Iraq. In 2009, a year after the end of the surge, McCain said, "Everybody knows that it succeeded."[30] In other words, Petraeus saved Iraq by doing something fundamentally different operationally than Casey. Nothing could be further from reality.

General Casey took command in Iraq in summer 2004, when the senior American political leadership believed that its effort in Iraq was adrift, especially amid the Abu Ghraib scandal, which had broken months before Casey's arrival.[31] After about a month of settling into the command position and making numerous trips around the country visiting American military units and Iraqi political and military leaders, Casey decided on a strategy to eventually turn over security and governing responsibilities to the Iraqis. The operational framework that supported this strategy combined counterinsurgency operations against various Shia and Sunni insurgent groups with efforts to build up Iraqi institutions. The idea was that as Iraqi institutions progressed, the Americans would gradually turn things over to them. To provide a common framework for understanding nation-building operations, General Casey established the Counterinsurgency Academy in the Iraqi city of Taji in late 2005 to teach counterinsurgency to the leaders of his tactical outfits.[32]

By the beginning of 2006, General Casey believed that over the course of the two previous years, Iraqi elections had laid the foundations of an independent government, which, combined with efforts to build up Iraqi security forces, would allow the army and marines to start drawing down their forces that summer. After the al Qaeda bombing of the Shia al-Askari shrine in Samarra, General Casey realized that his drawdown timeline was too ambitious. Before that, Casey had seen as his primary threat the Sunni insurgents made up of former Saddam regime members who refused to accept the American occupation of their country in support of a Shia-dominated government.[33]

But by 2005 a sectarian civil war was brewing in Iraq between various Sunni fighters and the Iraqi government and its Shia militia allies. The al-Askari bombing in late February 2006 brought that civil war into clear view, enraging the Shia to the point where they began attacking Sunni civilians as well as insurgents. The U.S. military was caught in between the warring factions, at times supporting one side against the other and at other times trying to broker peace agreements. The civil war was an incredibly complex and violent situation, one that did not offer easy operational solutions for the U.S. military.[34]

From where I was based, in southwestern Baghdad, it took me a couple of weeks after the Samarra shrine bombing to realize that the cavalry squadron I commanded was caught in the middle of a civil war. During those three weeks after the bombing, my squadron pinged back and forth from Sunni mosque to Sunni mosque under vicious attacks by roving Shia militias, often supported by Iraqi police and sometimes even the Iraqi army. Many discussions with Sunni religious leaders, or imams, made it clear that they were being attacked by militias supported by Iraqi security forces.

No longer was I dealing with only a simple Sunni insurgency. As the weeks passed, other signs of the burgeoning civil war appeared on a daily basis: dead bodies dropped on the streets and the near-constant relocation of Sunni and Shia families from areas that had previously been either mixed or dominated by one sect or the other. The same process was happening in other parts of Iraq as well.[35]

As the situation in Iraq in 2006 grew in complexity with the increasing violence of the civil war, certain members of the American army, along with a battery of retired military and civilian experts, were constructing what they saw as a potential military-operational solution to the problem. A meeting of sorts was held in February 2006 at Fort Leavenworth, Kansas, to discuss the writing of what would become the army's new counterinsurgency doctrinal manual. Headed by then Lieutenant General Petraeus, the commander at Leavenworth, this two-day meeting brought together a number of high-profile civilian and military experts and media luminaries. In the months after this initial meeting, a small writing group led by retired army officer and historian Conrad Crane drafted the army's "new" doctrine on counterinsurgency, or armed nation building.[36]

A group of senior officers from the Fourth Infantry Division, which had responsibility for Baghdad in 2006, offered a thorough critique of the new COIN manual based on their year's experience in the middle of Iraq's civil war. Their opening statement was simple: "Sectarian conflict [civil war] presents an additional battlefield dynamic to the already complex situation of counterinsurgency operations in Iraq." The critique recounted the "imperatives" of counterinsurgency as outlined in FM 3-24 and then also noted that combat units throughout Iraq had been "routinely employing these imperatives." Although the officers appreciated the value of the new counterinsurgency doctrine for a simple problem of insurgency, what they had experienced in Baghdad in

2006 was too complicated for the simplistic methods and solutions called for. The report shrewdly noted that in simple counterinsurgency operations the emphasis was on those "trying to control the government." In civil war, however, "the competing actors are frequently more interested in exerting primacy over one another than interest in sole control of the government." In short, these senior 4ID leaders saw the complex situation in Baghdad as defying the simplistic, cookie-cutter solutions offered by FM 3-24.[37]

Like his subordinate commanders in the Fourth Infantry Division, General Casey was wondering whether Iraq was truly experiencing a civil war. The informal journal that he kept shows a senior commander constantly challenging his planning assumptions and conceptions about the war and his strategy. The assumption that his staff and his commanders always returned to was that the country was not in civil war, because the major institutions had not squared off against each other. Iraq, in their words, was experiencing violent "sectarian conflict," not "technically" civil war. Yet the fundamental problem that General Casey identified by spring and early summer of 2006 was, in his words, that the violence was over the "division of political and economic powers among Iraq's ethnic and sectarian groups." He noted that this evolving conflict was moving away from "an insurgency" against the American occupation toward one fought among the Iraqi people.[38] General Casey had assessed the root problem: this was a conflict over who would hold political and economic power. Yet to acknowledge formally that Iraq was in civil war would call the entire American military effort into question, including the possibility of its developing a means to stop the fighting.[39] Yet civil war was exactly what was happening in Iraq in 2006.

General Casey could not officially describe what he was seeing as civil war, but his assessment of what the U.S. military could and could not accomplish in Iraq was tempered with an acute sense of the limits of American power. Casey knew that in the end the Iraqis had to solve their problems for themselves. He noted in late 2006 that the greatest problem in Iraq was sectarian violence and noted that until it was reduced the chance for reconciliation was slim to none. Anticipating what would come with Petraeus and the surge of troops in 2007, Casey argued that the United States troops should not walk away from the violence and withdraw into their forward operating bases to await a precipitous withdrawal. Instead, the American military had to help curb the violence so reconciliation could occur.[40]

By the end of 2006, Casey faced not only an extremely difficult situation in Iraq, but also an internal insurgency of sorts within the highest reaches of the American defense establishment, campaigning to discredit his strategy and remove him from command. This movement started with the writing of the new counterinsurgency manual, which was published in draft form in October 2006. The manual offered an ostensible alternative to what the U.S. Army had been doing, and a bevy of voices on the National Security Council and among military experts and retired army officers were arguing Iraq was burning in civil war because the American army under Casey had failed to do counterinsurgency operations correctly. In this view, Iraq demanded a new strategy, because Casey's was apparently failing.[41]

Over the course of about four months, from October 2006 to January 2007, there were a number of high-level visits by members of the National Security Council to Baghdad to review and assess the situation, along with studies and analyses being conducted back in Washington. General Casey often found himself spending a good deal of time addressing these visiting groups and explaining his strategy over video teleconference links (VTCs) to President Bush. Bush constantly prodded Casey with questions about whether the United States was winning or losing. In one VTC in late summer 2006, as the stirrings in D.C. for a "new strategy" were just getting started, General Casey, after listening to the president, noted that he needed to define "win" and especially "kick ass." The common theme in these meetings was a belief that what was being done was not working.[42]

The November 2006 congressional elections, in which the Republicans lost both houses to the Democrats, were seen as a referendum against the war in Iraq. Secretary of Defense Donald Rumsfeld's quick resignation after the elections only furthered the sense among administration defense officials that something needed to be done to turn the war around.[43] An ostensible radical shift in strategy and operations created an aura of change. One summary of a high-level study noted that new missions would be required as part of a surge of troops in 2007, such as an improved counterinsurgency campaign in the west, a faster transition to the Iraqi security forces, and a stepped-up fighting campaign against al Qaeda. When General Casey reviewed this summary, he noted dryly, and rightly, that he and his command had already been doing such things under his existing strategy.

In his official memoirs of his tenure of command in Iraq, General Casey made a profound observation about the relationship between strategy and policy during American wars. Looking back on the final months of his command, the general noted that in all of the VTCs, discussion groups, and NSC visits, what his president was really looking for was something that *appeared different*. He said this "was an intense period as it was clear that Washington was looking for something different from what I was recommending to them." In the end, Casey offered the president his best plan for achieving American objectives in Iraq. But a few years later, as he reflected on those final days in 2006, it became clear to him that he "should have offered the President a broader range of options . . . in Iraq." These would not have been different strategic approaches, but instead variations on an existing operational method that created the appearance of doing something different on the ground. It was the appearance of difference that the president needed in order to maintain domestic support for the war, to convince skeptics that the violence in Iraq could be managed.[44]

At the end of 2006, in a high-level strategic planning document, General Casey acknowledged that reduction of sectarian violence and "protection of the Iraqi population" were key requirements in order to continue transitioning control of security operations to the Iraqis. Casey also fully accepted that he might need at least two to three more combat brigades as a surge of forces to help quell the violence. American military presence would need to remain in large numbers, as Casey viewed things, well into 2008 and beyond. To be sure, Casey's planners believed that any additional American surge brigades should come with agreements from the Iraqi government in terms of reconciliation and other forms of progress. But by late 2006, on the eve of the Petraeus surge, General Casey and his staff were not looking to abandon Iraq anytime soon.[45]

In contrast to the counterinsurgency narrative as it became applied to the Iraq War, there was much continuity between the generalships of Casey and Petraeus. Dispersal of combat forces throughout cities in Joint Security States manned by American and Iraqi security forces, protection of the population, suppression of sectarian violence, reduction of al Qaeda, and the transition of security responsibilities to Iraqis were efforts that were in full force under Casey and continued by Petraeus. The NSC staffers believed that new strategy after Casey departed would "operationalize our forces and the Iraqi forces which would be different from the past." Yet at the tactical level of platoons, companies, and battalions, the surge troops used the same operational methods as those who came before them. The only significant difference was the additional five combat brigades.[46]

In order to sell the idea that the surge was more than simply an addition of combat troops, the National Security Council members went through strenuous efforts to make the "new strategy" seem a radical strategic change of direction. They did this by setting up a straw man, depicting Casey's command as guided by the premise that Iraqis should stop the sectarian violence while the Americans remained on the sidelines. Although this may have been the attitude among a minority of military officers at the time, it was not reflected in any of the planning or directing documents from General Casey and his staff. Other purported changes or "shifts" were fabrications that constructed misleading caricatures of the operational framework and strategy under Casey. For example, the NSC study contrasted "modest" pre-surge coalition efforts at embedding with Iraqi security forces to assist them with training and other matters with a "significant increase in the embedding program."[47] Yet a key component under General Casey's strategy was direct and sustained involvement by American combat units in training and supporting the Iraqi security forces. To suggest that embedding coalition forces with Iraqis during the Casey years was "modest," especially in 2006, was misinformed and misleading.

Another "shift" was the notion that the new strategy would focus on "providing protection" to the Iraqi population. Petraeus himself pushed this line of analysis in early January 2007, saying to newly appointed secretary of defense Robert Gates that if he took the job as commander in Iraq, the general wanted the main operational emphasis to be the security of the Iraqi people.[48] In fact, the American military in Iraq prior to Petraeus's arrival was intensely engaged in establishing that. Any combat commander on the ground in 2006 would have acknowledged that, for reconciliation to proceed and for the Iraqis to assume security responsibilities, sectarian violence had to be quelled and the population protected. My personal card, which I handed out to Iraqis in my area of operations in 2006, clearly stated that my squadron's purpose was to provide "security and protection" to the people of western Baghdad—and that is precisely what most of my operations focused on. The *Los Angeles Times* reporter Borzou Daragahi was embedded with my squadron in early October 2006. While observing our operations in Amriya, Daragahi quoted one woman from Amriya saying that electricity was still a problem but, as she gestured toward a group of soldiers from my squadron, added, "Thank God, security has gotten better." General Casey certainly noted the need for population security in his final high-level strategic planning document, from December 2006, which stated that the primary mission for coalition forces was to "stabilize Iraq by protecting the population."[49]

The mantra repeated by the NSC and Petraeus, that there was to be a significant strategic and operational shift with the surge as population protection became the primary function for coalition forces, drew on the principles laid out in the recently published counterinsurgency doctrinal manual. By the end of 2007, those principles and the ostensibly successful application of them during the surge would come to be seen as the main cause for the lowering of violence. Another "better war" within the counterinsurgency narrative had been born, and another enlightened counterinsurgency general christened a "maverick savior."

It is entirely possible, however, that if President Bush had never appointed General Petraeus as commander in Iraq but had kept General Casey in command, violence would have declined in the same way that it did by the end of 2007. This conclusion is based on extending the trajectory of the conditions that were already developing—the Sunni Awakening and the climax of sectarian violence in December 2006. Because Casey was not advocating a quick withdrawal from Iraq and because the operational framework for the military in Iraq before 2007 was and continued to be counterinsurgency, it is certainly possible that the level of violence would have fallen in the same way as it did after the actual Petraeus surge. Extending this hypothetical to Afghanistan, it is also entirely possible that without the surge triumph narrative constructed around Petraeus's surge and the mythical belief that COIN worked in Iraq, the discussions surrounding "Surge II" in the Hindu Kush in 2009 might have been tempered by focusing on other, more limited options. Had these options been seriously presented to President Obama in fall 2009 by his military, a different course of action might well have been taken. But the reality was that in 2008 and 2009, the surge triumph narrative arrived in full force, dominated thinking on what had happened in Iraq, and convinced key policy makers and military planners that something similar could be applied in Afghanistan.

# 5

# AFGHANISTAN: ANOTHER BETTER WAR
# THAT WASN'T

*The only way to prevent al-Qaeda from returning to Afghanistan [McChrystal argued] was to protect the people.*
— Rajiv Chandrasekaran[1]

*I heard the explosion at around 11.45 in the morning. A few minutes later my wife called my mobile phone. She was very upset and difficult to understand. She told me that my 14-year old son had been buying ice at the scene when the detonation occurred. She told me she could see his blood on the road but did not know where he was. I went to the hospital. After some time searching among the injured and the dead I found his body. A piece of shrapnel had gone through his head. I passed out and was taken home by friends. My son is dead and his loss is killing me and my wife. He was the only son I had.*
— father of a victim of an IED attack in the
Dasht-i-Shor area of Mazar-i-Sharif,
Balkh Province, July 20, 2011[2]

The reality of counterinsurgency warfare—despite all its high-minded, moralistic bromides of "protecting the population" and "serving" the local peoples—is revealed in the anguish of an Afghan father who lost his son in a Taliban IED attack against NATO troops. Counterinsurgency war is ultimately about death and destruction produced by the fighting between the insurgent enemy and counterinsurgent forces. Yet many people continue to believe in the promise of counterinsurgency. In the spring of 2009, Secretary of Defense Robert Gates boasted that the previous commanding general, David McKiernan, had been replaced by the COIN-savvy General Stanley McChrystal because the United States needed "new leadership and fresh eyes," implying that a significant shift in strategy would arrive with McChrystal. Typical of the mainstream American press's uncritical reporting of the counterinsurgency narrative, the *Wall Street Journal* stated blandly that the Pentagon appointed McChrystal "in an attempt to jump-start a new war strategy that relies more on counterinsurgency tactics and less on conventional warfare."[3] But Gates and the superficial reporting were wrong. There was no change in strategy and military mission in Afghanistan. From early 2002, it had been fundamentally one of nation building at the barrel of a gun.

American counterinsurgency in Afghanistan has not worked.[4] Violence in the country has steadily risen over the years, and it rose even more after the Afghanistan surge under General McChrystal began in late 2009.[5] The notion that the U.S. military was not doing counterinsurgency correctly in Afghanistan from 2002 to 2009, then suddenly started to under McChrystal, is specious and not supported by evidence.[6] In fact, since early 2002, the U.S. military in Afghanistan has been carrying out armed nation building. Yet after ten years of nation building, something resembling democracy in the Hindu Kush will take generations and generations to create. Former *New York Times* reporter Dexter Filkins noted that "after eleven years, more than four-hundred billion dollars spent and two thousand Americans dead, this is what we've built: a deeply dysfunctional, predatory Afghan state that seems incapable of standing on its own—even when we're there."[7]

Nevertheless, the proponents of counterinsurgency in Afghanistan continue to emphasize its purported promise. One such proponent, U.S. Army Colonel Robert Cassidy, argues that in 2009 with the arrival of General Stanley McChrystal, the army had finally figured out how to do counterinsurgency correctly. Paula Broadwell's biography of Petraeus summarized the essence of the narrative perfectly: get the right guy in charge, namely Petraeus, protect "the indigenous population," and success is almost guaranteed. In a passage reminiscent of the *Star Wars* epic, Broadwell told her readers that in July 2010 there was a "new strategic *force* loosed in Kabul: Petraeus's will."[8]

Petraeus has often been quoted as saying that after he arrived in command, and even one year before, with the arrival of General McChrystal in spring 2009, the American effort in Afghanistan had finally gotten the "inputs right." The expression betrayed a deep-seated American military assumption that by getting organization, systems, and procedures working correctly wars can be won. An army lieutenant colonel who served in Afghanistan in 2007 and 2008, Lewis G. Irwin, recently published a book titled *Disjointed Ways, Disunified Means: Learning from America's Struggle to Build an Afghan Nation*. His argument—largely accepted in military policy circles—is typical of the American army's belief that organizational and procedural adjustment can produce victory in war.[9]

In Vietnam, the American army also refined and improved its organizational structures and methods. The classic example was the introduction of Civil Operations and Revolutionary Development Support (CORDS), which efficiently channeled resources toward Vietnamese reconstruction and state-building efforts. Initiated by General Westmoreland, CORDS showed the army's ability to learn and adapt when the situation demanded. Drawing on this historical precedent, contemporary counterinsurgency experts like David Kilcullen have argued that America needs a "global CORDS" to fight radical Islamism based on the Vietnam model.[10] But in the end, the United States lost the war in Vietnam even with improved organizational structures like CORDS. It lost because it failed at strategy. Tactical and organizational improvements do not save wars fought under failed strategy.

In his new book on Afghanistan, *Washington Post* reporter Rajiv Chandrasekaran describes an American war that has seen buckets and buckets of wasted energy and effort, bungled military operations, dysfunctional command and organizational structures, and naive, misguided priorities. But wars and the militaries that fight them are never models of efficiency—far from it. Writing over two centuries ago, the Prussian philosopher on war Carl von Clausewitz, in his seminal book *On War*, introduced the idea of "friction" in war.[11] Because wars are fought between peoples and militaries with opposing wills, operating in a realm of death and destruction, "friction" makes otherwise smooth-running military organizations quite imperfect and at times dysfunctional, Clausewitz argued. The American military in Afghanistan in this regard is no different.

Consider some examples from military history. During the American Civil War, the Union army's command structure never produced efficient staffs at the higher levels to adequately convey orders and plans to subordinate units, and the Confederates were even worse. And the Union army arguably never really got its organizational structures for combat right. It never developed a powerful striking force of all arms that could exploit victories in battle to make them truly decisive. General George Meade at Gettysburg had soundly defeated Lee's army, but because he lacked a powerful counteroffensive force of cavalry and infantry and artillery, he could not exploit the victory to destroy Lee's army. In World War II, before the Normandy invasion, the American army under General Omar Bradley had badly conceived the use of airpower to destroy German defensive positions on the bluffs overlooking Omaha Beach. There was an assumption that high-flying strategic bombers would pulverize the beach defenses, so that when the Twenty-ninth and First Infantry Divisions landed, they would easily move off the beach and on to the high ground. But air-power did not have the intended effect, and the plan went dread-fully wrong.[12]

In both cases, however, the wars were fought under a broader strategic framework that made sense. When a state gets its strategy right in war, tactical problems tend to be subsumed and improved within it. The Union army in the Civil War and the American army in World War II encountered their fair share of "friction," but good strategy smoothed those problems out in the end. What Chandrasekaran exposes in his new book on the Americans in Afghanistan is nothing new in war: friction. But when a state fights a war under a botched strategy—as the United States is cur-rently doing in Afghanistan—that friction is exposed and laid bare with nothing higher for cover.

The impact of tactics without strategy was evident in Afghani-stan's Garmsir District in 2010, where a civilian, Carter Malka-sian, reportedly became one of the most respected civilian advisers to the American military in Afghanistan and a trusted friend of many Afghan leaders. He provided advice to American military commanders on the socioeconomic factors in the area and became a key link with Afghan local leaders. Yet larger questions of strat-egy did not seem especially relevant to Malkasian and his work. "I haven't spent a lot of time thinking if there was value in being here—I just assumed there was value. . . . To me, it's like being in a boxing match: If you're not going in with a mind-set that you're go-ing to win, there's no point being in the ring."[13] But what if fighting in the ring in Afghanistan in the way that the American military has chosen—armed nation building—is not worth the effort? How can the American military ask the hard questions of strategy when it is trapped in the belief that it can make nation building work?[14]

General Douglas MacArthur famously said in 1949 that in war "there is no substitute for victory." It is not uncommon today to hear American generals repeat MacArthur's problematic maxim.[15]

But sometimes, in a war that involves limited policy aims, there may well be alternatives to victory. Moreover, as was the case with MacArthur, it is not ultimately a general's call to decide that in war there is no substitute for victory. That decision rests with political leaders. If the American military believes there is no substitute for victory in Afghanistan, then the United States ends up with a military's operational solution defining the war's objective. In Afghanistan, that means victory is defined as allowing the army to make long-term nation building work. One American general recently suggested to his political masters that the United States was at war for the "long haul" in Afghanistan, and "political patience" needed to be maintained in order for the U.S. military to succeed there.[16] Such thinking by military leaders produces a situation in which the military's tactical methods eclipse strategy and even policy. As a result of this commitment by the American military to make counterinsurgency work, America has backed into a botched strategy in Afghanistan.

That botched strategy has sought to further a very limited and singular policy aim—the destruction of al Qaeda in Afghanistan—via a maximalist operational method, armed nation building. In war, strategy sits in the middle of two other components: policy and tactics. Policy directs what the war is to accomplish, then strategy applies the resources to achieve policy aims. In Afghanistan, good strategy has been absent from the start. Instead of using limited military force to get after the core policy objective, the American defense establishment has said that the only way to achieve that goal is to build up an Afghan government and economy that would win the population over to its side and thus prevent the return of al Qaeda. "The only way to defeat al Qaeda" in Afghanistan, argued General McChrystal in fall 2009, was to do proper counterinsurgency and "protect the people." Such thinking represents the death of good American strategy and a waste of good American blood and treasure.[17]

From the earliest days of the American war in Afghanistan, the core political objective has remained the same: the destruction of al Qaeda. During the early months of fighting after 9/11, the Taliban was targeted because it had assisted al Qaeda by allowing it to use Afghanistan as a base of operations to coordinate the attack against the United States. As the years progressed, the goal of defeating al Qaeda remained, even as its numbers of fighters in Afghanistan dwindled to somewhere between fifty and a hundred.[18] The Taliban also remained a target of American military operations, but only because the means to achieve the core policy objective of defeating al Qaeda was to build a new Afghan nation to prevent its return. Defeating the Taliban is not and never has been America's core political objective in Afghanistan, a position that has been reiterated by American presidents George W. Bush and Barack Obama and affirmed over and over again by senior military leaders and other civilian officials.

In the early months of 2002, the United States military carried out Operation Anaconda to complete the removal of the Taliban from power in Afghanistan and to destroy al Qaeda. General Tommy Franks reported to the House Armed Services Committee in February 2002, just months into combat operations, that "today, the Taliban have been removed from power and the al Qaeda network in Afghanistan has been destroyed." In an early indication of how American military operations would conform to a nation-building template, General Franks, restating what President George Bush had said only weeks earlier, argued that the way to keep al Qaeda at bay was to commit to a "permanent solution . . . based on strengthening Afghanistan's capacity."[19] (A popular term among the proponents of nation building, *capacity* means the sum total of a state's resources and institutions, such as governance, security forces, infrastructure, and economy.) General Franks's early testimony to Congress shows that United States has been in the nation-building business from the start.

From 2002 to 2004, the Taliban withdrew into eastern Afghanistan and parts of Pakistan and licked its wounds after a severe drubbing from American military operations. Those first two years saw an early American commitment to building up the capacity of Afghan institutions in order to prevent the return of the Taliban and al Qaeda. One report from the United States Agency for International Development (USAID) noted in 2003 that its efforts to "reconstruct Afghanistan" had helped to "improve the harvest by 82%" over the previous year. The report also noted that USAID had assisted in building up local governing institutions, had rebuilt "121 health clinics," and had provided close to "25 million textbooks to Afghan school children." The American army was also playing a significant role in the campaign to build a new Afghan state. The army had started a program called the Provincial Reconstruction Teams (PRTs), each composed of about eighty military and civilian personnel and providing expertise needed in rebuilding Afghan infrastructure, governing bodies, and the economy. A senior civilian adviser to one of the PRTs in 2004 described the team's function as rebuilding infrastructure and governance, engaging with political figures, and improving agriculture. He also complimented the American military, saying that they were not so much interested in destroying things but instead toward "building things up" and making "this country more viable economically and otherwise."[20]

The bulk of the American army's effort during these early years was dedicated to hunting down and capturing or killing the Taliban and any lingering al Qaeda fighters. By the end of 2004, U.S. Army troop strength in Afghanistan was about fifteen thousand. Most of those troops were in three combat brigades, with additional support personnel under an evolving command structure. Although the combat brigades were involved during these early years with nation-building endeavors—for example, building schools and using Commander's Emergency Response Program

(CERP) funds to improve local infrastructure—for the most part, they were carrying out combat missions against the Taliban and remaining al Qaeda.[21] Yet the overall American effort in Afghanistan was premised on nation building. Other elements of the U.S. Army deployed as PRTs, American agencies like USAID, and multiple civilian groups were actively involved with building a new Afghan state. The American army's combat mission was embedded in a larger campaign of nation building.[22]

The United States invaded Iraq in March 2003. Once the U.S. military toppled the Hussein regime, by early April, the U.S. Army and Marines quickly shifted to occupation duties and counterinsurgency operations. At the small-unit level of platoons, companies, and battalions, the army integrated combat operations with efforts to rebuild Iraqi institutions. On any given day, part of a combat unit might conduct a search operation to capture insurgents while other elements of that same outfit might meet with local leaders to work on infrastructure and security.

The experiences of the American army conducting counterinsurgency–nation building operations in Iraq inevitably migrated to Afghanistan. A clear indication of that transfer of experience can be seen in the Afghanistan command of Lieutenant General David Barno. From May 2003 to May 2005, Barno combined discrete American military operations into a more comprehensive approach to counterinsurgency involving a closer cooperation between American military personnel and civilians involved in reconstruction, as well as the direct involvement of army combat brigades in activities designed to win over the local population. One of Barno's subordinate officers noted that in order to win in Afghanistan, his outfit began to see its "role" as "separating the insurgents from the population." Another commanding officer under Barno noted that to be "victorious," his soldiers "must win the trust and confidence" of the Afghan people. Tacking perfectly with the counterinsurgency principles that would later be codified in FM 3-24, the commanding officer said that if the actions of his task force "ultimately did not foster the government's capacity and its legitimacy within the eyes of the population," then their "campaign could not be considered successful."[23]

The changes brought about by Barno, however, should not be seen as any kind of radical shift in American strategy in Afghanistan. He did put in place some significant tactical adjustments, but they were only that—tactical adjustments. The overall strategic framework for the United States had remained unchanged since the start of the war: armed nation building to create a new Afghan state that would prevent al Qaeda from using Afghanistan to conduct future attacks against America. A year into Barno's command, the chairman of the House Armed Services Committee, Duncan Hunter, made clear that the overriding political goal of the United States in Afghanistan was to "eliminate Afghanistan as a safe harbor . . . for al Qaeda." Hunter argued that the way to do that was, as President Bush said at the beginning of the war in 2002, by "laying the foundations for stable countries whose governments reflect the will of the people." Undersecretary of State Nancy Powell agreed. She told the House Armed Services Committee that the American strategy for "winning the peace in Afghanistan" was by "improving governance; defeating the terrorist threat and improving security, improving rule of law and justice; [and] enhancing economic and social development."[24]

Heavy American investment in Afghanistan has been the norm since 2002. That investment has come in the form of military operations and reconstruction aid. As of 2011, the total U.S. expenditure for fighting the Taliban and rebuilding Afghanistan came to nearly $444 billion. Overall expenditures began to increase significantly by 2007 due to an increase in insurgent activity and then again in 2009 with President Obama's Afghanistan surge. However, from the earliest days of American occupation, the amount of treasure spent has been substantial: in 2006 to 2011, with the increases, $352 billion; but even in the comparable period of 2002 to 2006, $90 billion—and this at a time when the insurgency was at a low idle.[25]

When the Taliban government was overthrown by American military power in December 2001, Taliban survivors retreated to the eastern reaches of the country and into sanctuaries in Pakistan. But after years of recovery in those areas, by the summer of 2006, the Taliban returned in force to fight against the American-led occupation and the government it installed, headed by Hamid Karzai. Total U.S. troop strength was at about twenty-two thousand, plus a smattering of foreign forces from Britain, Canada, the Netherlands, and others. These U.S. and NATO forces fought back against the reinvigorated Taliban insurgency. And the way it fought back was in conformity to its strategy from the beginning: build a new Afghan nation as the means to achieve America's core political goal of the destruction of al Qaeda. The Taliban had continued to be America's enemy because of its resistance to nation building. As the Combined Forces commander in Afghanistan in 2006, Lieutenant General Karl Eikenberry, explained, combat operations were only a part of a "longer-term goal of strengthening good governance, the rule of law, reconstruction and humanitarian assistance, and economic development. This emphasis on governance and development is indicative of our overall approach to the Afghan campaign."[26]

According to Defense Secretary Robert Gates, by the end of 2007, the campaign to deny al Qaeda safe haven in Afghanistan was making definite progress. Although the secretary pointed out that there remained significant problems with the "mission" and that Taliban attacks against state-building efforts had increased, he asserted that the efforts by the United States and its Afghan allies had produced "solid results." Gates noted in testimony to

Congress that the United States had spent $10 billion on reconstruction projects, along with additional billions for training the Afghan security forces. He went so far as to say that the restive valley along Afghanistan's eastern border with Pakistan, Khost Province, had been a "model counterinsurgency campaign" brought about by the "integration of hard and soft power." It was an example, Gates boasted, of "potential gains" in other areas of the country. In conclusion, the secretary maintained that the key to American security in Afghanistan was a rebuilt and "stable" country. At the same testimony, Eric Edelman, undersecretary of state for policy, was asked if the United States was involved in "nation building" in Afghanistan. Edelman replied in the affirmative that the United States was involved in an "effort at state building" by "getting the fundamental institutions of a functioning state."[27]

As violence subsided in Iraq, the U.S. Army and Marines began transferring combat brigades to Afghanistan. By the end of 2008, the total number of American troops in Afghanistan had risen to almost forty thousand. In 2007 and 2008, along with the increase in American troops came heightened levels of insurgent violence against American and NATO forces, as well as civilians. The year 2008 saw the arrival of another American commanding general, David McKiernan.[28] Like his predecessors, McKiernan committed himself and his command to a large-scale nation-building campaign to achieve the core policy objective, the defeat of al Qaeda.

McKiernan was the consummate counterinsurgency general. Reflecting on his time in command, he noted that once the United States had broken the Taliban regime in late 2001 and early 2002, it incurred a "moral responsibility" to stay and clean up the mess. General McKiernan believed that the way to prevent al Qaeda's return was to commit to a long-term effort of building up new Afghan governing, security, and economic institutions. Drawing on his understanding of history, General McKiernan noted that classic counterinsurgency campaigns—the kind that he believed he was conducting in Afghanistan in 2008 and 2009—required a very long time to be successful. And success would come when the United States and NATO reached a tipping point in Afghanistan, when "government at all levels, economy, and security [forces] in Afghanistan are strong enough that we can stand back and provide support and mentorship." The general submitted a report to Congress in June 2008 stating that his command's "counterinsurgency approach demonstrates how a combination of military and non-military resources can be integrated to create a stable and secure environment and connect the Afghan people with their government." In October 2008, on the eve of the American presidential election, General McKiernan requested additional troops from President Bush, a response to rising levels of insurgent violence that produced, in the words of the general, "a tough counterinsurgency fight."[29]

Just one month before the general would be relieved from command in Afghanistan, Representative Ike Skelton told the House Armed Services Committee that the counterinsurgency strategy that McKiernan was carrying out "largely gets it right." Skelton went on to add that President Obama also "got it right" when he pointed out that the ultimate focus of "our efforts was to eliminate al Qaeda and remove sanctuaries from which they are constantly planning attacks against us. That's the right goal. We should always remember that." Of course, from the beginning of U.S. military operations in Afghanistan, the operational framework had always been counterinsurgency—armed nation building—to achieve the core policy goal of destroying al Qaeda; Skelton was merely reiterating the continuity of American strategy in Afghanistan. At the same hearing, Michelle Flournoy, undersecretary of defense for policy, agreed with Skelton that the core American policy objective was to "disrupt, to dismantle and defeat al Qaeda and its extremist allies in the region."[30]

General David Petraeus had left Iraq after the surge had ended in the middle of 2008 and was appointed commanding general of Central Command (CENTCOM), which had Afghanistan as one of its areas of responsibility. Petraeus reported on the status of American operations in Afghanistan in April 2009 to the House Armed Services Committee. He spoke in very positive terms about the counterinsurgency campaign:

> Achieving our objectives in Afghanistan requires a comprehensive counterinsurgency approach, and that is what General David McKiernan and ISAF [the International Security Assistance Force] are endeavoring to execute with the additional resources being committed. The additional forces will provide an increased capability to secure and serve the people, to pursue the extremists, to support the development of host-nation security forces, to reduce the illegal narcotics industry and to help develop the Afghan capabilities needed to increase the legitimacy of national and local Afghan governance.[31]

Then just one month after Petraeus's laudatory testimony to Congress on McKiernan's "comprehensive counterinsurgency approach," General McKiernan was relieved of command and replaced by General Stanley McChrystal.

Andrew Exum is a counterinsurgency expert and former U.S. Army Ranger in Iraq and Afghanistan. Exum appeared giddy in the spring of 2009, with the prospect of the appointment of Stanley McChrystal as commanding general in Afghanistan. Exum emphasized in a television interview with talk show host Rachel Maddow that McChrystal had all of the right qualities to turn the situation in Afghanistan around and get the American army on the correct path to proper counterinsurgency methods. Comparing McChrystal favorably to McKiernan, Exum considered McChrystal the "right person" to do counterinsurgency focused on "population protection." McChrystal was clearly the better general, with a reputation for being one of the "smartest" in the American army—a "rare bird," he said.[32]

McKiernan's abrupt sacking demonstrates that the counterinsurgency narrative was shaping American actions in Afghanistan. What faults, mistakes, or failures caused him to be cashiered so abruptly and in such a publicly demeaning way? McKiernan had put in place a counterinsurgency campaign plan that differed little from McChrystal's. McKiernan was not a failed and fumbling general. One month before he was fired, his boss, General Petraeus, had affirmed that McKiernan was carrying out a "comprehensive counterinsurgency campaign" that would "protect and serve" the Afghan people. FM 3-24 could not have asked for a better general.

Relieving McKiernan focused attention and energy on the tactics, techniques, and methods of counterinsurgency rather than the strategy that decided where and when to apply them. Now that the right general was in command, with a surge in troops that McChrystal would soon ask for, the "right inputs" were there.

The counterinsurgency narrative posits that savior generals have game-changing effects, but it overstates their influence on the course of war. In Iraq, if Petraeus's arrival had "revolutionized" the way the war was being fought, giving Iraqis, to use Petraeus's words, "a new hope," then one would expect to see this change reflected in how Iraqis remember the war. But they don't remember such a change. The same is true for McChrystal and later Petraeus in Afghanistan. If these two generals fundamentally altered American strategy there, then it would be reasonable to expect the enemy to acknowledge as much. But a review of the letters captured in the Osama bin Laden raid reveals that while bin Laden and his lieutenants discussed many issues, there was never any mention made of the supposed game-changing adjustments in strategy that McChrystal and Petraeus had made in Afghanistan.[33]

The issue of operational *continuity* or *discontinuity* is critical here. The narrative of counterinsurgency as it is currently applied to Afghanistan posits that there must have been operational discontinuity once the better general, McChrystal, took over in 2009 and redirected his army toward correct counterinsurgency methods. As a result of this operational discontinuity, "winning" the war in Afghanistan was therefore finally in the realm of the possible. But what if there was operational continuity rather than discontinuity? Continuity exposes the myth of counterinsurgency. If the U.S. Army and supporting civilian agencies were doing nation-building counterinsurgency as early as 2002 in Afghanistan, why haven't we already won and departed? Why hasn't it worked? The blunt answer is that hearts-and-minds counterinsurgency carried out by an occupying power in a foreign land doesn't work, unless it is a multigenerational effort. It didn't work as touted in Malaya, Vietnam, or Iraq. Yet the narrative has become so hardened and dominant that folks continue to believe that progress can be made in Afghanistan because finally a better general has ridden onto the scene and his army is supposedly doing something different.

Comments from soldiers and officers serving in Afghanistan from 2002 to 2012 confirm continuity, not discontinuity. In early 2004, just as the counterinsurgency campaign was getting under way, one American combat soldier emphasized that his unit was "not like the Russians. We don't come here and bomb everything." His battalion commander noted that he and his men were not "down in the firebases" but instead were out among the civilian population. In the middle of 2005, an American reporter saw that the army believed it vital "to be seen working alongside Afghan soldiers or police to reinforce the idea that the United States is not an occupying force, but a partner with Karzai's government." Two years later, an infantry company commander operating in Kunar Province reflected on over a year of COIN operations, saying that one of the first things his company did was to "live with the people. . . . I didn't fully realize its importance until I did it for a while. You read about it in counterinsurgency. But it doesn't really click in your mind until you actually do it." An infantry battalion commander in eastern Afghanistan in 2008 remembered his fifteen-month deployment and the criticality of "living and working with the population."[34] The experiences of American commanders and soldiers in Afghanistan from late 2002 to 2009 clearly indicate that the army understood and was carrying out the principles of classic counterinsurgency—but they weren't working.

After General McChrystal assumed command, he offered an initial assessment of the situation in an August 2009 report to Secretary of Defense Robert Gates. His language closely resembled the instructions Petraeus issued to his troops in Iraq during the surge two years earlier. Moreover, McChrystal's assessment of what his troops needed to do to win the war in Afghanistan were remarkably similar to the announcements and public statements that his predecessor David McKiernan made on army operations in the year leading up to his relief. Yet McChrystal asserted that "we must change the way we think, act, and operate." The "mindset" of operations must be changed, and "we need to think and act very differently to be successful." The general stated forthrightly that "protecting the population from insurgent coercion demanded persistent presence. . . . The situation in Afghanistan is serious. The mission is achievable, but success demands a fundamentally new approach." It was not enough to just add more troops, argued the general; instead what was needed was a whole new strategy to achieve the president's core objective of destroying al Qaeda. Over the course of the next year, a common theme from McChrystal's headquarters and staff was that they finally had the "right inputs" in place.[35]

McChrystal's "strategic review" ultimately brought about, with President Obama's approval, an additional thirty thousand

American troops in Afghanistan; by the end of 2010, the total topped out at approximately one hundred thousand.[36] McChrystal also made organizational changes and some adjustments to tactics. For example, he increased overall unity of effort by bringing together a number of disparate command functions under one authority. He also issued command guidance that aimed to reduce the numbers of Afghan civilians injured or killed inadvertently. But whatever tactical and organizational refinements he put in place, and however many troops were added in the end, these were only changes in *degree* and not in *kind*. America's overall strategy, armed nation building, had not changed.

The arrival of Stanley McChrystal in Afghanistan in spring 2009 was a show of faith in the promise of the counterinsurgency narrative. Just as owners often believe a new manager will turn a failing sports team around, administrations have faith that better generals can turn a war around and save it from failure. McChrystal's abrupt relief a little more than a year into his command (after unprofessional remarks uttered by his immediate staff in his presence about American political leaders were reported in a *Rolling Stone* magazine article) caused no disruption in the counterinsurgency narrative.[37] As the new commanding general in Afghanistan, David Petraeus was very quick to compliment McChrystal and the operational changes that he purportedly put into place. Petraeus said that he admired what "General McChrystal had achieved in terms of input and output and will take much of his work forward."[38]

The "inputs" at times could be quite destructive for Afghanistan and its people. An American combat battalion reduced to rubble the village of Tarok Kolache in Kandahar Province in 2010. The tactical rationale for destroying the village made perfect sense for the combat battalion that fought there: it had become a haven for the Taliban and was laced with booby traps and mines that maimed and killed many soldiers in the battalion. Apparently, all of the civilians who lived there had left. Yet the commanding officer of the unit justified his actions by arguing that as a result of razing the village and eliminating it as a base for Taliban operations, the local people could now be linked to the government. "As of today," claimed the battalion commander, "more of the local population talks to us and the government than . . . the Taliban, who provide no services to the people."[39]

The tactical rationale for the destruction of Tarok Kolache is similar to that which led to the infamous destruction of the Vietnamese village of Ben Tre. During the Tet Offensive in early 1968, Ben Tre had become infested with Viet Cong fighters, who had dug themselves into the town with barricades, mines, and booby traps, causing significant casualties among the American infantrymen who were tasked to clear it. Instead of losing more men to clear the village, the commanding officer decided to level it with American firepower, to the tune of about 550 Vietnamese deaths and 1,200 injuries. A few days later at a press briefing, an officer from the infantry battalion that had been in charge of pummeling the town was pressured by American journalists to explain why he did it. Frustrated with the pressure and flurry of hard-biting questions, the officer blurted out that his unit had to "destroy Ben Tre to save it." The journalists in attendance ate it up like catnip and the phrase went viral. Since then, destroying something to save it has come to represent everything that was wrong with the war in Vietnam and other wars.[40] It did so because by the time of the Tet Offensive, the myth that the American people had been told about the Vietnam War, that it was in their vital interest and worth their blood and treasure, had been brought into serious question. Without the myth for cover, actions like the destruction of Ben Tre were laid bare and seen for what they were: brutal industrialized warfare. But with the myth of counterinsurgency in place in Afghanistan, destroying Tarok Kolache to link the people to the government was acceptable because it was carried out under a "comprehensive counterinsurgency strategy," led by an enlightened general who was "protecting the population" and had the right inputs in place. Petraeus's biographer Paula Broadwell made the explicit link between the destruction of the village and the belief that counterinsurgency works when she glibly noted that the residents of Tarok Kolache were "pissed about the loss of their mud huts but that is why the build story is important here."[41]

Independent sources show that violence in Afghanistan has progressively risen since 2009, when McChrystal took over and put into place a supposedly different strategy. The Afghanistan NGO Safety Office (ANSO) report for 2011 argued that the Taliban had increased its activity since 2009, including its ability to establish "shadow governments" in areas where the Afghan government was trying to gain control. The "momentum" of the Taliban and other insurgent forces appeared "unaffected by US led counterinsurgency efforts," and taking the country as a whole, there was "indisputable evidence that conditions are deteriorating. If [Taliban] losses are taken in one area they are simply compensated for in another." But the most critical statement in the report was directed at the never-ending stream of positive reports from American political and military leaders that progress is occurring in Afghanistan. The ANSO report blasted such optimism, saying that NATO and American proclamations of success were "solely intended to influence American and European public opinion . . . and are not intended to offer an accurate portrayal of the situation for those who live and work here."[42]

American strategy has failed in Afghanistan because it has become trapped by the promise that counterinsurgency can work if only it is given enough time and tactical tweaking. But in war, time is a factor in the overall calculation of strategy, and lots and lots of time is needed for American counterinsurgency to succeed in Afghanistan.

Successful long-term nation building in Afghanistan would involve a number of hypothetical "inputs." First, the United States would have to conjure the political will to commit to a multigenerational, sustained effort. After all, it took the United States almost a hundred years to solve the fundamental social and political issue that divided it—slavery. And even after 1865, much work was still to be done. In Europe, it took centuries to overcome feudalism and warlordism and transform fiefdoms into modern nation-states. Afghanistan today, with its competition for political power among its various warlords and political leaders, resembles European states in the late Middle Ages. Why do Americans think that Afghanistan can be taken from its current condition to that of a stable nation in only a handful of years? [43]

Once committed to a multigenerational nation-building effort in Afghanistan, the next step would be to develop the operational framework to carry it out. First, the size of American forces in Afghanistan would need to be doubled, if not trebled, toward a figure of around three hundred thousand soldiers and marines. At least a third of this force would be required to seal off the Pakistan-Afghanistan border, because the Pakistani government will do nothing to end the Afghan Taliban's use of the country for sanctuary. The other two thirds of this military force would flood the country with combat units, controlling the population and infrastructure. Of course, the Taliban would resist this through fighting, which is why large numbers of ground troops would be needed. Combined with the increased number of troops, the United States would have to take a more active role in governing the country, at least supporting Afghan leaders who would comply with the American program (with all of the challenges and contradictions such a move would imply for a country ostensibly on a path to democracy). Once the governmental structures were improved and stabilized, then foreign aid from America and elsewhere to build infrastructure, the economy, and local security forces would be used much more efficiently and effectively. Doing all of these things over decades would inevitably mean increasing the size of the American forces in Afghanistan, as well as civilian agency participation.[44]

This nation-building hypothetical is, of course, pure fantasy. There is no political will in the United States, either among the people or in government, to do anything of the sort. COIN expert John Nagl may be right when he says that in the future the American army and other government agencies will be able to build and "change entire societies."[45] But it won't be done on the cheap in a handful of years; it will be measured in generations. Such an endeavor would simply not be worth the effort, especially when we remember that the core policy goal in Afghanistan is the limited one of defeating al Qaeda.

In both Iraq and Afghanistan, the American military has achieved tactical gains. American service members have done their duty in Iraq, and they continue to do it in Afghanistan. They follow the orders of their civilian masters, and they are competent, professional servants and protectors of the United States and its people. But for war to work, all of that individual effort at the tactical level has to add up to something. Think about the German army in World War II, pound for pound one of the finest industrialized armies the world had ever seen, able to orchestrate huge amounts of tactical fighting power. Yet all of that tactical excellence on the part of the German army could not rescue it from a broken operational command structure and strategy and a morally perverse policy under Nazism. Then also consider the opposite case of the Soviet Union on the Eastern Front in World War II. Tactically, its army never really amounted to much and could never compare with the German one, but the Soviets developed excellent operational commanders who fought the war under a strategy that made sense for them.

There was a better strategy in Afghanistan available to American political and military leaders from the start. Our senior leaders could have discerned early the folly of trying to build Afghanistan into a modern state overnight and would have deduced that the core policy goal of destroying al Qaeda could have been done by a much smaller force concentrated against the few remaining al Qaeda left after the Taliban had been removed in early 2002.[46] Unfortunately, American strategy has failed in Afghanistan (and Iraq) because it was founded on an illusion—that American-style counterinsurgency could win Muslim hearts and minds at gunpoint and create viable nation-states on the Western model virtually from scratch in a short time. The idea that any of this ever made sense or has ever worked should be buried deep in the ground, yet the belief that counterinsurgency works persists like a vampire among the living.[47]

# AFTERWORD:
# TRUTH AS A CASUALTY OF COIN

*The first casualty when war comes is truth.*

—Senator Hiram Johnson, 1917

*Yemen is involved in three internal conflicts. The first conflict was the Houthi rebellion in the north. The Zaidiyyah Shia are more like the Sunnis than other Shia, but they're still Shia and they see themselves as being different from the rest of Yemen. They're looking for more autonomy. In the south, you have a secessionist movement. Those folks are basically saying that the north has been against them since unification in 1990 and they were abusing them a lot since the 1994 civil war. They think that they can do better on their own. They believe that they were better off alone in the 1970s and 1980s when they were supported by the Soviet Union, so they want to go back to the good old days. And the third insurrection . . . was . . . al Qaeda in the Arabian Peninsula—and its subsidiary Ansar al-Shariah. Throw the Arab Spring on top of all that and you have a bunch of different actors all vying for as much of the pie as they could possibly get.*

—Christopher Swift, "Observations on
Internal Conflict in Yemen," 2011[1]

*Military intervention in Syria offers the best hope for curtailing a long, bloody and destabilizing civil war.*

—Anne-Marie Slaughter,
February 23, 2012[2]

Christopher Swift's firsthand observations of internal conflict in Yemen in 2011 point to the reality of a place racked by a complex, violent civil war. Reading his description of Yemen's internal warring factions, I was reminded of my experiences in western Baghdad in 2006: multiple sides, violence, fear, hatred, death, and destruction and my foreign military force trying to stop it, all the while being a part of it. More recently, the decorated American combat veteran Michael Few said that, after reading reports of Syrian government suppression of rural villages, "it reminded [him] of the Diyala River Valley" in Iraq in 2007. When a foreign military force puts itself down in Yemen or Syria, places racked by civil war, it does so at the barrel of a gun, and the reality of such an intervention—even if the motive is to stop the fighting and protect civilian populations—is death and destruction.

Anne-Marie Slaughter, one of the leading advocates of foreign intervention in the Syrian civil war, sees the application of military force as the "best hope" for the Syrian people. Others agree, including Senators John McCain, Lindsay Graham, and Joseph Lieberman, all of whom argue for a stepped-up American involvement. I see it in a realistic light: even though the policy goals of such an intervention are noble—protecting innocent civilians from a predator government—the truth of such an intervention means that the foreign military force will inevitably end up taking sides in the civil war. That in turn will result invariably (even if unintentionally) in the killing of civilians and the destruction of parts of the country to an extent that no one can predict today. The president of the Council on Foreign Relations, Richard Haass, sums the problem up accurately: "The United States has an obligation to act to mitigate human suffering. But humanitarian responsibility—what the world terms the responsibility to protect—must be balanced against the projected human, military, political, and economic costs of acting, other calls on American resources, and the likelihood that the action would result in a demonstrably better political and humanitarian outcome."[3]

The notion that these kinds of interventions, especially if ground troops are involved, can be done in a precise and clean way must be jettisoned. In making the argument to intervene militarily in Syria, Slaughter says that it would be "defensive" in nature, involving only the minimum amount of force to protect vulnerable civilians. But her conception of how such a foreign military intervention in Syria to protect the population would go is a fantasy: wars are never clean. Wars are ugly, and soldiers fight and destroy things in the process; people die; the passions of hatred, fear, anger, and revenge resonate and multiply, producing exponential actions and reactions in infinite numbers and combinations; and once these wars start they have a momentum and logic all their own and become difficult to end.

American political leaders and the people they represent should have a clear idea of what will actually occur if the United States intervenes militarily to "protect populations" in the troubled spots of the world. Unfortunately, it seems that instead of learning from Iraq and Afghanistan that there are limits to what applied American military power can accomplish, especially in the middle of a virulent foreign civil war, civilian experts and government leaders have come away from these wars believing that COIN is an effective tool for the projection of American forces into new conflicts.

The myth that COIN works is catnip for advocates of U.S. intervention overseas because it promises the possibility of successful "better wars." American counterinsurgency has developed a language all of its own, and because of the faith in the myth that it works, the language rings in people's ears as factual truth. When generals, colonels, and policy makers say that they are "providing security" to a local population or are in a place like Afghanistan to "protect and serve" the Afghan people, many people have come to hear such utterances as accurate statements, despite the overwhelming evidence to the contrary. But saying the U.S. Army is "providing security" in Afghanistan—as if security were some kind of physical commodity that can be divvied out when the army is doing counterinsurgency correctly—does not mean that is what actually is happening.

The counterinsurgency narrative also provides moral sustenance to an American military—especially the army and marines—that has bled in these recent wars and wants to know that their sacrifice has been worth it. The narrative of counterinsurgency practiced by the U.S. military in Iraq and Afghanistan proves to be a story of failure and redemption. The moral righteousness embedded in the tactics of counterinsurgency casts the loss of American soldiers within an operational framework that has the ostensible moral objective of protecting innocent civilians and making their lives better. I lost five men from my cavalry squadron in western Baghdad in 2006—I understand this moral need. But I also understand the need for truth, and in the end, to me, the truth about these wars and exposing the myth of counterinsurgency is more important for the American military and the American people than the maintenance of the myth, even if that means losing the moral sustenance that goes along with it.

There are cracks in the myth of counterinsurgency, however. At the policy level, President Obama's nomination of Senator Chuck Hagel for secretary of defense suggests an end to nearly twenty years of military interventions from Somalia to Afghanistan. Hagel's Vietnam War experience has given him a cautionary view of the use of American military power to transform foreign societies—a notable change from the dominant view of counterinsurgency.[4]

The cracks are also seen in the sharp end of American counterinsurgency operations. In 2010, after a year of command in Afghanistan, General Stanley McChrystal visited a combat outpost in Kandahar Province to talk to an infantry platoon that a few days prior had a fellow soldier killed in action from an IED strike. General McChrystal spent about twenty minutes explaining the theory and practice of FM 3-24 counterinsurgency to the grieving soldiers. In his talk, he lectured the men, saying that they had to continue to concentrate on the imperatives of counterinsurgency: protecting the Afghan population, providing them with goods, and winning them over to the side of the Afghan government so that insurgents could be separated and captured or killed. Nobody other than McChrystal, a strident proponent of American counterinsurgency who declared he kept David Galula's *Counterinsurgency Warfare* (the operational template for FM 3-24) at his bedside, could have explained it any better. But the soldiers listening to the general were not moved by the sermon. One soldier responded angrily that, despite the general's assertion that their platoon "had stopped the momentum of the insurgency," he didn't "believe that was true in" his area: "The more we pull back, the more we restrain ourselves" from killing the enemy in order to protect and secure the population and "the stronger" the Taliban was becoming. *Rolling Stone* reporter Michael Hastings observed this exchange and noted that, at least from his view, General McChrystal "may have sold President Obama on counterinsurgency, but many of his men aren't buying it."[5]

If American combat soldiers in Afghanistan can see through the myth of COIN, it is time for the American people and especially policy makers to see it too. Sir Michael Howard, the eminent military historian and decorated World War II combat veteran, says that it is the historian's duty to shine light on things that are not compatible with "myth." "To do so is necessary," he argues, "not simply to conform to the values which the war was fought" but "to preserve military efficiency for the future." As the American army looks toward the future in a very uncertain world, and as it devises strategy for American security, it should do so with a clear eye to the recent past—and not one clouded with myth.[6]

# A NOTE ON SOURCES

As a historian, I tried as much as possible to support my argument using primary evidence.

For the chapter on Malaya, most of the primary evidence comes from two archival collections on British Army operations in Malaya: the British National Archives at Kew Gardens and the Templer Study Centre at the British Army Museum in London. At Kew Gardens I relied primarily on the documents and records from the War Office and the Colonial Office. The Templer Study Centre had a treasure trove of papers from senior British Army officers who served in Malaya, along with numerous interviews with soldiers who served there, daily journals of British officers, and historical reports from British field outfits in Malaya. I also drew on numerous published memoirs by British officers and soldiers who had served in Malaya. Also useful was the published three-volume collection of Malayan Emergency documents edited by S.R. Ashton, D.A. Low, and A.J. Stockwell.

For the chapter on Vietnam, I did research in three archival repositories. At the National Archives in College Park, Maryland, I drew mostly from Record Group 472, which contained valuable operational records of the U.S. Army in Vietnam. At the Center for Military History (CMH) in Washington, D.C., the MAC-V's Historians File had a wealth of documents, especially campaign plans and other operational documents. Also useful was the Westmoreland Message Traffic File at CMH, which contained General William Westmoreland's daily correspondence between MAC-V and outside agencies and commands. The archives at the Army Heritage and Education Center at the U.S. Army War

College in Carlisle Barracks, Pennsylvania, contained many sets of papers from American officers and civilians who served in Vietnam. These papers provided a broad range of documentary evidence on American combat operations and efforts at pacification, along with analyses and criticism of the American effort in Vietnam. I also relied on Gareth Porter's multivolume documentary history of the Vietnam War, the Gravel Edition of the Pentagon Papers, and Lewis Sorley's very helpful transcription of the audiotapes of General Creighton Abrams's weekly meetings.

The digital age is presenting problems for researchers in that so much of the primary evidence is contained on computer discs and hard drives, many of them already out of date and unreadable. I confronted these problems while writing the chapters on Iraq and Afghanistan. For the primary evidence in these chapters, I relied on a mix of archival material and sets of documentary evidence provided to me by other researchers; and, since these wars are current, I treated as primary evidence many of the articles, blog posts, and interviews that have been published in journals or in various places on the Internet. General George W. Casey (retired) gave me access to his papers from Iraq stored at the National Defense University, a very useful trove of the general's daily journals, notes from discussions with the national command authority, analyses done by himself and his staff on the situation in Iraq, and documents on his campaign planning and assessments. I also benefited greatly from several compact discs full of documentary evidence of American army operations in Iraq by scholar James Russell based on the research he did for his own book on military innovation in Iraq. Over the past few years a number of databases of important primary evidence have been made available, such as Iraq Body Count. A large number of interviews with American military personnel who served in Iraq in various capacities are available, as are equally important interviews of Iraqis, both military and civilian. For the Afghanistan chapter, I also relied heavily on interviews not only of Afghans but also of American military and civilian personnel involved with the war. Many of these interviews can be found in various online locations. Other important sources of data and evidence are the quarterly reports produced by the United Nations and other agencies on security conditions in Afghanistan. A substantial number of campaign plans and assessments by American senior commanders have also been made available online. Congressional testimony by senior American military and civilian leaders was a very important source for this chapter. Lastly, Daniel Weggelend provided me a significant batch of reports, databases, and briefing slides from his time spent in Afghanistan as an adviser to USAID.

The specifics of these sources are contained in the endnote citations in this book.

# NOTES

## Preface: A Personal Note—the Hell of Baghdad

1. For an excellent view of the Iraqi people's experience of the war and its destructiveness, see Mark Kukis, *Voices from Iraq: A People's History, 2003–2009* (New York: Columbia University Press, 2011). Kukis offers close to seventy interviews of Iraqi civilians who tell stories of their hard experiences during the American war of occupation. Another excellent view of the Iraqi side is Victoria Fontan's *Voices from Post-Saddam Iraq: Living with Terrorism, Insurgency, and New Forms of Tyranny* (Westport, CT: Praeger International Security, 2008). When I read accounts of the war from the Iraqi point of view, I find myself looking for connections to the Iraqis I knew during my years there, like the ones I describe above. Alas, I don't find them.

2. Headquarters, Department of the Army, Field Manual (FM) 3-24, *Counterinsurgency* (Washington, DC: 2006), pp. 1–26 to 1–28; the genesis to the Paradoxes Section in FM 3-24 is an article by Conrad Crane, Eliot Cohen, Jan Horvath, and John Nagl, "The Principles, Imperatives, and Paradoxes of Counterinsurgency," *Military Review*, March–April 2006.

3. See, for example, my "Eating Soup with a Spoon: Missing from the New COIN Manual Is the Imperative to Fight," *Armed Forces Journal*, September 2007; "Our COIN Doctrine Removes the Enemy from the Essence of War," *Armed Forces Journal*, January 2008; and "In the Middle of a Civil War," *Washington Post*, August 7, 2007.

4. David Kilcullen, "Understanding Current Operations in Iraq," *Small Wars Journal*, June 26, 2007, smallwarsjournal.com/blog/understanding-current-operations-in-iraq.

5. On Kagan's position, see his January 2007 plan for the surge, "Choosing Victory: A Plan for Success in Iraq," available at aei.org/files/2007/01/05/20070111_ChoosingVictoryupdated.pdf, and his comments on "Assessing the Surge" at the American Enterprise Institute, July 7, 2007, aei.org/files/2007/07/09/Assessing-the-Surge-in-Iraq.html; and Michael E. O'Hanlon and Kenneth M. Pollack, "A War We Just Might Win," *New York Times*, July 30, 2007.

## Introduction: The Conceit of American Counterinsurgency

1. Victor Davis Hanson, "Winning in Afghanistan: We Have Everything but a Confident Commander in Chief," *Morning Journal*, November 6, 2009, morning -journal.com/articles/2009/11/06/opinion/doc4af428c8801d9888871579.txt; see also Hanson's "Victory and the Savior Generals," Private Papers, February 10, 2011, victorhanson.com/articles/hanson021011.html.

2. Rajiv Chandrasekaran, *Little America: The War Within America's War in Afghanistan* (New York: Random House, 2012), 118.

3. Scott A. Cuomo and Brandon A. Gorman, "CSIS's Afghanistan IED Metrics Report Does Not Tell the Whole Story," *Small Wars Journal*, October 26, 2010, smallwarsjournal.com/blog/journal/docs-temp/586-cuomo.pdf.

4. "Petraeus: Afghan Army, Police, Making Progress, but Retention Lags," interview on *PBS Newshour* with Charles Sennott, February 2, 2011.

5. Samantha Power, "Our War on Terror," *New York Times*, July 29, 2007.

6. Sarah Sewall, John A. Nagl, David A. Petraeus, and James F. Amos, *The U.S. Army/Marine Corps Counterinsurgency Manual* (Chicago: University of Chicago Press, 2007).

7. For an explanation of the logic of American counterinsurgency and the importance of winning the people over to the side of the government and COIN force in order to separate them from the rebels, see Peter R. Mansoor and Mark S. Ulrich, "Linking Doctrine to Action: A New COIN Center of Gravity Analysis," *Military Review*, September–October 2007.

8. Robert M. Citino, *From Blitzkrieg to Desert Storm: The Evolution of Operational Warfare* (Lawrence: University of Kansas Press, 2004), 102.

9. "The Philosophy Behind the Iraq Surge," an interview with General (ret) Jack Keane by Octavian Manea, *Small Wars Journal*, April 5, 2011, smallwarsjournal .com/journal/iss/v7n4.pdf; and Victor David Hanson, "Winning in Afghanistan."

10. George W. Bush, *Decision Points* (New York: Random House, 2010), 365.

11. On McChrystal teaching at Yale and the issue of academic freedom, see Elisabeth Bumiller, "After War Room Heading Ivy League Classroom," *New York Times*, May 6, 2012; Gian P. Gentile, "Why Is General McChrystal Teaching an Off-the-Record Course at Yale?" *The Atlantic* (online), May 24, 2012, theatlantic .com/national/archive/2012/05/why-is-general-mcchrystal-teaching-an-off-the-record-course-at-yale/257626; Stephen Walt, "Yale Flunks Academic Freedom," *Foreign Policy*, May 29, 2012, walt.foreignpolicy.com/posts/2012/05/29/yale_flunks_academic_freedom. For a view of the kind of lucrative consulting firm General McChrystal runs, see his advertisement here: mcchrystalgroup.com/?q=content

/crosslead_executive_course; a three-day course per individual, according to the webpage, is $4,700.

12. *Decade of War*, vol. 1, *Enduring Lessons from the Past Decade of Operations*, Joint and Coalition Operational Analysis (JCOA), June 15, 2012. In this report, see pages 1, 4, 11–12, 19–20.

13. On the number of army combat brigades, see "The Army Strategy," August 22, 2008, 12–13; on the issue of the declining importance of heavy armor and mechanized brigades, see my "Death of the Armor Corps," *Small Wars Journal*, April 17, 2010, smallwarsjournal.com/jrnl/art/the-death-of-the-armor-corps; on the argument that the active heavy brigades (tanks and mechanized infantry) should be moved to the National Guard, see Andrew Krepinevich, "An Army at the Crossroads," Center for Strategic and Budgetary Assessments, 2008, xiii–xvi.

14. Douglas A. Wissing, *Funding the Enemy: How US Taxpayers Bankroll the Taliban* (Amherst, NY: Prometheus Books, 2012), 267.

15. Christina Lamb, "War: The World Tour," *Weekend Australian Magazine*, September 4, 2010, 5, 6.

16. Bob Woodward, *Obama's Wars* (New York: Simon & Schuster, 2010), 332, 338.

17. Chandrasekaran, *Little America*, 125–26. Vice President Biden has been identified in Woodward's book *Obama's Wars* and now in Chandraskaran's as a rare voice of dissent against a backdrop of lockstep agreement among senior army generals and defense officials, like Petraeus and Secretary of Defense Gates, toward the promise of counterinsurgency working in Afghanistan. During the run-up to major American escalation in Vietnam by the Johnson administration, George Ball was one of the few voices recommending restraint and caution; so too was Biden with regard to Afghanistan many years later.

18. Iraq Body Count, iraqbodycount.org; and Nir Rosen, *Aftermath: Following the Bloodshed of America's Wars in the Muslim World* (New York: Nation Books), 277.

19. The best work on army transformation is in Douglas Macgregor's two seminal books, *Breaking the Phalanx: A New Design for Landpower in the 21st Century* (Westport, CT: Praeger, 1997), and *Transformation Under Fire: Revolutionizing How America Fights* (Westport, CT: Praeger, 2003); see also my "The Imperative for a General Purpose Army That Can Fight," *Orbis*, Summer 2009.

20. For example, former secretary of defense Robert Gates stated at a speech at West Point in February 2011 that any future secretary of state who advocates sending a "large American army" to the Middle East or other places ought to have his "head examined."

21. The most vocal advocate for R2P interventions in places like Syria is Anne-Marie Slaughter: see her "How to Halt the Butchery in Syria," *New York*

*Times*, February 23, 2012. For a thoughtful argument suggesting that R2P is becoming the next COIN, see Mark Sanfranski's blog entry "R2P Is the New COIN: Slaughter's Premises," Zenpundit, zenpundit.com/?p=4327.

## 1. The Construction of the Counterinsurgency Narrative

1. Senator John McCain, jacket cover endorsement of Kimberly Kagan's *The Surge: A Military History* (New York: Encounter Books, 2009).

2. FM 3-24, *Counterinsurgency*, 1–14, 1–15; for two similar views of how the army must shape the narrative through what it calls "information operations," see Richard B. Leap, "Strategic Communication: An Imperative for the Global War on Terror Environment," in *Information as Power: An Anthology of Selected Army War College Student Papers*, ed. Dennis M. Murphy et al. (Information Warfare Group, US Army War College, 2006); and Ralph O. Baker, "Information Operations: From Good to Great," *Military Review*, July–August, 2011.

3. For a recent example of the power of the counterinsurgency narrative, see Fred Kaplan's *The Insurgents: David Petraeus and the Plot to Change the American Way of War* (New York: Simon & Schuster, 2013); and Michael Gordon, "The Iraq Red Team," *Foreign Policy*, September 24, 2012, foreignpolicy.com/articles/2012/09/24/the_iraq_red_team. The Iraq war, argues Gordon, could have been put on a path to success in 2005 if only the commanding general, George Casey, had listened to some of his experts, who were proposing a "classic" counterinsurgency campaign. see also a very effective counter to Gordon by General George Casey, "About That Red Team Report," *Foreign Policy*, September 27, 2012, foreignpolicy.com/articles/2012/09/27/about_that_iraq_red_team_report.

4. Sir Robert Thompson, *Defeating Communist Insurgency: The Lessons of Malaya and Vietnam* (New York: Praeger, 1966), 20.

5. *The Pentagon Papers: The Defense Department History of United States Decision Making on Vietnam*, Senator Gravel edition, vol. 2 (Boston: Beacon Press, 1971), 139–43.

6. The best review of the complex and competing interpretations of America's loss in Vietnam is Garry R. Hess, *Vietnam: Explaining America's Lost War* (Malden, MA: Blackwell Press, 2009).

7. John Whiteclay Chambers II, "Counterinsurgency," in *The Oxford Companion to American Military History*, ed. John Whiteclay Chambers II, 189–90; John Mackinlay, *The Insurgent Archipelago: From Mao to Bin Laden* (New York: Columbia University Press, 2009), 19–21.

8. For a good general history of guerrilla warfare, see Robert B. Asprey's encyclopedic *War in the Shadows: The Guerrilla in History*, vol. 1 (New York: Double-

day, 1975) and vol. 2 (New York: Morrow, 1994); C.E Callwell offers excellent summaries of a multitude of small wars and engagements from the nineteenth century in his classic *Small Wars: Their Principles and Practice* (1906; Lincoln: University of Nebraska Press, 1996); for a useful set of analytical essays on modern insurgencies, see Ian Beckett's *Modern Counterinsurgency* (Aldershot, UK: Ashgate, 2007) and my "Counterinsurgency and War," in *The Oxford Handbook of War,* ed. Julian Lindley-French and Yves Boyer (New York: Oxford University Press, 2012).

9. Rupert Smith, *The Utility of Force: The Art of War in the Modern World* (New York: Vintage, 2008), 1–5, 148–49.

10. Lieutenant General William B. Caldwell IV and Lieutenant Colonel Steven Leonard, "Field Manual 3-07, *Stability Operations: Upshifting the Engine of Change,*" *Military Review* (July–August 2008), 6.

11. A common refrain among COIN analysts over the years has been that the American army has been committed to fighting wars in conventional operations and large-scale battles of annihilation, preventing it, according to this line of thinking, from effectively fighting counterinsurgencies. In this regard, see Robert Cassidy, *Counterinsurgency and the Global War on Terror: Military Culture and Irregular War* (Westport, CT: Praeger, 2006), 21–23, and James S. Corum, *Bad Strategies: How Major Powers Fail in Counterinsurgency* (Minneapolis: Zenith Press, 2008), 147. For an argument that supports the idea of an American way of war being one of adaptation and flexibility, see Brian Linn's "The American Way of War Revisited," *Journal of Military History,* April 2002, 530; and Robert M. Citino, *From Blitzkrieg to Desert Storm: The Evolution of Operational Warfare* (Lawrence: University of Kansas Press, 2004), 226.

12. For example, FM 3-24 says that there is a more limited way to fight counterinsurgencies, yet it offers only one five-sentence paragraph in the entire manual to explain this alternative: FM 3-24, pp. 5–25; for an excellent analysis of contemporary strategy, see Colin Gray, *Fighting Talk: 40 Maxims on War, Peace, and Strategy* (Westport, CT: Praeger, 2007).

13. Robert D. Kaplan, "Counterinsurgency Forever?" *Global Affairs,* October 3, 2012, stratfor.com/analysis/counterinsurgency-forever?0=ip_login_no_cache%3D 6c334f58eebcfcc20b2917437330b907; and John Nagl, "Invisible Armies: The American Revolution was a Guerilla War," *Wall Street Journal,* January 21, 2013.

14. On the development of French antirevolutionary warfare doctrine see Peter Paret, *French Revolutionary Warfare from Indochina to Algeria: The Analysis of Political and Military Doctrine* (New York: Praeger, 1964); on the French in Indochina, see Bernard B. Fall, *Street Without Joy* (1961; Mechanicsburg, PA: Stackpole Books, 1994); for a good primary source that gives a view of the thinking of counterrevolutionary practitioners like David Galula, Frank Kitson, and Edward

Lansdale, see *Counterinsurgency: A Symposium* (Santa Monica: RAND Corporation, 1962). For an excellent explanation of the historical roots of Western counter-Maoist methods, see John Mackinlay, *The Insurgent Archipelago*.

15. *Pentagon Papers*, vol. 2, 128–60; Thompson, *Defeating Communist Insurgency*, 128–40; Andrew Birtle, *U.S. Army Counterinsurgency and Contingency Operations Doctrine, 1942–1976* (Washington, DC: U.S. Army Center of Military History, 2006), 319.

16. This is the core argument in Nagl's *Learning to Eat Soup with a Knife*—that if the U.S. Army had only learned and adapted toward proper counterinsurgency methods, as the British did in Malaya, it very well might have won; for similar arguments saying that the United States lost in Vietnam because it did not "learn" counterinsurgency correctly, see Michael Schafer, *Deadly Paradigms: The Failure of U.S. Counterinsurgency Policy* (Princeton, NJ: Princeton University Press, 1988); and for an account of army "learning" after Vietnam, see Robert Downie, *Learning from Conflict: The U.S. Military in Vietnam, El Salvador, and the Drug War* (Westport, CT: Praeger, 1998). Nagl published his doctoral dissertation in 2002 with Praeger as *Counterinsurgency Lessons from Malaya and Vietnam: Learning to Eat Soup with a Knife*, then three years later the University of Chicago Press republished it with the title and subtitle reversed. The same press published David Galula's *Counterinsurgency Warfare* in 2006 and then FM 3-24 in 2007.

17. Early examples of the better-war thesis are Kevin Buckley, "General Abrams Deserves a Better War," *New York Times Magazine*, October 5, 1969; and Sir Robert Thompson, *No Exit from Vietnam*, rev. ed. (New York: McKay, 1970), 144. An army officer and long-serving adviser in Vietnam, John Paul Vann, became an early and vocal advocate of "the other war," or hearts-and-minds counterinsurgency; see Neil Sheehan's biography of Vann, *Bright and Shining Lie: John Paul Vann and America in Vietnam* (New York: Random House, 1988), 3–10, 783–87. Also see Edward Lansdale, *In the Midst of Wars: An American's Mission to Southeast Asia* (New York: Harper & Row, 1972).

18. The newest rendition of the Vietnam better-war thesis is Lewis Sorley's hypercritical and unfair biography, *Westmoreland: The General Who Lost Vietnam* (New York: Houghton Mifflin, 2011). For a set of critical reviews of Sorley's *Westmoreland*, see Gregory Daddis, "On Lewis Sorley's *Westmoreland: The General Who Lost Vietnam*," *Parameters*, Autumn 2011, 99–105; Dale W. Andrade's review, *Journal of Military History*, April 2012, 549–52; Andrew J. Birtle, "In Pursuit of the Great White Whale: Lewis Sorley's *Westmoreland: The General Who Lost Vietnam*," *Army History*, Summer 2012, 26–31; Gregory A. Daddis, *Westmoreland's War: Reassessing American Strategy in Vietnam, 1964–1968* (New York: Oxford University Press, forthcoming); and my "The Better War That Never Was," *National Interest*, March 8, 2012.

19. See Lewis Sorley, *Vietnam Chronicles: The Abrams Tapes, 1968–1972* (Lubbock: Texas Tech University Press, 2004). I will develop this argument fully using primary evidence in chapter 3.

20. Cited in Birtle, "In Pursuit of the Great White Whale."

21. See my "Vietnam: The Lost War," in *Between War and Peace: How America Ends Its Wars*, ed. Matthew Moten (New York: Free Press, 2011); George Herring, *The Longest War: The United States and Vietnam, 1950–1975*, 2d ed. (New York: McGraw Hill, 1986), ix; and John Prados, *Vietnam: The History of an Unwinnable War, 1945–1975* (Lawrence: University Press of Kansas, 2009).

22. Larry Cable, *Conflicts of Myths: The Development of American Counterinsurgency Doctrine and the Vietnam War* (New York: New York University Press, 1986), 88–92; Guenter Lewy, *America in Vietnam* (New York: Oxford University Press, 1978), 430–41; Andrew Krepinevich, *The Army and Vietnam* (Baltimore: Johns Hopkins University Press, 1988), 9, 170–71.

23. The best examples of this line of thought are in the works of analysts John T. Fishel and Max Manwaring, among others. See Manwaring's *Uncomfortable Wars: Toward a New Paradigm of Low Intensity Conflict* (Boulder, CO: Westview Press, 1991).

24. General John R. Galvin, "Uncomfortable Wars: Toward a New Paradigm," *Parameters*, Winter 1986.

25. This idea of lack of preparation and planning for counterinsurgency wars is a constant refrain by the COIN experts. A recent emblematic presentation of this refrain is David Ucko, *The New Counterinsurgency Era: Transforming the U.S. Military for Modern Wars* (Washington, DC: Georgetown University Press, 2009), 12–15. In typical fashion, Nagl also pounds this relentless theme in his introduction to the University of Chicago Press edition of FM 3-24; see also Max Boot, *The Savage Wars of Peace: Small Wars and the Rise of American Power* (New York: Basic Books, 2002); and Paula Broadwell with Vernon Loeb, *All In: The Education of General David Petraeus* (New York: Penguin, 2012), 65.

26. H.R. McMaster, *Dereliction of Duty: Lyndon Johnson, Robert McNamara, the Joint Chiefs of Staff, and the Lies That Led to Vietnam* (New York: HarperCollins, 1997), 332–35. For a critical review of McMaster that accuses him of "ethnocentrism," see Ronald Spector, "Cooking Up a Quagmire: Army Scholar Assesses Responsibility for the Vietnam War," *New York Times*, July 20, 1997. For a critical view of American generalship in Vietnam that also conforms to the counterinsurgency narrative, see David Hackworth and Julie Sherman, *About Face: The Odyssey of an American Warrior* (New York: Simon & Schuster, 1989).

27. Lewis Sorley, *A Better War: The Unexamined Victories and Final Tragedy of America's Last Years in Vietnam* (New York: Harcourt Brace, 1999), 17, 217.

28. David Cloud and Greg Jaffe, *The Fourth Star: Four Generals and the Epic Struggle for the Future of the United States Army* (New York: Crown, 2009), 197–98; Fred Kaplan, "The End of the Age of Petraeus: The Rise and Fall of Counterinsurgency," *Foreign Affairs*, January–February 2013, 79.

29. Broadwell with Loeb, *All In*, 69.

30. David Kilcullen, "Twenty-eight Articles: Fundamentals of Company-Level Counterinsurgency," *Military Review*, May–June 2006, 134; Andrew Krepinevich, "How to Win in Iraq: A Faltering Effort," *Foreign Affairs*, September–October 2005; and Nigel R.F. Aylwin-Foster, "Changing the Army for Counterinsurgency Operations," *Military Review*, November–December 2005.

31. David Brooks, "Winning in Iraq," *New York Times*, August 28, 2005.

32. "Is There a Way to Win in Iraq (8 Letters)," *New York Times*, August 28, 2005.

33. For a summary of the conference and the key events leading up to it, see John A. Nagl's foreword to the University of Chicago Press edition of FM 3-24; see also Nagl's "Constructing the Legacy of FM 3-24," *Joint Forces Quarterly*, 3d quarter, 2010; and Colin Kahl, "COIN of the Realm," *Foreign Affairs*, November–December 2007.

34. For a succinct argument that the British had developed this way of counterinsurgency, see Thomas R. Mockaitis, *British Counterinsurgency, 1919–1969* (New York: St. Martin's Press, 1990), 13–14. Since Mockaitis wrote his book in 1990, there has been a good deal of scholarly literature that calls into question if there ever really was such a way; see, for example, John Newsinger, *British Counterinsurgency: From Palestine to Northern Ireland* (London: Palgrave, 2002); Huw Bennett, "Soldiers in the Court Room: The British Army's Part in the Kenya Emergency Under the Legal Spotlight," *Journal of Imperial and Commonwealth History* 39, no. 5 (2011): 717–30; Douglas Porch, "The Dangerous Myth and Dubious Promise of COIN," *Small Wars and Insurgencies* 22, no. 2 (2011): 249; and M.L.R. Smith, "A Tradition That Never Was: Critiquing the Critique of British COIN," *Small Wars Journal*, August 9, 2012, smallwarsjournal.com/jrnl/art/a-tradition-that-never-was.

35. FM 3-24, pp. 1–20 to 1–21; David Galula, *Counterinsurgency Warfare: Theory and Practice*, (New York: Praeger, 1964), 75–76; a comprehensive history of the French in Algeria is Alistaire Horne, *A Savage War of Peace: Algeria 1954–1962* (New York: Viking Press, 1978).

36. Stathis N. Kalyvas, "Review Symposium, Counterinsurgency Manual," *Perspectives on Politics*, June 2008, 351–53; see also Wendy Brown's review essay in the same symposium.

37. See his foreword to the University of Chicago Press edition of FM 3-24.

38. Gregor Mathias, *Galula in Algeria: Counterinsurgency Practice Versus Theory* (Santa Barbara, CA: Praeger, 2011), 92–103; on the origins of Galula's thinking, see Thomas Rid "The 19th Century Origins of Counterinsurgency Doctrine," *Journal of Strategic Studies*, October 2010.

39. Thomas E. Ricks, *Fiasco: The American Military Adventure in Iraq* (New York: Penguin Press, 2006), 414–24.

40. Frederick W. Kagan, *Choosing Victory: A Plan for Success in Iraq* (Washington, DC: American Enterprise Institute, 2007), aei.org/files/2007/01/05/20070111_ChoosingVictoryupdated.pdf.

41. Some of the best analyses of the reasons for the lowering of violence are: Steven Simon "The Price of the Surge," *Foreign Affairs*, May–June 2008; Octavian Manea, "The Iraqi COIN Narrative Revised: An Interview with Douglas Ollivant," *Small Wars Journal*, July 24, 2011, smallwarsjournal.com/blog/journal/docs-temp/821-manea.pdf; my "Misreading the Surge Threatens US Army's Conventional Capabilities," *World Politics Review*, March 4, 2008; Judah Grunstein, "The Limits of the Surge: An Interview with Gian Gentile," *World Politics Review*, April 11, 2008, worldpoliticsreview.com/articles/1924/the-limits-of-the-surge-an-interview-with-gian-gentile; Nir Rosen's chapter on the surge in his *Aftermath: Following the Bloodshed of America's Wars in the Muslim World* (New York: Nation Books, 2010); and although the interpretation and use of evidence is problematic, see also Stephen Biddle, Jeffrey A. Friedman, and Jacob N. Shapiro, "Testing the Surge: Why Did Violence Decline in Iraq in 2007?" *International Security*, Summer 2012.

42. Clifford May, "Al Qaeda in Iraq on the Run," *National Review* Online, October 18, 2007, nationalreview.com/articles/222554/al-qaeda-iraq-run/clifford-d-may#; and "COIN Is Not Small Change," *National Review* Online, October 4, 2007, nationalreview.com/articles/222387/coin-not-small-change/clifford-d-may.

43. George W. Bush, *Decision Points* (New York: Crown, 2010), 365.

44. Evan Thomas and John Barry, "The Surprising Lessons of Vietnam: Unraveling the Mysteries of Vietnam May Prevent Us from Making Its Mistakes," *Newsweek*, November 16, 2009.

45. Bob Woodward, *Obama's Wars* (New York: Simon & Schuster, 2010), Petraeus quote 332–33, Tien quote 319; for quote by Petraeus's aide, see Rajiv Chandrasekaran, *Little America*, 322.

46. David Petraeus, "The Surge of Ideas: COINdinistas and Change in the U.S. Army in 2006," American Enterprise Institute, May 6, 2010, aei.org/article/foreign-and-defense-policy/regional/middle-east-and-north-africa/the-surge-of-ideas. Two years later, in 2012, Petraeus still holds the same view of what he sees as his and the surge's accomplishments; see Bruce Schreiner, "Former Commander

in Iraq Says Anti-Insurgency Strategy Behind Iraq Turnaround," Associated Press, September 12, 2012.

## 2. Malaya: The Foundation of the Counterinsurgency Narrative

1. John A. Nagl, *Learning to Eat Soup with a Knife: Counterinsurgency Lessons from Malaya and Vietnam* (Chicago: University of Chicago Press, 2005), 81, 87, 103.

2. Headquarters, Department of the Army, Field Manual (FM) 3-24, *Counterinsurgency* (Washington, DC: December 2006), pp. 6–21 to 6–22 (italics mine).

3. Templer Study Centre (hereafter referred to as Templer Center), British National Army Museum (hereafter NAM), Folder 1995-01-165-20, "Notebook containing handwritten notes taken at meetings 13 Nov 51 to 10 Jan 52," entry of November 15, 1951; see also entries of November 19, 20, and 23 and Lockhart's letter to Police Commissioner Young, November 20, 1951, Templer Center, NAM, Folder 1995-01-165-17.

4. The National Archives, Kew Gardens, London (hereafter TNA), War Office (hereafter WO), 216/874, "Director of Operations, Federation of Malaya, Planning Directive for 1955," August 11, 1954.

5. The best general histories of the Malayan Emergency are: Donald Mackay, *The Domino That Stood: The Malayan Emergency 1948–1960* (London: Brassey's, 1997); and John Coates, *Suppressing Insurgency: An Analysis of the Malayan Emergency* (New York: Westview Press, 1992). For a thorough explanation of the various histories and arguments surrounding the Malayan Emergency, see Karl Hack, "'Iron Claws on Malaya': The Historiography of the Malayan Emergency," *Journal of Southeast Asian Studies*, March 1999, 99–125. See also Christopher A. Bayly and Timothy N. Harper, *Forgotten Wars: The End of Britain's Asian Empire* (London: Allen Lane, 2007).

6. On the Japanese occupation of Malaya during World War II and the resistance against it, see Bert H. Cooper Jr., "Malaya, 1942–1945," and on the Emergency, "Malaya, 1948–1960," in *Challenge and Response in Internal Conflict*, vol. 1: *The Experience in Asia*, ed. Doris M. Condit et al. (Washington, DC: American University, 1968), 181–205; Huw Bennett, "'A Very Salutary Effect': The Counter-Terror Strategy in the Early Malayan Emergency, June 1948–December 1949," *Journal of Strategic Studies*, June 2009, 415–44; C.C. Chin and Karl Hack, *Dialogues with Chin Peng: New Light on the Malayan Communist Party* (Singapore: Singapore University Press, 2004), 150–51.

7. Richard Clutterbuck, *Conflict and Violence in Singapore and Malaya* (Singapore: Graham Brash, 1985), 358.

8. J. Robert Jackson, *The Malayan Emergency: The Commonwealth's Wars, 1948–1966* (London: Routledge, 1991), 115.

9. Bernard Fall, "South Vietnam 1956 to November 1963," in *Challenge and Response in Internal Conflict*, vol. 1, pp. 333–75.

10. Jackson, *Malayan Emergency*, 11.

11. Minutes of meeting with prime minister, May 3, 1951, TNA WO 32/16138; and "Summary of Conversation Between Lieutenant General Sir Nevil Brownjohn and General Sir Bernard Montgomery," January 3, 1952, TNA WO 216/806.

12. For an example of this kind of periodization of the Emergency that puts the breaking or tipping point at the end of 1951, when seemingly the war was lost and awaiting the arrival of Templer, see Richard Stubbs, "From Search and Destroy to Hearts and Minds: The Evolution of British Strategy in Malaya, 1948–1960," in *Counterinsurgency in Modern Warfare*, ed. Daniel Marston and Carter Malkasian (London: Osprey, 2008), 120. Nagl's argument that the British Army became a learning organization after Templer's arrival has been thoroughly refuted by Karl Hack in "The Malayan Emergency as Counterinsurgency Paradigm," *Journal of Strategic Studies* 32, no. 3 (2009): 383–414, at 394–96; and John Nagl, *Learning to Eat Soup with a Knife*, 79, 107. For a look at British Army operations that accedes to the notion of continuity, see David Ucko, "Countering Insurgents Through Distributed Operations: Insights from Malaya, 1948–1960," *Journal of Strategic Studies*, February 2007; Richard Stubbs, *Hearts and Minds in Guerrilla Warfare: The Malayan Emergency 1948–1960* (London: Oxford University Press, 1989), 159, 189–91; and F.A. Godfrey, "The Malayan Emergency—an Exhibition to Commemorate the Declaration of the State of the Emergency in Malaya on 18 June 1948," June 19, 1978, Templer Center, NAM 1978-07-20-1. For a contemporary analysis of British Army tactical action in Malaya that shows continuity rather than discontinuity, see Raffi Gregorian, "'Jungle Bashing' in Malaya: Towards a Formal Tactical Doctrine," *Small Wars and Insurgencies*, Winter 1994, 338–59.

13. "War Diary, 2nd Battalion, Coldstream Guards," December 1948, TNA WO 268/608. For other combat battalion reports that indicate the same kind of operations as the Coldstream Guards, see Historical Report, 4th Queens Own Hussars, December 31, 1948, TNA WO 268/597; and Historical Report, 1st Battalion, Devonshire Regiment, January 1, 1949–December 31, 1949, TNA WO 268/614.

14. John B. Oldfield, *The Green Howards in Malaya, 1949–1952: The Story of a Post-war Tour of Duty by a Battalion of the Line* (London: Gale & Polden, 1953), 53; see also Arthur Campbell, *Jungle Green* (Boston: Little, Brown, 1953); Historical Report, 1st Battalion, Scottish Rifles, April 1, 1950–June 31, 1950, TNA WO 305/223; and "Transcript of Interview with Les Sedge on His Service in Malaya

1951–1952 with Royal West Kents," compiled by Adrian Walker, Templer Center, NAM 2002-07-359-4.

15. Annual Historical Report, 26th Field Regiment, RA, April 1, 1950–April 1, 1951, TNA WO 305/58; Jackson, *Malayan Emergency*, 19–23; Hack, "Malayan Emergency as Counterinsurgency Paradigm," 397; Chin and Hack, *Dialogues with Chin Peng*, 155–56; Chin Peng, *Alias Chin Peng: My Side of History* (Singapore: Media Masters, 2003), 268–71; and Letter from General Sir Charles F. Keightley to Field Marshal Slim, January 20, 1952, TNA WO 216/806.

16. *The Conduct of Anti-Terrorist Operations in Malaya*, Prepared Under the Direction of H.Q. Malaya, Kuala Lampur, 1952, U.S. Military Academy, History Department Library.

17. "Index to a Study of the Military Aspects of the Malayan Emergency 48–60," ed. John P. Veys, 2009, Templer Center, NAM 2004-06-67-1; for casualty statistics for the British Army in Malaya, see "Malaya Army Casualties," February 18, 1963, TNA WO 162/303.

18. Historical Report, 1st Battalion, 6th Gurkha Rifles, April 1, 1950–March 31, 1951, TNA WO 305/249; see also Historical Report, 48th Gurkha Brigade, January–March 1950, TNA WO 268/672; and Historical Report, 1st Battalion, 7th Gurkha Rifles, January–March 1950, TNA WO 268/788.

19. Historical Reports, 1st Battalion, 6th Gurkha Rifles," by year from 1950–1955, TNA WO 305/249.

20. Ibid., April 1, 1950–March 31, 1951. For an excellent overview of British Army counterinsurgency operations, see Riley Sunderland, *Organizing Counterinsurgency in Malaya, 1948–1960* (Santa Monica, CA: RAND Corporation, 1964); see also Historical Report, 3rd Battalion, The King's African Rifles, 1952–53, Templer Center, NAM 1988-08-57-7; Historical Record, 1st Battalion, The Queen's Own Royal West Kent Regiment," April 1, 1951–April 1, 1952, TNA WO 305/237; Robert A. Bonner, *Jungle Bashers: A British Infantry Battalion in the Malayan Emergency 1951–1954* (Knutsford, UK: Flur de Lys, 2002); John Scurr, *Jungle Campaign: A King's Own Yorkshire Light Infantryman* (Salisbury, UK: Owl Press, 1994); and E.T. Boddye, *Malayan Patrol* (Edinburgh: Pentland Press, 1993).

21. The numerous historical reports at the Kew National Archives and the Templer Center show this to be the case. Riley Sunderland's "Organizing Counterinsurgency in Malaya, 1948–1960" also supports this view, as does David Ucko's more current analysis in his "Countering Insurgents Through Distributed Operations: Insights from Malaya, 1948–1960." There was never a breaking or tipping point nor a tectonic shift when the British Army went from not getting counterinsurgency operations, as Nagl argues, to one that did. For more nuanced and nonlinear explanations of how armies learn and adapt in combat, see Dennis Showalter,

"Military Innovation and the Whig Perspective of History," in *The Challenge of Change: Military Institutions and New Realities, 1918–1941*, ed. Harold R. Winton and David R. Mets (Lincoln: University of Nebraska Press, 2000); and Paddy Griffith, *Battle Tactics of the Western Front: The British Army's Art of Attack, 1916–1918* (New Haven, CT: Yale University Press, 1996).

22. Letter from General Keightley to Field Marshal Slim, July 27, 1951, TNA WO 216/395; see also Hugh Fraser, "Report to the Ministers on the Situation in Malaya," January 16, 1952, TNA Colonial Office (hereafter CO), 1022/22; Letter from Lieutenant General Sir Robert Lockhart to Field Marshal Sir William Slim, January 14, 1952, TNA WO 216/806; Letter from General Slim to General Harding, November 21, 1951, TNA WO 216/835; and Mackay, *The Domino That Stood*, 102.

23. On Vietnam, see William Colby with James McCargar, *Lost Victory: A Firsthand Account of America's Sixteen-Year Involvement in Vietnam* (Chicago: Contemporary Books, 1989), 185–87. On Malaya see Richard Clutterbuck, *The Long, Long War: The Emergency in Malaya 1948–1960* (London: Cassell, 1966), 51–52; James S. Corum, *Bad Strategies: How Major Powers Fail in Counterinsurgency* (Minneapolis: Zenith Press, 2008),148–50; and Thomas E. Ricks, *Fiasco: The American Military Adventure in Iraq* (New York: Penguin Press, 2006), 194–95.

24. General Robert Lockhart, "Assessment of Operations Warbler/Grasshopper /Sedge," Templer Center, Lockhart Papers, NAM 1995-01-165-33; see also Bennett, "'A Very Salutary Effect,'" 424; and Jackson, *Malayan Emergency*, 29–31.

25. Lucian W. Pye, *Guerrilla Communism in Malaya: Its Social and Political Meaning* (Princeton, NJ: Princeton University Press, 1956), 95–99; and Chin and Hack, *Dialogues with Chin Peng*, 148.

26. For the actual Briggs Plan, see the collection of documents compiled by Anthony Stockwell, *Malaya*, vol. 2 (London: Her Majesty's Stationery Office, 1995), 217–21. For good summaries of the Briggs Plan, see Mackay, *Domino That Stood*, 88–89; and Anthony Short, *The Communist Insurrection in Malaya, 1948–1960* (Plymouth, UK: Frederick Muller, 1975).

27. Mackay, *Domino That Stood*, 50.

28. Ibid., 89–91.

29. Letter from Ministry of Defence to Prime Minister Churchill, May 2, 1951, TNA WO 32/16138; and Mackay, *Domino That Stood*, 106–8;

30. For a sophisticated historical argument and analysis, see Karl Hack's "The Malayan Emergency as Counterinsurgency Paradigm," *Journal of Strategic Studies* 32, no. 3 (2009): 383–414. Hack argues that the insurgency was broken between 1950 and 1952 and that the Briggs Plan played a crucial part. Hack rightly points out that the arrival of Templer in early 1952 mattered, but more in terms of optimizing the decisive strategy that had already been put into place.

31. HQ FARELF, Weekly Situation Reports on Bandit Activity in Malaya, July 7, 1952, January 7, 1953, September 29, 1952, and August 11, 1952, TNA CO 1022/11; "The Security Forces Weekly Intelligence Summary for the Week of 26 June 1952," TNA CO 1022/15; Mackay, *The Domino That Stood*, 115–18; and Jackson, *Malayan Emergency*, 39–41. For a contemporaneous summary by British Intelligence of the content of the October Directives, see "The Security Forces Weekly Intelligence Summary for May 1952," TNA CO 1022/15.

32. Chin Peng, *Alias Chin Peng*, 270, 272–73, 279; see also Chin and Hack, *Dialogues with Chin Peng*, 144–56. Chin's conclusion was ultimately the same as that of the British; see "Personal Estimate by Directory of Operations," July 17, 1954, TNA WO 216/874.

33. Mackay, *Domino That Stood*, 111–14. Chin Peng confirms that it was a lucky strike: Chin and Hack, *Dialogues with Chin Peng*, 156.

34. Coates, *Suppressing Insurgency*, 110; Short, *Communist Insurrection in Malaya*, 305–6; and John Cloake, *Templer, Tiger of Malaya: The Life of Field Marshall Sir Gerald Templer* (London: Harrap, 1985), 199.

35. Coates, *Suppressing Insurgency*, 111.

36. This cause-and-effect relationship is the premise of most of the counterinsurgency literature on Malaya; see, for example: Nagl, *Learning to Eat Soup with a Knife*; Stubbs, *Hearts and Minds in Guerrilla Warfare*; and Parkinson, *Templer in Malaya*. The same type of syllogism has been applied to explaining Petraeus and the surge and the reduction of violence in Iraq in late 2007.

37. Malaya Emergency Correspondence with U.S. Student, December 3, 1968, Templer Center, Papers of D.L. Lloyd Owens (hereafter Owens Papers), NAM 1980-11-132-1.

38. Chin Peng, *Alias Chin Peng*, 299–301.

39. Francis Loh Kok Wah, *Beyond the Tin Mines: Coolies, Squatters and New Villagers in the Kinta Valley, Malaysia, 1880–1980* (Singapore: Oxford University Press, 1988), 135–61; see also Cheah Boon Kheng, review of Richard Stubbs, *Hearts and Minds*, in *Journal of Southeast Asian Studies* 22, no. 2 (1991), 427–30; for an argument by an American scholar in agreement with Wah, see Wade Markel, "Draining the Swamp: The British Strategy of Population Control," *Parameters*, Spring 2006.

40. Press Statement, by Lieutenant General Sir Robert Lockhart, October 27, 1952, Templer Center, NAM 1995-01-165-77.

41. "The Security Forces Weekly Intelligence Summary for 1 April 1952" and "The Security Forces Weekly Intelligence Summary for 15 April 1952," TNA CO 1022/15; see also HQ FARELF, Weekly Situation Reports on Bandit Activity, May 20, 1952, TNA CO 1022/11. Donald Mackay argues rightly in *The Domino That Stood* (116–17) that the reason it took four to six months before the security forces

started to see the effect of the October Directives was simply because it took weeks and sometimes months for the word to get from Chin Peng out to isolated insurgent groups of ten to twenty men in a jungle hideout.

42. The indication that it was found in March comes from the June report where it was mentioned, "The Security Forces Weekly Intelligence Summary for the Week Ending 12 June 1952," TNA CO 1022/15.

43. HQ FARELF Weekly Situation Report on Bandit Activity in Malaya, July 7, 21, and 28, TNA CO 1022/11.

44. Hack, "Malayan Emergency as Counterinsurgency Paradigm," 404.

45. "Appreciation of the Situation in Malaya," September 22, 1952, appendix A, TNA WO 216/561.

46. Ibid.

47. Press Conference at the Colonial Office, London, June 19, 1952, "Templer Speeches"; see also Federal Government Press Release, July 29, 1952; and speech by General Templer in Australia in *Malaya Today*, September 29, 1952, all in Templer Center, NAM 1974-10-29-1-90, 1–6 .

48. For these articles, see Templer Center, NAM 1974-10-29-7.

49. On World War II historiography, see R.J. Bosworth, *Explaining Auschwitz and Hiroshima: History Writing and the Second World War* (London: Routeledge, 1993). See also Kevin Blackburn and Karl Hack, *War Memory and the Making of Modern Malaysia and Singapore* (London: Eurospan, 2012); for a heroic account of Templer comparing him to Montgomery, see C. Northcote Parkinson, *Templer in Malaya* (London: D. Moore, 1954).

50. Allington Kennard, *Straights Times*, May 4, 1954.

51. Alex Jossey, "Malayan Affairs," *Straights Times*, February 13, 1954.

52. David French, *The British Way in Counter-Insurgency, 1945–1967* (New York: Oxford University Press, 2011), 5.

## 3. Vietnam: The First Better War That Wasn't

1. Lewis Sorley, *A Better War: The Unexamined Victories and Final Tragedy of America's Last Years in Vietnam* (New York: Harcourt Brace, 1999), 17. On page 17, Sorley puts in quotation marks "The tactics changed within fifteen minutes of Abrams taking command," and attributes the remark directly to General Weyand. However, I use the quote to represent one of the basic argument's in *A Better War*, that there was a radical transformation in the tactics of counterinsurgency that Abrams put into place. It's interesting that the senior intelligence officer in Vietnam, General Phillip Davidson, who served under both Westmoreland and Abrams, and Robert Komer, who became the highest-ranking American civilian in charge

of pacification and also served under both generals, both say that Abrams did not change the tactics of the war; see Phillip Davidson, *Vietnam at War: The History, 1946–1975* (Novato, CA: Presidio Press, 1988), 512; and Robert Komer, quoted in *The Lessons of Vietnam*, ed. W. Scott Thompson and Donaldson D. Frizzell (New York: Crane, Russak, 1977).

2. Octavian Manea, interview with General (ret) Jack Keane, *Small Wars Journal*, April 5, 2011, smallwarsjournal.com/jrnl/art/an-interview-with-general -jack-keane.

3. George C. Herring, *America's Longest War: The United States and Vietnam, 1950–1975* (New York: McGraw-Hill, 1986), ix.

4. For the better-war thesis as it applies to Vietnam, see three books by Lewis Sorley: *Thunderbolt: General Creighton Abrams and the Army of His Times* (New York: Simon & Schuster, 1992), *A Better War: The Unexamined Victory and Final Tragedy of America's Last Years in Vietnam*, and *Westmoreland: The General Who Lost Vietnam* (Boston: Houghton Mifflin, 2011). See also Rufus Phillips, *Why Vietnam Matters: An Eyewitness Account of Lessons Not Learned* (Annapolis: Naval Institute Press, 2008), 286–90; and Max Boot, *The Savage Wars of Peace: Small Wars and the Rise of American Power* (New York: Basic Books, 2002). For an excellent scholarly critique of Sorley's work, see Andrew J. Birtle, "PROVN, Westmoreland, and the Historians: A Reappraisal," *Journal of Military History*, October 2008, 1213–47; and Andrew J. Birtle, "In Pursuit of the Great White Whale: Lewis Sorley's *Westmoreland: The General Who Lost Vietnam*," *Army History*, Summer 2012, 26–31. Colonel Gregory A. Daddis's *Westmoreland's War: Reassessing American Strategy in Vietnam, 1964–1968* (New York: Oxford University Press, forthcoming) is a tour de force that overturns conclusively the better-war thesis. The best summary of the various competing interpretations of the Vietnam War is Gary Hess, *Vietnam: Explaining America's Lost War* (Oxford, UK: Blackwell, 2009).

5. Julian J. Ewell and Ira A. Hunt Jr., *Sharpening the Combat Edge: The Use of Analysis to Reinforce Military Judgement* (Washington, DC: Department of the Army/U.S. Government Printing Office, 1974), 165, 175.

6. Another contemporaneous term applied in a pejorative way to the military arm of the National Liberation Front (NLF), the PLAF, was "Viet Cong." Throughout this chapter, unless referenced in a primary source, I will use the initials PLAF to represent Viet Cong.

7. "Combat After-Action Report of Operation Speedy Express," June 14, 1969, Center for Military History (hereafter CMH), Historian Files; see also Message to M.G. Bolton, ODCSOPS, January 17, 1972, CMH, Historian Files. Because of the high number of enemy kills but low number of weapons found, Speedy Express generated interest by investigative journalist Kevin Buckley, who wrote "Pacification's

Deadly Price," *Newsweek*, June 19, 1972. Buckley originally made it clear that the operation slaughtered many civilians, but the piece was truncated by the editors. For a recent relook at Speedy Express by investigative reporter Nick Turse, see "A My Lai Month: How the U.S. Army Fought the Vietnam War," *The Nation*, December 1, 2008; see also Turse's "The Pentagon Book Club," *The Nation*, May 17, 2010.

8. "Excerpts of a Diary of a VC Company Commander," Delta Military Assistance Command, 9th Division, Papers of John Paul Vann, Box 1, U.S. Army Heritage and Education Center (hereafter AHEC), Carlisle Barracks, PA; see also General Ewell's discussion of his operations in the Mekong Delta, "Senior Officer Debriefing Program, Conversation Between Lieutenant General Julian J. Ewell and Robert Crowley," undated, Papers of Julian J. Ewell (hereafter Ewell Papers), Box 1, AHEC.

9. Central Office for South Vietnam (COSVN), Directive No. 01/CT71, "Development of the Situation, and Our Leadership Since [the issue of] Resolution 9," October 1971, in *Vietnam: The Definitive Documentation of Human Decisions*, ed. Gareth Porter (Stanfordville, NY: Earl M. Coleman Enterprises, 1979), 551.

10. Andrew J. Birtle, *U.S. Army Counterinsurgency and Contingency Operations Doctrine, 1942–1976* (Washington, DC: U.S. Army Center of Military History, 2006), 361–68.

11. For facts and statistics regarding the Vietnam War, see Michael Clodfelter, *Vietnam in Military Statistics: A History of the Indochina Wars, 1772–1991* (Jefferson, NC: McFarland & Co., 1995); Sir Robert Thompson, "A Just Peace in Vietnam: The Meaning of Victory," draft of an article submitted to *Readers Digest*, March 18, 1970, Papers of Donald A. Seibert (hereafter Seibert Papers), Box 26, AHEC; and Nick Turse, *Kill Anything That Moves: The Real American War in Vietnam* (New York: Metropolitan Books, 2013), 13.

12. For a good and current general history of the Vietnam War, see John Prados, *Vietnam: The History of an Unwinnable War, 1945–1975* (Lawrence: University of Kansas Press, 2009); and my "Vietnam: The Lost War," in *Between War and Peace: How America Ends Its Wars*, ed. Matthew Moten (New York: Free Press, 2011).

13. For North Vietnam, see Lien-Hang T. Nguyen, *Hanoi's War: An International History of the War for Peace in Vietnam* (Chapel Hill: University of North Carolina Press, 2012). On the NLF in the South, see William J. Dukier, *Sacred War: Nationalism and Revolution in a Divided Vietnam* (New York: McGraw Hill, 1995) and David Hunt, *Vietnam's Southern Revolution: From Peasant Insurrection to Total War* (Amherst: University of Massachusetts Press, 2008).

14. On the early years of American involvement, see Ronald Spector, *Advice and Support: The Early Years, 1941–1960* (Washington, DC: U.S. Army Center of Military History, 1985); and Mark Moyar, *Triumph Forsaken: The Vietnam War, 1954 to 1965* (New York: Cambridge University Press, 2006).

15. On U.S. escalation and major commitment, see Lloyd C. Gardner and Ted Gittinger, eds., *Vietnam: The Early Decisions* (Austin: University of Texas Press, 1997); and George C. Herring, *LBJ and Vietnam: A Different Kind of War* (Austin: University of Texas Press, 1994).

16. For excellent operational histories of the Vietnam War, see John M. Carland, *The U.S. Army in Vietnam: Stemming the Tide, May 1965 to October 1966* (Washington, DC: U.S. Army Center of Military History, 2001); and George L. MacGarrigle, *The United States Army in Vietnam, Taking the Offensive, October 1966 to October 1967* (Washington, DC: U.S. Army Center of Military History, 1998). See also Shelby Stanton, *The Rise and Fall of an American Army: U.S. Ground Forces in Vietnam, 1965-1973* (Novato, CA: Presidio Press, 1985). On pacification, see Richard A. Hunt, *Pacification: The American Struggle for Vietnam's Hearts and Minds* (Boulder, CO: Westview Press, 1995). For the air war over North Vietnam, see Mark Clodfelter, *The Limits of Air Power: The American Bombing of North Vietnam* (New York: Free Press, 1989).

17. Andrew J. Birtle, *U.S. Army Counterinsurgency and Contingency Operations Doctrine, 1942-1976*, 364-65.

18. Memorandum for Record, Commander's Conference, MACV, October 3, 1966," CMH, Historian Files; Briefing to Mission Council, MACV, August 1966, CMH, Historian Files; Memorandum, "Concept for Operations in the Republic of Vietnam," MACV for distribution, August 30, 1965, CMH Historian Files; Westmoreland to Commanding General 1st Infantry Division, December 8, 1965, AHEC, Papers of Jonathan O. Seaman (hereafter Seaman Papers), Box 35; William C. Westmoreland, *A Soldier Reports* (New York: Dell, 1976), 85; "A Program for the Pacification and Long-Term Development of South Vietnam," March 1966, CMH, Historians File, 4, 5-10, 23-25. PROVN has been wielded like an ax by adherents of the better-war thesis (Sorley, *A Better War*; Nagl, *Learning to Eat Soup with a Knife*; Krepinevich, *The Army and Vietnam*; Lewy, *America in Vietnam*) to slay Westmoreland by arguing that PROVN repudiated Westmoreland's strategy of going after main-force units with American conventional forces. It did nothing of the sort, as the above quotes, taken directly from PROVN, indicate. For a primary source–based, thorough critique of this flawed line of historical argument, see Andrew Birtle, "PROVN, Westmoreland, and the Historians"; and Dale Andrade, "Westmoreland Was Right: Learning the Wrong Lessons from the Vietnam War," *Small Wars and Insurgencies*, June 2008, 145-81. For a new, refreshing, and fair treatment of Westmoreland's strategy in Vietnam, see Daddis, *Westmoreland's War*.

19. Birtle, *U.S. Army Counterinsurgency and Contingency Operations Doctrine*, 368-82.

20. Lance A. Betros, *Carved from Granite: West Point Since 1902* (College Station: Texas A&M University Press, 2012), 230; and Gian P. Gentile, "The Better War That Never Was," *National Interest*, March–April 2012.

21. Birtle, *U.S. Army Counterinsurgency and Contingency Operations Doctrine*, 249–50.

22. Message from General Westmoreland to General Wheeler, October 30, 1966, CMH, Westmoreland Message Files, COMUSMACV; see also Message from General Westmoreland to Admiral Sharp, February 17, 1967.

23. Combat Operation After-Action Report, Operation Summerall, May 21, 1967, NA RG 472, 101st Airborne Division, 1st Brigade, ACofS (assistant chief of staff) S-3, AARs, Box 2; see also After-Action Report, 1st Brigade, 101st Airborne Division, September 8, 1966, Box 2; Message from General Westmoreland to General Wheeler, August 25, 1967, CMH, Westmoreland Message Files, COMUS-MAC, April 1–September 30, 1967.

24. Combat Operations After-Action Report, April 25, 1967, NA RG 472, 4th Infantry Division, 1st Brigade, ACofS S-3, Box 1; see also "Summary of Engagement, NVA Battalion in Prepared Bunker Positions," March 12, 1967, Box 2; Combat Operation After-Action Report, Operation Francis Marion, October 24, 1967, NA RG 472, 4th Infantry Division, 1st Brigade, ACofS S-3, Box 1; and George L. MacGarrigle, *Taking the Offensive*, 287–96.

25. David W.P. Elliot, *The Vietnamese War: Revolution and Social Change in the Mekong Delta, 1930–1975*, vol. 2 (New York: M.E. Sharpe, 2003), 970, 979; and Warren Wilkins, *Grab Their Belts to Fight Them: The Viet Cong's Big-Unit War Against the U.S., 1965–1966* (Annapolis: Naval Institute Press, 2011), 206–12.

26. U.S. MACV, Military History Branch, "Vietnam Command History, 1969," CMH; and Birtle, *U.S. Army Counterinsurgency and Contingency Operations Doctrine*, 367.

27. Graham A. Cosmas, MACV, *The Joint Command in the Years of Withdrawal, 1968–1973* (Washington, DC: U.S. Army Center of Military History, 2007), 129.

28. Operational Guidance, July 27, 1968, and September 28, 1968, CMH, CO-MUS MACV Actions File (courtesy of Colonel Gregory A. Daddis); J3 Briefer and Abrams, October 5, 1968, in Lewis Sorley, *Vietnam Chronicles: The Abrams Tapes, 1968–1972* (Lubbock: Texas Tech University Press, 2004), 59; Cosmas, MACV, 244, 410; and Dale Andrade, "Westmoreland Was Right," 164.

29. Operational Report, 1st Brigade, 4th Infantry Division, January 31, 1969, and August 4, 1969, NA RG 472, ACofS S-3, Box 1; 4th Infantry Division G3 Operations, Duty Officer's Log, February 21 and 24, 1969, NA RG 472, ACofS G-3, Box 8; see also Colonel Volney Warner, End of Tour Report, July 21, 1969–January 14, 1970, AHEC, Papers of Volney Warner (hereafter Warner Papers), Box 1.

30. Letter from Volney Warner to Robert Komer, July 10, 1968, AHEC, Warner Papers, Box 1; Ministry of Revolutionary Development, "The Village Self-Development Program," February 24, 1969, AHEC, Papers of Robert A. Montague (hereafter Montague Papers), Box 7; HQ MACV, "1969 Accelerated Pacification Campaign," June 28, 1969, AHEC, Montague Papers, Box 7. On HES and American metrics in Vietnam, see Gregory Daddis, *No Sure Victory: Measuring American Effectiveness and Progress in the Vietnam War* (New York: Oxford University Press, 2011).

31. Elliot, *Vietnamese War*, 1281–88; see also Elliot's 1968 RAND Corporation study, coauthored with W.A. Stewart, "Pacification and the Viet Cong System in Dinh Tuong, 1966–1967"; Richard A. Hunt, *Pacification*, 208–9; and Truong Nhu Tang, *A Vietcong Memoir* (New York: Harcourt Brace, 1985).

32. Colonel Hoang Ngoc Lung, *Strategy and Tactics* (Washington, DC: U.S. Army Center of Military History, 1980), 129; Military History Institute of Vietnam, *Victory in Vietnam: The Official History of the People's Army of Vietnam* (Hanoi, 1988), trans. Merle L. Pribbenow (Lawrence: University of Kansas Press, 2002), 254; see also COSVN Directive No . 01/CT71, January–February 1971, in Gareth A. Porter, *Vietnam: The Definitive Documentation of Human Decisions*, vol. 2 (Stanfordville, NY: E.M. Coleman Enterprises, 1979), 551–55.

33. Quoted in Eric Bergerud, *The Dynamics of Defeat: The Vietnam War in Hau Nghia Province* (Boulder, CO: Westview Press, 1993), 314–15. For observations very similar to Herrington's from a year prior, see Charles Benoit, *Conversations with Rural Vietnamese* (Santa Monica, CA: RAND Corporation, 1970).

34. Elliot, *Vietnamese War*, 1127–28, 1133–35; and Hunt, *Vietnam's Southern Revolution*, 203–11.

35. "Viet Cong Evaluation of the Situation in Quang Dien," October 18, 1968, AHEC, Seibert Papers, Box 26; Director, CORDS, "MACORDS After-Action Report," March 9, 1973, MACV Command Historian's Collection, Series 2, Staff Sections, J3 CORDS, Reports, Briefings, 1967–1973, AHEC; Allan E. Goodman and Lawrence A. Franks, *Between War and Peace: A Profile of Migrants to Saigon* (New York: Asia Society, 1974). On refugees and immigration of ARVN soldiers and their families, see Robert A. Brigham, *ARVN: Life and Death in the South Vietnamese Army* (Lawrence: University Press of Kansas, 2006), 126–30; for a still classic account of revolution and war in rural South Vietnam, see Jeffrey Race, *War Comes to Long An* (Berkeley: University of California Press, 1973).

36. Elliot, *Vietnamese War*, 1278–81.

37. For typical hagiographic portrayals of CAPs as the potential key to overall success in Vietnam, see Krepinevich, *Army and Vietnam*, 172–77; and Nagl, *Learning to Eat Soup with a Knife*, 156–58. For an objective analysis of CAPs, see Michael

E. Peterson, "The Combined Action Platoons: The Marines' Other War in Vietnam" (MA thesis, University of Oregon, 1988). The classic firsthand account of a CAPs platoon is Bing West, *The Village* (1972; New York: Pocket Books, 2003). For detailed primary-source reporting on CAPs operations, see 3rd Combined Action Group, "Command Chronology," May 19, 1969, June 10, 1969, July 5, 1969, and May 22, 1970, in NA RG 127, 3rd Combined Action Group, October 1968–September 1970, Box 300. For the effects of CAPs action on the village of My Thuy Thong, see James Walker Trullinger Jr., *Village at War: An Account of Revolution in Vietnam* (New York: Longman, 1980), 118–20.

38. Lewis Sorley, *Vietnam Chronicles*: "28 June 1969, WEIU," 214–17; "20 November 1971, WEIU," 696–701; "10 January 1972 Secretary of the Army Froehkle Briefing," 745–49; and "10 July 1971, WEIU," 647–50. See also William Colby, *Lost Victory*, 306; and David Richard Palmer, *Summons of the Trumpet: US-Vietnam in Perspective* (San Rafael, CA: Presidio Press, 1978), 226. Historian Jeffrey J. Clarke in his *Advice and Support: The Final Years* (Washington, DC: U.S. Army Center of Military History, 1988), 508, supports the assertion that Vietnamization and pacification were of secondary importance to fighting the NVA and VC main-force units for Abrams. Clarke notes that Abrams "regarded Vietnamization as an unfortunate policy that had to be carred out, rather than as a challenge to be met."

39. Hunt, *Pacification*, 263, 268; Elliot, *Vietnamese War*, 1270, 1281–88; Thomas L. Ahern, *Vietnam Declassified: The CIA and Counterinsurgency* (Lexington: University of Kentucky Press, 2010), 357–58.

40. Lien-Hang Nguyen, *Hanoi's War: An International History of the War for Peace in Vietnam* (Chapel Hill: University of North Carolina Press, 2012), 259–60.

41. Elliot, *Vietnamese War*, 1214.

42. House Committee on Armed Services, Hearings on Military Posture, 91st Congress, 2nd Session, 1970, 7023–24; for a thorough coverage of Vietnamization, see James H. Willbanks, *Abandoning Vietnam: How America Left and South Vietnam Lost Its War* (Lawrence: University Press of Kansas, 2004).

43. See Jeffrey Kimball, *Nixon's Vietnam War* (Lawrence: University of Kansas Press, 1998), 93.

44. On the Easter Offensive, see Dale Andrade, *Trial by Fire: The 1972 Easter Offensive, America's Last Vietnam Battle* (New York: Hippocrene Books, 1995); Willbanks, *Abandoning Vietnam*, 122–63; and Cosmas, MACV, 345–77.

45. Henry A. Kissinger, *White House Years* (Boston: Little, Brown, 1979), 1006; Richard M. Nixon, *The Memoirs of Richard M. Nixon* (New York: Filmways, 1978), 606–7; "Conversation among President Nixon, the President's Assistant for National Security Affairs (Kissinger), and the Chairman of the Joint Chiefs of Staff (Moorer), Washington, April 3, 1972," and "Conversation Between President

Nixon and the President's Assistant for National Security Affairs (Kissinger), Washington, April 4, 1972," in *Foreign Relations of the United States, 1969–1976,* vol. 3, *Vietnam, January–October 1972* (Washington, DC: Government Printing Office, 2010), 171, 212.

46. See Kimball, *Nixon's Vietnam War,* 338–71.

47. Trullinger, *Village at War,* 193–95; William E. Le Gro, *Vietnam from Cease-Fire to Capitulation* (Washington, DC: U.S. Army Center of Military History, 1981).

48. Willbanks, *Abandoning Vietnam,* 259–63; Le Gro, *Vietnam from Cease-Fire to Capitulation,* 171; Nixon, *Memoirs,* 889.

49. Graham Cosmas, in *MACV: The Joint Command,* 422, argues that for the United States to have been successful in Vietnam, it "would have needed a generation or more to transform South Vietnam into an effective state."

# 4. Iraq: A Better War, Version 2

1. Thomas E. Ricks, "The Dissenter Who Changed the War," *Washington Post,* February 8, 2009; and Ricks's "A Military Tactician's Political Strategy," *Washington Post,* February 9, 2009; see also Ricks's interview with Charlie Rose on February 13, 2009, charlierose.com/view/interview/10080; for an example of reviewers who accepted the counterinsurgency narrative proffered by Ricks in the book, see Michiko Kakutani, "The War in Iraq," second in a series, *New York Times,* February 9, 2009.

2. Mark Bowden, "The Professor of War," *Vanity Fair,* May 2010; George W. Bush, *Decision Points* (New York: Random House, 2010), 365. For a similar argument to mine regarding the lionization of generals in COIN wars, see Joshua Rovner, "The Heroes of COIN," *Orbis* 56, no. 2 (Spring 2012).

3. Quoted in Nir Rosen, *Aftermath: Following America's Wars in the Muslim World* (New York: Nation Books, 2010), 241.

4. Paula Broadwell with Vernon Loeb, *All In: The Education of General David Petraeus* (New York: Penguin, 2012), 97–104, 165–69.

5. On the Anbar Awakening and firsthand accounts from its members, see the various interviews in *Al-Anbar Awakening,* vol. 2, *Iraqi Perpectives: From Insurgency to Counterinsurgency in Iraq, 2004–2009* (Quantico, VA: Marine Corps University Press, 2009); Khalid al Ansary and Ali Adeeb, "Most Tribes in Anbar Agree to Unite," *New York Times,* September 18, 2006; Peter Beaumont, "Iraqi Tribes Launch Battle to Drive al Qaeda Out of Troubled Province," *The Guardian,* October 3, 2006; and Dexter Filkins, "US and Iraq Retake Ramadi One Neighborhood at a Time," *New York Times,* June 27, 2006.

6. Aymen Jawad, "Assessing the Surge in Iraq," *Middle East Review of International Affairs*, December 2011, 31; Bing West, *The Strongest Tribe: War, Politics, and the Endgame in Iraq* (New York: Random House, 2008), 130–34; Rosen, *Aftermath*, 230–34; Dale Andrade, *Surging South of Baghdad: The Third Infantry Division and Task Force Marne in Iraq, 2007–2008* (Washington, DC: U.S. Army Center of Military History, 2010), 209–41; Carter Malkasian, "Counterinsurgency in Iraq, May 2003–January 2007," in *Counterinsurgency in Modern Warfare*, ed. Daniel Marston (New York: Osprey Publishing, 2008), 257; and David Kilcullen, "Anatomy of a Tribal Revolt," *Small Wars Journal*, August 29, 2007. E-mail discussions in early August 2012 with scholar Austin Long of Columbia University refined my thinking on the Anbar Awakening and other Sunni groups.

7. On the tactical actions of American combat units working with the various Sunni groups, see Andrade, *Surging South of Baghdad*; Sean MacFarland and Niel Smith, "Anbar Awakens: The Tipping Point," *Military Review*, March–April 2008; Andrew W. Koloski and John S. Kolasheski, "Thickening the Lines: Sons of Iraq, a Combat Multiplier," *Military Review*, January–February 2009; and Michael Gordon, "The Former Insurgent Counterinsurgency," *New York Times*, September 2, 2007.

8. Alissa J. Rubin, "Shiite Rivalries Slash at a Once Calm Iraqi City," *New York Times*, June 21, 2007. See answers by Juan Cole, Shawn Brimley, Marina Ottaway, and Mathew Duss to "How Important Was the Surge?" *American Prospect*, July 25, 2008, prospect.org/article/how-important-was-surge; and Stephen Farrell, "50 Die in Fight Between Shia Groups in Karbala," *New York Times*, August 29, 2007.

9. Lawrence Korb, Mark Katulis, Sean Duggan, and Peter Juul, *How Does This End? Strategic Failures Overshadow Tactical Gains in Iraq* (Washington, DC: Center for American Progress, 2008); John Agnew, Thomas W. Gillespie, Jorge Gonzalez, and Brian Min, "Baghdad Nights: Evaluating the US Military Surge Using Nighttime Light Signatures," *Environment and Planning*, October 2008; Patrick Cockburn, "Who Is the Enemy?" *London Review of Books*, March 2008. For a useful essay that attempts to analyze using various databases the role the surge played in the lowering of violence, see Stephen Biddle, Jeffrey A. Friedman, and Jacob N. Shapiro, "Testing the Surge: Why Did Violence Decline in Iraq in 2007?" *International Security*, Summer 2012.

10. *Measuring Stability in Iraq*, March 2008, Report to Congress in Accordance with the Department of Defense Appropriations Act 2008, 18, defense.gov/pubs /pdfs/Master%20%20Mar08%20-%20final%20signed.pdf; Joshua Thiel, "The Statistical Irrelevance of American SIGACT Data: Iraq Surge Analysis Reveals Reality," *Small Wars Journal*, April 12, 2011, smallwarsjournal.com/blog/journal/docs -temp/732-thiel1.pdf; see also Carl Prine, "David Ucko Is Wrong (Mostly)," *Line of*

*Departure*, November 30, 2011, lineofdeparture.com/2011/11/30/ucko-is-wrong-mostly.

11. Mark Kukis, *Voices from Iraq: A People's History, 2003–2009* (New York: Columbia University Press, 2011); see also Victoria Fontan, *Voices from Post-Saddam Iraq: Living with Terrorism, Insurgency, and New Forms of Tyranny* (Westport, CT: Praeger International Security, 2008); and Stephen Farrell, "Iraqis Judge America's Seven Years in Their Country," *New York Times*, August 31, 2010. On casualty figures see Iraq Body Count, iraqbodycount.org; Nir Rosen in *Aftermath*, 277, has somewhat different figures for American-produced casualties, with 250 in 2006 and 940 in 2007.

12. "General Petraeus's Second Letter to MNF-I," March 15, 2007, at *Small Wars Journal*, council.smallwarsjournal.com/showthread.php?p=10347; Chris Rogers, "More Soup Please: COIN Manual Provides Guidance for Modern Day Tactical Commanders," *Armed Forces Journal*, January 2008.

13. Greg Jaffe and David Cloud, *The Fourth Star: Four Generals and the Epic Struggle for the Future of the Army* (New York: Crown, 2009), 282–83; and David Finkel, *The Good Soldiers* (New York: Sarah Crichton Books, 2009), 273. Other recently published examples of books that tack perfectly with surge/Petraeus triumphalism are Michael R. Gordon and Bernard E. Trainor, *The Endgame: The Inside Story of the Struggle for Iraq, from George W. Bush to Barack Obama* (New York: Pantheon, 2012); Broadwell with Loeb, *All In*; and Fred Kaplan, *The Insurgents: David Petraeus and the Plot to Change the American Way of War* (New York: Simon & Schuster, 2013).

14. David Kilcullen, *The Accidental Guerrilla: Fighting Small Wars in the Midst of a Big One* (New York: Oxford University Press, 2009), 116–17; Janine Davidson, *Lifting the Fog of Peace: How Americans Learned to Fight Modern Wars* (Ann Arbor: University of Michigan Press, 2010); David Ucko, *The New Counterinsurgency Era: Transforming the U.S. Military for Modern Wars* (Washington, DC: Georgetown University Press, 2009), 117, 125–27; and Broadwell with Loeb, *All In*, xxviii.

15. Donald P. Wright and Timothy R. Reese, *On Point II: Transition to the New Campaign, the United States Army in Operation Iraqi Freedom, May 2003–January 2005* (Fort Leavenworth, KS: Combat Studies Institute Press, 2008), 87–88, 567–68; and James A. Russell, *Innovation, Transformation, and War: Counterinsurgency Operations in Anbar and Ninewa, Iraq, 2005–2007* (Stanford, CA: Stanford University Press, 2011), 7–11.

16. See my "The Risk of Velvet Gloves," *Washington Post*, January 19, 2004.

17. Ralph O. Baker, "The Decisive Weapon: A Brigade Combat Team Commander's Perspective on Information Operations," *Military Review*, May–June 2006; Peter A. Mansoor, *Baghdad at Sunrise: A Brigade Commander's War in Iraq*

(New Haven: Yale University Press, 2008), 356–57; Douglas A. Ollivant and Eric D. Chewning, "Producing Victory: Rethinking Conventional Forces in COIN Operations," and Paul D. Stanton, "Unit Immersion in Mosul: Establishing Security in Transition," *Military Review*, July–August 2006; and Ross A. Brown, "Commander's Assessment: South of Baghdad," *Military Review*, January–February 2007.

18. "State of the Insurgency in al-Anbar, I MEF G-2," *Washington Post*, August 17, 2006, media.washingtonpost.com/wp-srv/nation/documents/marines_iraq _document_020707.pdf; Russell, *Innovation, Transformation, and War*, 55–57; Michael Gordon, "Grim Outlook Seen in West Iraq Without More Troops and Aid," *New York Times*, September 12, 2006; and Bing West, *Strongest Tribe*, 185–86.

19. Thomas Ricks, for example, reprints the entire Devlin report in an appendix in *The Gamble: David Petraeus and the American Military Adventure in Iraq, 2006–2008* (New York: Penguin, 2009), 331–35. There was significant disagreement within higher echelons of American military command in Iraq over Devlin's report. But within the counterinsurgency narrative, as expressed by writers like Ricks, it becomes a point of evidence that the war was not going well and potentially on the path to "strategic defeat," words used by Thomas Ricks to explain the situation at the end of 2006.

20. "The Indirect Approach: Engaging the Tribes," interview with Colonel Michael M. Walker, in *Al Anbar Perspectives*, vol. 1, *American Perspectives*, ed. Timothy S. McWilliams and Curtis P. Wheeler (Quantico, VA: Marine Corps University, 2009), 72; and Andrew Lubin, "Counterinsurgency and Leadership," *Marine Corps Gazette*, December 2009. On 3ACR in Tall 'Afar, see Rick Herrera, "Brave Rifles at Talafar," in *In Contact: Case Studies in the Long War*, vol. 1, ed. William G. Robertson (Fort Leavenworth, KS: Combat Studies Institute Press, 2006); and Chris Gibson, "The Path Forward in Iraq," *Military Review*, September–October 2006.

21. Quoted in Daniel Davis, "Dereliction of Duty II: Senior Military Leaders' Loss of Integrity Wounds Afghan War Effort," *Rolling Stone*, January 27, 2012; and Niel Smith, "Anbar Awakens: The Tipping Point; Interview with Colonel Sean MacFarland," *Contemporary Studies Operations Team: On Point III* (Fort Leavenworth, KS: Combat Studies Institute Press, January 18, 2011). On 1/1 AD in Ramadi, see Jim Michaels, *A Chance in Hell: The Men Who Triumphed over Iraq's Deadliest City and Turned the Tide of the War* (New York: St. Martin's, 2011).

22. For Petraeus's quote on "commuting to the fight," see his March 2007 letter to MNF-I at *Small Wars Journal*, council.smallwarsjournal.com/showthread. php?p=10347.

23. Quoted in Daniel Davis, "Dereliction of Duty II," 69; e-mail exchange between the author and Dale Kuehl, October 27, 2008; Iraqi woman's quote from Nir

Rosen, *Aftermath*, 317. See also Julian E. Barnes, "Baghdad Outpost Plan Flawed, Some Troops Say," *Los Angeles Times*, July 8, 2007; and Dale Kuehl, "Testing Galula in Ameriyah: The People Are the Key," *Military Review*, March–April 2009.

24. Reidar Vissar, "An Unstable, Divided Land," *New York Times*, December 15, 2011.

25. "The Surge in Iraq: One Year Later," Lieutenant General Raymond Odierno, speech at Heritage Foundation, March 13, 2008, heritage.org/research/lecture /the-surge-in-iraq-one-year-later; "2007 Surge of Ground Forces in Iraq: Risks, Challenges, and Successes," *Fires: A Joint Professional Bulletin for US Field and Air Defense Artillerymen*, March–April 2008, 4–10.

26. Peter Mansoor, "How the Surge Worked," *Washington Post*, August 10, 2008.

27. E-mail exchange between author and Sterling Jensen, July 26, 2012; and Daniel Davis, "Dereliction of Duty II," 64–66. See also Sterling Jensen, "Lessons from an Anbar Sheik," *Washington Post*, September 29, 2007; Najim Abed al Jabouri and Sterling Jensen, "The Iraqi and AQI Roles in the Sunni Awakening," *Prism* 2, no. 1 (December 2012); Mark Wilbanks and Efraim Karsh, "How the 'Sons of Iraq' Stabilized Iraq," *Middle East Quarterly*, Fall 2010; and Joel Wing, "Re-Thinking the Surge in Iraq," *Musings on Iraq*, August 22, 2011, musingsoniraq. blogspot.com/2011/08/re-thinking-surge-in-iraq.html; Austin Long, "The Anbar Awakening," *Survival*, April–May 2008; and John McCary, "The Anbar Awakening: An Alliance of Incentives," *Washington Quarterly*, January 2009.

28. Aymenn Jawad al-Tamimi, "Assessing the Surge in Iraq," *Meria Journal* 15, no. 4 (December 2011): 33, available at Global Research in International Affairs (GLORIA) Center, Herzliya, Israel, gloria-center.org/2011/12/assessing-the-surge-in-iraq; Steven Simon, "The Price of the Surge," *Foreign Affairs*, May–June 2008; and Kimberly Strassel, "Rumsfeld's 'Slice of History,'" *Wall Street Journal*, February 8, 2008. On the importance of Fallujah in the Sunni Awakening, see analysis provided to me in a letter by scholar Austin Long, August 10, 2012. On the CIA, see Stephen Manning, "CIA Chief: Military Strikes Offer Lessons," Associated Press, September 17, 2008; Timothy S. McWilliams and Kurtis P. Wheeler, eds., *Al-Anbar Awakening*, vol. 2, 57, 122, 206–8; Seth Jones, *Hunting in the Shadows: The Pursuit of al Qaeda Since 9/11* (New York: Norton, 2012), 255. On the importance of special-operations forces in the reduction of al Qaeda, see Mark Urban, *Task Force Black: The Explosive True Story of the SAS and the Secret War in Iraq* (London: Little, Brown, 2010); and Christopher Lamb and Evan Munsing, "Secret Weapon: High-Value Target Teams as an Organizational Innovation" (Washington, DC: National Defense University, 2011). On the killing power of American special operations forces, see General Stanley McChrystal's newly published memoir, *My Share of the Task: A Memoir* (New York: Portfolio, 2013).

29. "Reassessing the Surge, and Recognizing Iraqi Agency in Ending the 2005–2008 Civil War in Iraq, and Interview with Douglas Ollivant," Musings on Iraq, February 27, 2012, musingsoniraq.blogspot.com/2012/02/reassessing-us-surge-and-recognizing.html; see also Ollivant's "Countering the New Orthodoxy," June 28, 2011, New America Foundation, newamerica.net/publications/policy/counter ing_the_new_orthodoxy.

30. David S. Cloud, "General Parries Attacks on Iraq Record," *New York Times*, February 2, 2007; "Senator John McCain Remarks on the Nomination of General Casey for Chief of Staff of the Army," February 8, 2007, mccain.senate.gov; CBS Television interview by Katie Couric with Senator John McCain, "McCain: 'We Will Come Home in Victory,'" June 8, 2009, cbsnews.com/2100-18563_162-4283813 .html.

31. "US Names General Casey as New Commander in Iraq," *China Daily*, June 16, 2006.

32. For Casey's Iraq strategy, see "Campaign Plan: Operation Iraqi Freedom; Partnership, from Occupation to National Elections," August 5, 2004; "Campaign Progress Review," Multi-National Forces Iraq, December 5, 2004; and "MNF Update," December 29, 2004, all in Papers of George W. Casey, National Defense University (hereafter Casey Papers, NDU); and General George W. Casey Jr., *Strategic Reflections: Operation Iraqi Freedom, July 2004–February 2007* (Washington, DC: National Defense University Press, 2012), 27.

33. "Campaign Progress Review," December 2004–December 2005, Multi-National Forces Iraq, December 20, 2005, Casey Papers, NDU.

34. Robert F. Worth, "Blast Destroys Shrine in Iraq, Setting Off Sectarian Fury," *New York Times*, February 22, 2006.

35. See my "In the Middle of a Civil War," *Washington Post*, August 7, 2007, and my "Legitimacy Was Step One," *Washington Post*, February 11, 2007; see also Joshua Thiel, "The Statistical Irrelevance of American SIGACT Data: Iraq Surge Analysis Reveals Reality," *Small Wars Journal*, April 12, 2011, smallwarsjournal. com/blog/journal/docs-temp/732-thiel1.pdf; and John Agnew, Thomas W. Gillespie, Jorge Gonzalez, and Brian Min, "Baghdad Nights: Evaluating the US Military Surge Using Nighttime Light Signatures," *Environment and Planning*, October 2008.

36. On the writing of FM 3-24, see John A. Nagl, "Constructing the Legacy of FM 3-24," *Joint Forces Quarterly*, no. 58, 3d quarter, 2010, 117–20.

37. Multi-National Division Baghdad, "Brigade Combat Team Commanders' Thoughts On: Applicability of COIN Doctrine to Sectarian Conflict; Dealing with Sectarian Conflict and the Complex Environment; What They Want to Pass on to Their Successors," November 3, 2006, Casey Papers, NDU.

38. See, for example, Pocket Day-Timer Notes, January 20, February 22, March 1, March 9, and March 11, 2006, Casey Papers, NDU; "Talking Points for POTUS SVTC," February 7, 2007; and David Cloud and Greg Jaffe Interview with General Casey, September 27, 2008, Casey Papers, NDU.

39. "Americans Debate Whether to Call Crisis in Iraq 'Civil War,' " PBS News-Hour, November 28, 2006, pbs.org/newshour/bb/middle_east/july-dec06/civilwar_11-28.html.

40. "Guiding Principles," November 11, 2006, Casey Papers, NDU; and "MNF-I Commanders Conference," December 15, 2006, Casey Papers, NDU.

41. Thomas E. Ricks praises certain individuals, like General (retired) Jack Keane, for circumventing military command channels by going directly to the president and other key officials, arguing for the surge and calling Casey's strategy a failure; see The Gamble, "Keane Takes Command," 74–105. For a better explanation of the machinations by Keane and others in putting together the surge, see Bob Woodward, The War Within: A Secret White House History, 2006–2008 (New York: Simon & Schuster, 2008); also see Peter Feaver, "The Right to Be Right: Civil-Military Relations and the Iraq Surge Decision," International Security, Spring 2011.

42. "Pocket Day-Timer Notes," June 12 and August 17, 2006, Casey Papers, NDU.

43. Sheryl Gay Stolberg and Jim Rutenberg, "Rumsfeld Resigns as Secretary of Defense After Big Election Gains for Democrats," New York Times, November 8, 2006.

44. Casey, Strategic Reflections, 144; and interview by author with General Casey, May 5, 2011; see also David Cloud and Greg Jaffe interview with Casey, July 28, 2008, and Tom Ricks interview with Casey, October 13, 2008—all in Casey Papers, NDU.

45. "Joint Campaign Plan: Transition of Security Responsibility," January 2007; "Campaign Progress Review, June 2006–December 2006," United States Mission Iraq and Multi-National Force Iraq Papers; and "MNF-I Commanders Conference," December 15, 2006—both in Casey Papers, NDU.

46. "Joint Security Station Snapshot," 1st Cavalry Division, February 4, 2007; "Meeting Notes from VTC" [early December 2006]; and "VTC," December 11, [2006]—all in Casey Papers, NDU.

47. "Iraq Strategic Review," January 8, 2007, Casey Papers, NDU.

48. Petraeus quoted in Ricks, The Gamble, 128.

49. "Campaign Progress Review," June–December 2006, Casey Papers, NDU; Borzou Daragahi, "Under U.S. Patrol, Once Tough District Revives," Los Angeles Times, October 11, 2006.

## 5. Afghanistan: Another Better War That Wasn't

1. Rajiv Chandrasekaran, *Little America: The War Within America's War in Afghanistan* (New York: Random House, 2012), 120.

2. *Afghanistan Annual Report 2011: Protection of Civilians in Armed Conflict* (Kabul: United Nations Assistance Mission, Afghanistan, February 2012); for a narrative account of the effects of the war on the Afghan people, see Anna Bad-khen, *Afghanistan by Donkey: A Year in a War Zone* (Washington, DC: Foreign Policy /Pulitzer Center on Crisis Reporting, 2012).

3. Yochi Dreazen and Peter Spiegel, "U.S. Fires Afghan War Chief: Four-Star General Replaced by Counterinsurgency Expert as Campaign Stumbles," *Wall Street Journal*, May 12, 2009; see also Elisabeth Bumiller and Thom Shanker, "Commander's Ouster Is Tied to Shift in Afghan War," *New York Times*, May 11, 2009; and Ann Scott Tyson, "General McKiernan Ousted as Top U.S. Commander in Afghanistan," *Washington Post*, May 12, 2009.

4. Lakhdar Brahimi, former United Nations special representative for Afghanistan, and Thomas R. Pickering, former ambassador and undersecretary of state, argued in a March 22, 2011, op-ed in the *New York Times* that "despite the US-led counterinsurgency in Afghanistan, the Taliban endures." Investigative reporter Douglas Wissing in his new book, *Funding the Enemy: How US Taxpayers Bankroll the Taliban* (Amherst, NY: Prometheus Books, 2012), repeats what many soldiers in Afghanistan said to him, that "COIN wasn't working." Wissing goes on to say in his own words in assessing the overall American COIN strategy in Afghanistan that "none of it looks promising." Scholar Hugh Gusterson says in a July 1, 2010, article in the *Bulletin of the Atomic Scientists* that "it is vital to make the argument that counterinsurgency has failed in Afghanistan." See also David Wood, "Counterinsurgency in Afghanistan Not Working, Critics Say," *Politics Daily*, January 11, 2011, politicsdaily .com/2011/01/11/counterinsurgency-strategy-not-working-in-afghanistan-critics-s.

5. Daniel Davis, "Dereliction of Duty II: Senior Military Leaders' Loss of Integrity Wounds Afghan War Effort," *Rolling Stone*, January 27, 2012, 9–13; Alissa J. Rubin, "Fatal Attack Shows Plan to Unsettle Afghanistan," *New York Times*, August 8, 2012; United Nations Assistance Mission, Afghanistan, "Conflict Continues to Take Devastating Toll on Civilians," August 8, 2012, unama.unmissions.org/default.aspx?.

6. David Kilcullen in his book *Counterinsurgency* (p. 9) suggests that prior to 2009 and the arrival of General McChrystal with a so-called new counterinsurgency strategy, the American military in Afghanistan was "enemy-centric," meaning that its main priority was killing the enemy, not on proper counterinsurgency methods focused on winning the hearts and minds of the local population.

7. Dexter Filkins, "Have Obama and Romney Forgotten Afghanistan?" *New Yorker*, Daily Comment, August 13, 2012, newyorker.com/online/blogs/comment/2012/08/have-obama-and-romney-forgotten-afghanistan.html.

8. Robert M. Cassidy, *War, Will, and Warlords: Counterinsurgency in Afghanistan and Pakistan, 2001–2011* (Quantico, VA: Marine Corps University Press, 2012), vii–viii, 3, 45–51, 57–59, 232–35; and Paula Broadwell with Vernon Loeb, *All In: The Education of General David Petraeus* (New York: Penguin, 2012), 33. The *Star Wars* theme has been played up in the COIN narrative at various times. For example, Nagl when writing on Templer's arrival in Malaya says, "The Empire Strikes Back." Petraeus himself said that his surge of troops in Iraq gave the Iraqis a "new hope," *A New Hope* being the new title of the original *Star Wars* movie. And now Broadwell, in *All In*, uses the term *force* as seemingly another *Star Wars* link to the counterinsurgency narrative. Fred Kaplan's recently published book *The Insurgents*, which glowingly portrays Petraeus and his fellow "coindinistas" as innovators who transformed the American army for the better, has a chapter on the February 2006 COIN conference at Fort Leavenworth titled "The Workshop at Tatooine." Tatooine is of course the home planet of Luke Skywalker. For some reason many mainstream American journalists have been unable to see through the myth of American counterinsurgency and instead have taken all of it as truth and fact. For a recent example of this, see the review of Kaplan's book by the American journalist Thanassis Cambanis, "How We Fight: Fred Kaplan's 'Insurgents' on David Petraeus," *New York Times Book Review*, January 24, 2013. The American investigative journalist Carl Prine has noted that it was "odd" that the COIN myth "has infected so many American journalists." He went on to note that "Arabists" often point out "that you would never read these stories in Arab press, and surely not in Iraq."

9. Testimony by General David Petraeus to U.S Senate Committee on Armed Services, "Hearing to Receive Testimony on the Situation in Afghanistan," March 15, 2011, 10; and Lewis G. Irwin, *Disjointed Ways, Disunified Means: Learning from America's Struggle to Build an Afghan Nation* (Carlisle, PA: Strategic Studies Institute Books, 2012), x–xi.

10. For an assessment and explanation of CORDS, see Dale Andrade and James H. Willbanks, "CORDS: Counterinsurgency Lessons from Vietnam for the Future," *Military Review*, March–April 2006; and David Kilcullen, *Counterinsurgency* (New York: Oxford University Press, 2010), 217.

11. Chandrasekaran, *Little America*, 3–11; Carl von Clausewitz, *On War*, ed. and trans. Michael Howard and Peter Paret (Princeton, NJ: Princeton University Press, 1984), 119–22; for a provocative and new interpretation of Clausewitz, see Jon Tetsuro Sumida, *Decoding Clausewitz: A New Approach to* On War *(Law-*

rence: University Press of Kansas, 2008); and for a good history of military thought and theory, see Azar Gat, *A History of Military Thought: From the Enlightenment to the Cold War* (New York: Oxford University Press, 2001).

12. Paddy Griffith, *Battle Tactics of the Civil War* (New Haven, CT: Yale University Press, 1989), 64–72; Adrian Lewis, *Omaha Beach: A Flawed Victory* (Chapel Hill: University of North Carolina Press, 2001), 163.

13. Rajiv Chandrasekaran, "In Afghanistan's Garmser District, Praise for U.S. Official's Tireless Work," *Washington Post*, August 13, 2011; see also Chandrasekaran, *Little America*, 184–88.

14. Richard N. Haass, *War of Necessity, War of Choice: A Memoir of Two Iraq Wars* (New York: Simon & Schuster, 2009), 272–79.

15. For use of this quote by contemporary general officers, see Raymond T. Odierno, "Prevent, Shape, and Win," Army Live: The Official Blog of the United States Army, December 12, 2011, armylive.dodlive.mil/index.php/2011/12/prevent-shape-win.

16. William B. Caldwell IV and Nathan K. Finney, "Building the Security Force That Won't Leave," *Joint Forces Quarterly*, 3d quarter, 2011, 80.

17. Leslie Gelb, "Why Obama Won't Speed U.S. Troop Withdrawal in Afghanistan," TheDailyBeast.com, March 19, 2012; see also my "Death of American Strategy," *Infinity Journal*, Summer 2011; Jeffrey Scahill "America's Failed War of Attrition in Afghanistan," *The Nation*, November 22, 2010; Andrew Bacevich, "Afghanistan Surge Not Worth Cost in Blood and Treasure," *U.S. News and World Report*, February 23, 2009. For an excellent argument that debunks the "domino theory" for Afghanistan, which posits if the United States doesn't do nation building successfully there, then al Qaeda will return in large numbers and attack the United States from there again, see Joshua Rovner and Austin Long, "Dominoes on the Durand Line: Overcoming Strategic Myths in Afghanistan and Pakistan," *Cato Institute Journal*, Foreign Policy Briefing No. 92, June 14, 2011.

18. David Sanger and Mark Mazzetti, "New Estimate of Strength of al Qaeda Is Offered," *New York Times*, June 30, 2010; Paul Cruickshank, "Brennan on bin Laden Raid and 'Dangerous Yemen,'" CNN Security Clearance blog, April 20, 2012, security.blogs.cnn.com/2012/04/20/brennan-on-bin-laden-raid-and-dangerous-yemen. For an excellent analysis of the events leading up to the World Trade Center attack, see Lawrence Wright, *The Looming Tower: al Qaeda and the Road to 9/11* (New York: Vintage Books, 2006).

19. Testimony by General Tommy R. Franks, "Operation Enduring Freedom," Hearing Before the Committee on Armed Services, U.S. Senate, February 7, 2002; on Operation Anaconda, see Sean Naylor, *Not a Good Day to Die: Chaos and Courage in the Mountains of Afghanistan* (New York: Penguin, 2005); for a good

general military history of Afghanistan, see Stephen Tanner, *Afghanistan: A Military History from Alexander the Great to the War Against the Taliban* (Philadelphia: Da Capo Press, 2009).

20. Andrew S. Natsios, "Reconstructing Iraq and Afghanistan: Address to the National Defense University," PowerPoint slides, October 2, 2003; documents on Afghanistan provided to author by Daniel Weggeland (hereafter Weggeland documents); Interview no. 2, Oral Histories: Afghanistan Provincial Reconstruction Teams, 2004–2005, October 12, 2004, usip.org/files/file/resources/collections/histories/afghanistan/2.pdf, and Interview no 3; for a detailed description of the amount of money and effort spent by agencies like USAID in the early years of the war, see Wissing, *Funding the Enemy*, 62–105.

21. Donald Wright with the Contemporary Operations Study Team, *A Different Kind of War: The United States Army in Operation Enduring Freedom, October 2001–September 2005* (Fort Leavenworth, KS: Combat Studies Institute Press, 2010), 181–275, 279.

22. See, for example, interview with Lieutenant General Karl Eikenberry, November 27, 2006, on his experience as chief of Office of Military Cooperation, Afghanistan, 2002–2003; and interview with Colonel Mark Miley, June 6, 2007, on his experience training Afghan security forces in 2003; both interviews in *Eyewitness to War*, vol. 3: *US Army Advisers in Afghanistan*, ed. Michael G. Brooks (Fort Leavenworth, KS: Combat Studies Institute Press, 2009).

23. David W. Barno, "Jihad and the Global War on Terrorism: Counterinsurgency in Afghanistan, 2003–2005," PowerPoint briefing at National Defense University, November 15, 2005, Weggeland documents; Combined Forces Command Afghanistan, "How to Fight a Counterinsurgency," PowerPoint briefing, November 1, 2005, Weggeland documents; Barno's subordinates quoted in Donald Wright, *A Different Kind of War*, 283.

24. Opening Statement by Duncan Hunter, chairman, Committee on House Armed Services, "Afghanistan Security and Reconstruction," April 29, 2004; Statement by Undersecretary of State Nancy Powell to House Armed Services Committee, "Situation in Afghanistan," June 22, 2005.

25. See Amy Belesco, "The Cost of Iraq, Afghanistan, and other Global War on Terror Operations Since 9/11," Congressional Research Service, March 29, 2011; Curt Tarnoff, "Afghanistan: US Foreign Assistance," Congressional Research Service, August 12, 2010. Douglas Wissing, in *Funding the Enemy* (17), notes that of this total, at least $31 billion of American "taxpayer money has been lost to fraud and waste."

26. For vignettes on the way different combat battalions took part in this nation-building campaign during the years 2003 to 2009, see Jerry Meyerle, Megan

Katt, and Jim Gavrilis, *On the Ground in Afghanistan: Counterinsurgency in Practice* (Quantico, VA: Marine Corps University Press, 2010). See also Statement to House Armed Services Committee by Lieutenant General Karl Eikenberry, "Status of Security and Stability in Afghanistan," June 28, 2006; on the increased activity of the Taliban during this period, see Ahmed Rasheed, *Descent into Chaos: The United States and the Failure of Nation Building in Pakistan, Afghanistan, and Central Asia* (New York: Viking, 2008), 349–74; and Antonio Giustozzi, *Koran, Kalashnikov, and Laptop: The Neo-Taliban Insurgency in Afghanistan, 2002–2007* (London: Hurst, 2007).

27. Testimony by Secretary of Defense Robert Gates and Undersecretary of State for Policy Eric Edelman to House Armed Services Committee, "Status of US Strategy and Operations in Afghanistan," December 11, 2007.

28. Curt Tarnoff, "Afghanistan: US Foreign Assistance"; and Seth G. Jones, *In the Graveyard of Empires: America's War in Afghanistan* (New York: Norton, 2009), 306–10.

29. Patrick Brennan, "The Dog Days of War: General David McKiernan Maps Out Our Way Forward," *National Review* Online, April 24, 2012, nationalreview .com/articles/296823/dog-days-war-drag-patrick-brennan; "Report on Progress Toward Security and Stability in Afghanistan," June 2008, Report to Congress in Accordance with the 2008 National Defense Authorization Act, Section 1230, Public Law 110–181; and Woodward, *Obama's Wars*, 70–71.

30. Remarks by Representative Ike Skelton and Testimony by Undersecretary of Defense for Policy Michelle Flournoy to House Armed Services Committee, April 2, 2009, "New Strategy for Afghanistan and Pakistan."

31. Ibid.

32. *The Rachel Maddow Show*, May 12, 2009, msnbc.msn.com/id/30766509/ns/ msnbc_tv-rachel_maddow_show/t/rachel-maddow-showfor-tuesday-may. Conforming to the counterinsurgency narrative of generals fumbling at COIN being replaced by enlightened ones who bring about radical shifts, Thomas Ricks on his blog on May 11, 2009, wrote that he equated the relief of McKiernan to the "firing" of Casey in Iraq, and that it foreshadowed big "changes" in the works: ricks.for eignpolicy.com/posts/2009/05/11/on_the_defenstration_of_gen_mckiernan_in_ afghanistan.

33. On the bin Ladin letters, see *Letters from Abbottabad: bin Ladin Sidelined*, ed. Don Rassler et al. (West Point, NY: Center for Combating Terrorism, May 3, 2012), ctc.usma.edu/posts/letters-from-abbottabad-bin-ladin-sidelined.

34. Ann Scott Tyson, "Going in Small in Afghanistan," *Christian Science Monitor*, January 14, 2004; Paul Wiseman, "Taliban on the Run but Far from Vanquished," *USA Today*, July 26, 2005; "Afghan Counterinsurgency: In the Words of

the Commanders," Company Command, companycommand.army.mil/index.htm, August 2007; William B. Ostlund, "Tactical Leader Lessons Learned in Afghanistan: Operation Enduring Freedom VIII," *Military Review*, July–August 2009, 7.

35. Headquarters, International Security Force Assistance, Kabul, "COMISAF's Initial Assessment" for Secretary of Defense Robert Gates, August 30, 2009, Weggeland documents; "Press Roundtable with General McChrystal in Istanbul, Turkey," February 4, 2010, defense.gov/transcripts/transcript.aspx?transcriptid=4559; Cassidy, *War, Will, and Warlords*, 227; and Michael Hastings, *The Operators: The Wild and Terrifying Inside Story of America's War in Afghanistan* (New York: Blue Rider, 2012), 71.

36. Amy Belasco, "The Cost of Iraq, Afghanistan, and other Global War on Terror Operations Since 9/11," Congressional Research Service, March 29, 2011, fas.org/sgp/crs/natsec/RL33110.pdf.

37. Michael Hastings, "The Runaway General," *Rolling Stone*, June 22, 2010; see also Hastings, *The Operators*.

38. Testimony by General David Petraeus to Senate Armed Services Committee, June 29, 2010, "Nomination of General David Petraeus to Be Commander, International Security Assistance Force and Commander of US Forces, Afghanistan"; and Broadwell with Loeb, *All In*, 33.

39. Battalion Commander Lieutenant Colonel David Flynn quoted in Paula Broadwell, "Travels with Paula (I): A Time to Build," *Best Defense*, January 24, 2011, ricks.foreignpolicy.com/posts/2011/01/13/travels_with_paula_i_a_time_to_ build; for a searing critique of Broadwell's reporting on Tarok Kolache, see Joshua Foust, "The Unforgivable Horror of Village Razing," Registan, January13, 2011, registan.net/index.php/2011/01/13/the-unforgivable-horror-of-village-razing; for Lieutenant Colonel Flynn's response to Foust, see "A Battalion Commander Responds to a Blogger on How to Operate in Afghanistan," *Best Defense*, January 20, 2011, ricks.foreignpolicy.com/posts/2011/01/20/a_battalion_commander_responds_ to_a_blogger_on_how_to_operate_in_afghanistan; for additional background on this debate, see Spence Ackerman, "25 Tons of Bombs Wipe Afghan Town Off Map," *Wired*, January 19, 2011.

40. On the origins of the phrase from the Vietnam War, see Michael D. Miller, "About the Famous Quote of the Vietnamese 1968 Tet Offensive, 'We Had to Destroy Ben Tre in Order to Save it,'" October 25, 2009, nhe.net/BenTreVietnam; and Kathy Shaidle, "Myths of the Vietnam War, Part II, 'We Had to Destroy the Village . . .'" Examiner.com, February 13, 2009, examiner.com/article/myths-of-the-vietnam-war-part-2-we-had-to-destroy-the-village; for a fulminating explanation of the quote's origins, see Victor David Hanson, "Misplaced Metaphors: The Conventional Wisdom Reveals More About Us than Iraq," *National Review* On-

line, November 24, 2004, nationalreview.com/articles/212984/misplaced-metaphors /victor-davis-hanson.

41. Quoted in Ackerman, "25 Tons of Bombs Wipe Afghan Town off Map."

42. Nick Lee, "ANSO Quarterly Data Report, Q4, 2011" Afghanistan NGO Safety Office, January 2012, and Nick Lee, "ANSO Quarterly Data Report, Q4 2010," Afghanistan NGO Safety Office, January 2011; UN Office of the High Commissioner for Human Rights, "Annual Report 2011: Protection of Civilians in Armed Conflict," Kabul, February 2012; C.J. Chivers et al., "View Is Bleaker than Official Portrayal of War in Afghanistan," *New York Times*, July 25, 2010; and Davis, "Dereliction of Duty II."

43. Joshua Rovner and Austin Long, "Dominoes on the Durand Line." For an excellent exploration of the driving forces behind America's role in the world and its propensity to use military force to solve the world's problems, see Richard Immerman, *Empire for Liberty: A History of American Imperialism from Benjamin Franklin to Paul Wolfowitz* (Princeton, NJ: Princeton University Press, 2010); and Walter McDougall, *Promised Land, Crusader State: The American Encounter with the World Since 1776* (Boston: Houghton Miflin, 1997). Some army officers have acknowledged that to make COIN work in Afghanistan will take generations; the director of the army COIN Center, Lieutenant Colonel John Paganini, when asked in an interview how long it would take COIN to work in Afghanistan, said, "It could take generations. . . ." Kristina Wong, "10 Years of Counterinsurgency in Afghanistan: Is it Working?" ABC News, October 8, 2011, abcnews.go.com/blogs /politics/2011/10/10-years-of-counterinsurgency-in-afghanistan-is-it-working.

44. For an argument that the United States should bring back the draft, see Josh Rogin, "McChrystal: Time to Bring Back the Draft," *Foreign Policy*, July 3, 2012; for a counterargument that says the United States needs not a draft but a foreign policy that appreciates the limits of U.S. military power, see Bill Moyers interview with Andrew Bacevich, *Bill Moyers Journal*, July 15, 2008, pbs.org/moyers /journal/08152008/transcript1.html.

45. John Nagl, review of Brian Linn's *The Echo of Battle: The Army's Way of War*, in *RUSI*, April 2008, 82–89.

46. For an alternative operational framework to long-term nation building, see Austin Long, "Small Is Beautiful: The Counterterrorism Option in Afghanistan," *Orbis*, Spring 2010. Bob Woodward's *Obama's Wars* makes the case that a much reduced military footprint that concentrated its assets on al Qaeda was what Vice President Biden was aiming for and what President Obama deep down actually was wanting his military to give him.

47. See my "American Strategy in Afghanistan Flunks Sun Tzu," *Jerusalem Post*, July 2, 2012.

## Afterword

1. Carl Prine interview with Christopher Swift, June 11, 2012, Line of Departure, lineofdeparture.com/2012/06/11. My concluding thoughts in this chapter are informed by Chris Hedges's brilliant and groundbreaking work *War Is a Force That Gives Us Meaning* (New York: PublicAffairs, 2002).

2. Anne-Marie Slaughter, "How to Halt the Butchery in Syria," *New York Times*, February 23, 2012.

3. Benjamin Bell, "Richard Haass Answers 8 Questions 'This Week,'" Yahoo! News, January 10, 2013, news.yahoo.com/richard-n-haass-answers-8-questions-week-205338875—abc-news-politics.html.

4. Douglas Macgregor, "Hagel: A Different Kind of Defense Secretary," *Time*, January 8, 2013.

5. Michael Hastings, "Runaway General," *Rolling Stone*, June 22, 2010; and Michael Hastings, *The Operators: The Wild and Terrifying Inside Story of America's War in Afghanistan* (New York: Blue Rider, 2012), 209.

6. Sir Michael Howard, "The Use and Abuse of Military History," in *The Causes of War and Other Essays* (Cambridge, MA: Harvard University Press, 1983)

# INDEX

Abrams, Creighton: cited regarding
  Afghanistan and Iraq, 22, 30;
  continuity with Westmoreland, 17, 66,
  68, 71–72, 74; Kissinger and Nixon
  displeasure with, 80–81; mythology, 3,
  17, 18, 20–21, 36, 59, 60, 71, 77–78
Abu Ghraib scandal, 102
Abu Risha al-Sattar. See Sattar, Abu
  Risha al-
The Accidental Guerrilla (Kilcullen), 91
Advice and Support: The Final Years
  (Clarke), 165n38
aerial bombing. See bombing, aerial
Afghani children. See children, Afghani
Afghanistan, 1, 2, 5, 6–7, 33, 98, 110–11,
  113–35, 139–41; Biden as voice of
  caution on, 7, 147n17; casualties, 113,
  114, 130, 141; Fivecoat in, 86–87; FM
  3–24 and, 26; Malayan Emergency as
  model for, 46; Obama memo on,
  30–31; Paganini on, 179n43; Petraeus
  and, 1–2, 30, 31, 115, 126, 127, 130;
  Provincial Reconstruction Teams, 120,
  121; pundits' overoptimism about, 15,
  29–30, 126–27; U.S. reconstruction
  aid, 122–23, 124
Afghanistan NGO Safety Office
  (ANSO), 132
Agincourt, battle of, 13
aid, international. See international aid
al-Askari shrine bombing, 2006, xiv, 31,
  103
Alexander the Great, 13
Algeria, 16, 22, 25, 26, 68, 94
All In: The Education of General David
  Petraeus (Broadwell and Loeb), 91, 115,
  174n8
al Qaeda: Afghanistan, 31, 113, 118–125,
  129, 134, 135, 175n17, 179n46; Iraq, 28,
  32–33, 87–88, 91, 95–97, 99–100, 107,

108; Yemen, 137. See also al-Askari
  shrine bombing, 2006
America in Vietnam (Lewy), 18–19,
  162n18
Amriya, Baghdad, xv, 90, 97, 110
Anaconda Operation. See Operation
  Anaconda
Anbar Awakening, 6, 28, 87, 88–89, 97,
  98, 99–100, 101, 110
Ansar al-Shariah, 137
ANSO. See Afghanistan NGO Safety
  Office (ANSO)
Armed Services Committee, U.S. House
  of Representatives. See House Armed
  Services Committee
The Army and Vietnam (Krepinevich),
  18–19, 21, 162n18
Army Field Manual 3–0. See Field
  Manual 3–0
Army Field Manual 3–07. See Field
  Manual 3–07
Army Field Manual 3–24. See Field
  Manual 3–24
Army Field Manual 31–22. See Field
  Manual 31–22
Aylwin-Foster, Nigel, 22

Baker, Ralph O., 93–94
Ball, George, 147n17
Barno, David, 121–22
battle of Agincourt. See Agincourt,
  battle of
battle of Fallujah, November–December
  2004. See Fallujah, second battle of
battle of Ia Drang. See Ia Drang, battle of
Ben Tre, Vietnam, 131
A Better War: The Unexamined Victories
  and Final Tragedies of America's Last
  Years in Vietnam (Sorley), 20–21, 71,
  159n1, 162n18

Biden, Joseph, 7, 147n17, 179n46
bin Laden, Osama, 127
Birtle, Andrew, 62
Boer War, 1899–1902. *See* Second Boer
    War
bombing, aerial, 66, 72, 80, 116–17
Bourne, Geoffrey, 36
Bowden, Mark, 85–86
Bradley, Omar, 116
Brahimi, Lakhdar, 173n4
Briggs, Harold, 35, 36, 40, 41, 45, 48, 52
Briggs Plan, 41–42, 48–49, 50, 52, 53, 54,
    57
Britain. *See* Great Britain
Broadwell, Paula, 132; *All In*, 91, 115,
    174n8
Brooks, David, 22–24
Brown, Ross, 94
Buckley, Kevin, 160–61n7
Bush, George W., 29, 85, 86, 110, 119,
    125; Casey relations, 102, 106–8;
    declares Iraq success prematurely, 11;
    on Petraeus, 4; quoted by Hunter, 122

Cable, Larry: *Conflict of Myths*, 18–19
Caldwell, William B., IV, 14
Cambodia, 63, 65, 66, 74, 78
Canada, 123
Casey, George, 28, 85, 101–3, 105–10,
    148n3, 172n41, 177n32
Cassidy, Robert, 114–15
casualties: Afghanistan, 113, 114, 130,
    141; Iraq, 89, 90, 168n11; Malaya, 63;
    Vietnam, 63, 70, 82, 131. *See also* child
    casualties; civilian casualties
Cedar Falls Operation. *See* Operation
    Cedar Falls
Central Command (CENTCOM), 126
Central Intelligence Agency (CIA),
    101
CERP. *See* Commander's Emergency
    Response Program (CERP)
Chandrasekeran, Rajiv, 1, 113, 116, 117,
    147n17
child casualties, xv, 113
children, Afghani, 6
China, 16, 37, 47, 68
Chinese Malayans, 37, 38, 41, 43–44, 48,
    49, 52; forced relocation, 35–36, 48, 52,
    54
Chin Peng, 38, 47, 49, 50, 52, 54
Churchill, Winston, 39

CIA. *See* Central Intelligence Agency
    (CIA)
Citino, Robert, 3
civilian casualties, 138; Afghanistan,
    113, 130; Iraq, xv–xvi, 28, 89, 90;
    Malaya, 63; Vietnam, 63, 73, 82
civilians, forced removal of. *See* forced
    removal of citizens
civilians, international aid to. *See*
    international aid
civilians, reimbursement. *See*
    reimbursement of civilians
civilians, relocation of. *See* relocation of
    civilians
Civil Operations and Revolutionary
    Development Support (CORDS), 74,
    76, 115
Civil War, 15, 116, 117
Clarke, Jeffrey J.: *Advice and Support*,
    165n38
Clausewitz, Carl von: *On War*, 116
Clemenceau, Georges, 30
Cloud, David, 91
Colby, William, 74
Coldstream Guards, 40
Cold War, 13, 64
Commander's Emergency Response
    Program (CERP), 120–21
compensation of civilians. *See*
    reimbursement of civilians
*Conflict of Myths* (Cable), 18–19
conscription. *See* military draft
continuity and discontinuity,
    operational, 6; Afghanistan, 114, 125,
    126–28; Iraq, 91–92, 93–94, 98, 101–2,
    107, 108, 127; Malaya, 17–18, 36,
    39–40, 42–43, 46; Vietnam, 17–18, 63,
    71–72, 91
CORDS. *See* Civil Operations and
    Revolutionary Development Support
    (CORDS)
corruption, 75, 81, 83
Cosmas, Graham, 71, 166n49
costs, 60, 138. *See also* casualties; U.S.
    spending
*Counterinsurgency* (FM 3–24). *See* Field
    Manual 3–24
*Counterinsurgency* (Kilcullen),
    175n6
*counterinsurgency* (word), 13
Counterinsurgency Academy, Taji, Iraq,
    103

*Counterinsurgency Warfare* (Galula), 25, 94, 141
Cuba, 68

Daragahi, Borzou, 110
Davidson, Janine: *Lifting the Fog of Peace*, 91
Davidson, Phillip, 159–60n1
D-Day, preparation for, 116–17
Dempsey, Martin, 4–5
*Dereliction of Duty: Lyndon Johnson, Robert McNamara, the Joint Chiefs of Staff, and the Lies That Led to Vietnam* (McMaster), 20
destruction of villages. *See* village destruction
Devlin, Peter, 95, 169n19
Diem, 12, 16, 65
Dien Bien Phu, 64
discontinuity and continuity, operational. *See* continuity and discontinuity, operational
*Disjointed Ways, Disunified Means: Learning from America's Struggle to Build an Afghan Nation* (Irwin), 115
*Dr. Strangelove* (Kubrick), 30
draft, military. *See* military draft

East African soldiers, 43
economies, local. *See* local economies
Edelman, Eric, 124
Eikenberry, Karl, 123
Eisenhower, Dwight, 39, 64
elections: Iraq, 33, 103; United States, 79, 100, 107, 125; Vietnam, 64
elephants, 72–73
Eliot, David, 78
euphemism and newspeak, 139–40
Ewell, Julian J., 61
Exum, Andrew, 126–27

Fall, Bernard, 38
Fallujah, second battle of, 101
Far East Land Forces (FARELF), 50
Few, Michael, 138
*Fiasco: The American Military Adventure in Iraq, 2003–2005* (Ricks), 26–27
Field Manual 3-0, 14
Field Manual 3-07, 14
Field Manual 3-24, xvi–xvii, 2, 13, 14–15, 24–26, 92, 106, 127; Bush on writing of, 85; cited by officer in Iraq,

90; Fourth Infantry leaders on, 104–5; Fred Kagan on, 27–28; on limited way to fight counterinsurgencies, 149n12; on "logical lines of operations," 93; Malaya Emergency as model for, 25, 35, 36, 58; McChrystal lectures soldiers on, 141; Petraeus summary of, 32; precedence for, 94–95, 96, 121–22; referred to as "new" in 2007, 99
Field Manual 31–22, 68
Filkins, Dexter, 114
Finkel, David: *The Good Soldiers*, 91
First Armored. *See* U.S. Army First Armored Division
First Cavalry. *See* U.S. Army First Cavalry Division
Fivecoat, David, 86–87
Flournoy, Michelle, 125
food aid, 71
food as a weapon, 35–36, 41, 42, 50, 55
forced removal of citizens, 35–36, 48, 70, 75, 76
Ford, Gerald, 83
foreign aid. *See* international aid
Fourth Infantry. *See* U.S. Army Fourth Infantry Division (4ID)
"framework operations," 48–49
France, 13, 68. *See also* Indochina War
Francis Marion Operation. *See* Operation Francis Marion
Franco-Prussian War, 13
Franks, Tommy, 119
French, David, 58
"friction" in war, 116, 117
*Funding the Enemy: How US Taxpayers Bankroll the Taliban* (Wissing), 6, 173n4, 176n25

Galula, David, 26, 68; *Counterinsurgency Warfare*, 25, 64, 141
Galvin, John R., 19–20
Gates, Robert, 109, 114, 123–24, 129, 147n17, 147n20
Geneva Accords, 1954, 64, 65
Gentile, Gian, xiii–xviii, 23–24, 93, 109–10, 138, 140
Germany, 116, 134
Giap, 64
*The Good Soldiers* (Finkel), 91
Gordon, Michael, 148n3
Graham, Lindsay, 138
Grant, Ulysses S., 15

Great Britain, 13, 123; colonial losses, 56–57. *See also* Malayan Emergency
Green Howards, 41, 42, 44
Guevara, Che, 68
Gurkhas, 43–44
Gurney, Henry, 48, 51, 95
Gusterson, Hugh, 173n4

Haass, Richard, 138–39
Hack, Karl, 157n30
Hagel, Chuck, 140
hamlet destruction. *See* village destruction
Hanson, Victor Davis, 1, 4
Hastings, Michael, 141
Henry V, 13
Herring, George, 60
Herrington, Stuart, 75
Hoang Ngoc Lung, 74
Ho Chi Minh, 63, 75
Ho Chi Minh Trail, 65, 80
House Armed Services Committee, 79, 119, 122, 125, 126
Howard, Michael, 141
Huk Rebellion, 68
Hunter, Duncan, 122

Ia Drang, battle of, 67, 69
improvised explosive device (IED) attacks, xiv, 113
India, 56–57
Indochina War, 16, 38, 63–64, 65, 79
*The Insurgents* (Kaplan), 176n8
intelligence gathering: Iraq, 93–94, 101; Malaya, 41, 49, 51, 53–54
international aid, 2, 120, 122–23, 124, 133–34, 176n25. *See also* food aid
Iraq War, 2, 4, 15, 21–29, 85–111, 135; Bush prematurely announces success, 11–12; casualties, 89, 90, 168n11; Dempsey report, 5; Devlin report, 95, 169n19; dissenting views, 174n8; Fred Kagan on, 27–28; Gentile experience and views, xiii–xviii, 23–24, 93; Malaya Emergency as model for, 22, 23, 28, 29, 36, 46; McCain on, 11; McMaster views, 6, 90–91, 93–94, 98, 101–2, 107, 108, 127; Petraeus on, 31–32, 32–33, 90; Petraeus role, 28–30, 85–86, 87, 90–91, 97, 99, 127, 129; press coverage, xiii, xviii; Ricks on, 27,

85, 169n19; Syria events compared to, 138; Vietnam War as model for, 12, 20, 22, 23, 28, 29, 84. *See also* Anbar Awakening
Irwin, Lewis G.: *Disjointed Ways, Disunified Means*, 115
Islam: Shia-Sunni relations. *See* Shia-Sunni relations
Islam, Zaidiyyah. *See* Zaidiyyah Shia

Jaffe, Greg, 91
Japan, 37, 38; atomic bombings, 1945, 14
Jensen, Sterling, 99–100
Jocks, J.S., 40–41
Johnson, Harold K., 67
Johnson, Hiram, 137
Johnson, Lyndon, B., 20, 65–66, 79
Jossey, Alex, 57
al-Juburi, Nadim, 100

Kagan, Fred, xviii, 27–28
Kagan, Kimberly: *The Surge*, 11
Kalyvas, Stathis, 25–26
Kaplan, Fred: *The Insurgents*, 174n8
Karzai, Hamid, 123, 128
Keane, Jack, 27, 59, 172n41
Keightley, Charles F., 42, 46
Kennard, Allington, 57
Kilcullen, David, xvii–xviii, 22, 115; *The Accidental Guerrilla*, 91; *Counterinsurgency*, 173n6
King Henry V. *See* Henry V
Kissinger, Henry, 80–81
Komer, Robert, 159–60n1
Korean War, 13–14, 37–38
Krepinevich, Andrew, 22, 23, 26; *The Army and Vietnam*, 18–19, 21, 162n18
Kubrick, Stanley: *Dr. Strangelove*, 30
Kuehl, Dale, 97
Kukis, Mark, *Voices from Iraq*, 89–90, 145n1
Kurds, 98

Laird, Melvin, 79
Laos, 63, 65, 66, 74, 78
*Learning to Eat Soup with a Knife: Counterinsurgency Lessons from Malaya and Vietnam* (Nagl), 21, 150n16, 162n18
Lee, Robert E., 116
Lewy, Gunther: *America in Vietnam*, 18–19, 162n18

Lieberman, Joseph, 138
*Lifting the Fog of Peace* (Davidson), 91
local economies, 2; Afghanistan, 117,
    118, 119, 120, 122, 123, 124, 125, 134;
    Iraq, 33, 93, 95, 105; Vietnam, 66, 75
Lockhart, Robert, 35–36, 47, 53
Loh Kok Wah, Francis, 52–53
Long, Austin, 175n17

MAC: *The Joint Command* (Cosmas),
    166n49
MacArthur, Douglas, 117–18
MacFarland, Sean, 96
Malayan Emergency, 2, 16, 19, 21, 35–58,
    63, 95; casualties, 63; Commonwealth
    regiments in, 42–44; as model for Iraq
    War, 22, 23, 28, 29, 36, 46; as model for
    Vietnam War, 12–13, 16, 36, 58, 68;
    October Directives, 50–51, 53, 57;
    operational continuity in, 6, 17–18, 36,
    39–40, 42–43, 46; as source for FM
    3–24, 25, 35, 36, 58
Malayans, Chinese. *See* Chinese
    Malayans
Malkasian, Carter, 117
Mansoor, Peter, 94, 99
Mao Tse-tung, 16, 47, 68
Marine Corps, U.S. *See* U.S. Marine
    Corps
May, Clifford, 28–29
McCain, John, 11, 102, 138
McChrystal, Stanley, 1, 5, 113, 114–15;
    Biden response to, 7; Kilcullen view,
    173n6; lectures soldiers in
    Afghanistan, 140–41; on "the only
    way to defeat al-Qaeda," 118; replaces
    McKiernan, 29, 33, 115, 126–28,
    129–30, 132; role at Yale, 4
McDonald, Charles B., 18
McKiernan, David, 29, 114, 124–25, 126,
    127, 129, 177n32
McMaster, H.R., 27, 96; *Dereliction of
    Duty*, 20
McNamara, Robert, 20
Meade, George, 116
media. *See* press; television
Middle Ages, 133
military draft, 179n44
militias, Shia. *See* Shia militias
Moltke, Helmuth von, 13
Montgomery, Bernard, 39, 57
Mosul, Iraq, 94

Mullen, Michael, 6
Muslims: Shia-Sunni relations. *See*
    Shia-Sunni relations

Nagl, John, 2, 26, 35, 39–40, 134, 174n8;
    *Learning to Eat Soup with a Knife*, 21,
    150n16, 162n18
National Security Council (NSC), 106,
    107, 108–9, 110
NATO, 123, 132
Nazis, 134
Nepalese Gurkhas. *See* Gurkhas
Netherlands, 123
*The New Counterinsurgency Era* (Ucko),
    91
newspeak and euphemism. *See*
    euphemism and newspeak
*Newsweek*, 29–30
*New York Times*, xiii, xviii, 22–24
Ngo Dinh Diem. *See* Diem
Nguyen Van Thieu. *See* Thieu
Ninth Infantry. *See* U.S. Army Ninth
    Infantry Division
Nixon, Richard, 79, 80–81, 83
Normandy invasion. *See* D-Day
North Atlantic Treaty Organization
    (NATO). *See* NATO
NSC. *See* National Security Council
    (NSC)

Obama, Barack, 6–7, 30–31, 111, 119,
    122, 125, 129–30, 141, 179n46
*Obama's Wars* (Woodward), 147n17,
    179n46
Odierno, Raymond, 85, 98–99,
    100
O'Hanlon, Michael, xiii, xviii
Oldfield, J.B., 41
Ollivant, Douglas, 94, 101–2
101st Airborne. *See* U.S. Army 101st
    Airborne Division
*On War* (Clausewitz), 116
operational continuity and discontinuity.
    *See* continuity and discontinuity,
    operational
Operation Anaconda, 119
Operation Cedar Falls, 67
Operation Francis Marion, 70
Operation Speedy Express, 160–61n7
Operation Summerall, 69
*Operations* (FM 3–0). *See* Field Manual
    3–0

Packer, George, 24
Paganini, John, 179n43
Pakistan, 120, 123, 124, 133
Palestine, 37, 56–57
Paris Peace Accords, 1973, 81
payments to tribes and civilians, xv–xvi, 87–88
perpetual war, 30, 33
Petraeus, David, 6, 15; Afghanistan and, 1–2, 30, 31, 115, 126, 127, 130; called "professor of war," 85–86; Casey anticipation of, 106, 108; dissenting views on, 147n17; FM-24 role, 24, 32, 85; on Iraq War, 31–32, 32–33, 90; Iraq War role, 28–30, 85–86, 87, 90–91, 97, 99, 127, 129; mentor of, 20; mythology, xvii–xviii, 4, 7–8, 12, 90–91, 97, 99, 101, 109, 110, 127; press coverage, xiii, 29–30; Vietnam War analysis of, 21
Philippines, 15, 68
Pickering, Thomas R., 173n4
political will, 60, 133, 134
Pollack, Kenneth, xiii, xviii
Powell, Nancy, 122
Power, Samantha, 2
press, 22–24, 130; on Afghanistan, 29–30, 114; on FM 3–24, 2; on Iraq, xiii, xviii, 22–23, 90–91, 110; on Malaya Emergency, 56, 57
Prine, Carl, 174n8
*A Program for the Pacification and Long-Term Development of South Vietnam* (PROVN), 67, 162n18
propaganda, 55, 132. *See also* euphemism and newspeak
protectionism doctrine. *See* responsibility to protect doctrine (R2P)
Pye, Lucien, 47

Ramadi, Iraq, 96
reconstruction aid, 122–23, 124
Reese, Timothy, 92
refugees, 73, 76
reimbursement of civilians, xv–xvi
relocation of civilians, 16, 104. *See also* forced removal of citizens
responsibility to protect doctrine (R2P), 8, 15
Ricks, Thomas, 85, 169n19, 172n41, 177n32; *Fiasco*, 26–27
Robinson, K.K., 27
Robinson, Linda, 90

*Rolling Stone*, 130, 141
Rovner, Joshua, 175n17
Rumsfeld, Donald, 107
Russell, James, 92

Sadr, Moqtada al-, 88–89
Samarra, xiv, 31
Sattar, Abu Risha al-, 100
Schoomaker, Peter, 32
search-and-destroy operations: Malaya, 40, 44; Vietnam, 18, 21, 62, 67, 69–72
Second Boer War, 48
Second Iraq War. *See* Iraq War
Sewell, Sarah, 24
Shia Islam, Zaidiyyah. *See* Zaidiyyah Shia
Shia militias, xiv, 6, 28, 88–89, 98, 103
Shia-Sunni relations, xiv–xv, xvii, 28, 88–89, 103
Skelton, Ike, 125
Slaughter, Anne-Marie, 137, 138, 139
Slim, William, 46
Smith, Rupert, 14
soldiers, East African. *See* East African soldiers
soldiers, Gurkha. *See* Gurkhas
Sorley, Lewis: *A Better War*, 20–21, 59, 71, 159n1, 162n18; *Vietnam Chronicles*, 78
Soviet Union, 19, 37, 64, 134, 137
Speedy Express Operation. *See* Operation Speedy Express
Spanish-American War, 15
spending, U.S. *See* U.S. spending
*Stability Operations* (FM 3–07). *See* Field Manual 3–07
strategy-tactics distinction, 115–17, 118, 130, 132, 134–35
Stubbs, Richard, 40
Summerall Operation. *See* Operation Summerall
Sunni Awakening. *See* Anbar Awakening
Sunni-Shia relations. See Shia-Sunni relations
*The Surge: A Military History* (Kagan), 11
Swift, Christopher, 137, 138
Syria, 8, 99, 137, 138, 139

tactics-strategy distinction. *See* strategy-tactics distinction
Taliban, 1, 119–21, 122–23, 124, 132, 133, 141, 173n4; IED attacks by, 113; Tarok Kolache, 130–31

Tall 'Afar, Iraq, 27, 96
tank destroyers, 3
Tarok Kolache, Afghanistan, 130–32
television, 126–27
Templer, Gerald, 36, 40, 42, 44, 45, 46,
    50, 53, 54–58; appointment as
    supremo, 49, 51–52; Nagl on, 174n8
Teng Meng, 43
Tet Offensive, 1968, 16, 71, 73, 79, 95,
    131
Thieu, 74, 81
Thompson, Robert, 12–13, 16, 19, 25–26
Thurman, James D., xiii
Tien, John, 31
Tikrit, Iraq, 93
troop strength: British in Malaya, 44;
    U.S. in Afghanistan, 120, 123, 124,
    129–30, 133; U.S. in Iraq, 103; U.S. in
    Vietnam, 66, 80; Viet Cong, 38

Ucko, David: The New Counterinsurgency
    Era, 91
United Kingdom. See Great Britain
University of Chicago Press, 2
U.S. Agency for International
    Development (USAID), 120, 121
U.S. Army Counterinsurgency Forces (FM
    31–22). See Field Manual 31–22
U.S. Army Field Manual 3–0. See Field
    Manual 3–0
U.S. Army Field Manual 3–07. See Field
    Manual 3–07
U.S. Army Field Manual 3–24. See Field
    Manual 3–24
U.S. Army Field Manual 31–22. See Field
    Manual 31–22
U.S. Army First Armored Division, 96
U.S. Army First Cavalry Division, 69,
    101
U.S. Army Fourth Infantry Division
    (4ID), 70, 72, 73, 104–5
U.S. Army Ninth Infantry Division,
    61–62
U.S. Army 101st Airborne Division,
    69–70
U.S. Civil War. See Civil War
U.S. House of Representatives, Armed
    Services Committee. See House
    Armed Services Committee
U.S. Marine Corps, 140; Afghanistan, 1,
    124, 133; Iraq, xiii, 86, 92, 95, 96, 97,
    101, 103, 121; Vietnam, 77

U.S. National Security Council (NSC).
    See National Security Council (NSC)
U.S. spending, 114, 122–23, 124, 176n25.
    See also payments to tribes and
    civilians
U.S.S.R. See Soviet Union
The Utility of Force (Smith), 14

Vann, John Paul, 150n17
Viet Cong (term), 160n6
Viet Minh, 63–64
Vietnam Chronicles (Sorely), 78
Vietnamization, 78, 79–80,
    165n38
Vietnam War, 2, 14, 16–24, 59–84, 91;
    Accelerated Pacification Campaign,
    73–74; aerial bombing, 66, 72, 80; Ball
    cautionary voice on, 147n17; Brooks
    on, 22–24; casualties, 63, 70, 82, 131;
    Clarke on, 165n38; Combined Action
    Program, 77; CORDS, 74, 76, 115;
    destruction of Ben Tre "to save it," 131;
    dissenting views, 159–60n1; Easter
    Offensive, 80, 81; Hagel experience,
    140; Hamlet Evacuation System, 73;
    Malayan Emergency as model for,
    12–13, 16, 36, 58, 68; as model for
    Afghan war, 30; as model for Iraq War,
    12, 20, 22, 23, 28, 29, 84; Nagl on, 21;
    "one-war strategy," 62, 70, 71–72, 74;
    operational continuity in, 6, 17–18, 63,
    71–72, 91; peace treaty, 81; Petraeus
    on, 21; PROVN, 67, 162n18;
    resettlement programs, 48, 70; as
    source for FM 3–24, xvi, 13, 25, 26;
    U.S. search-and-destroy operations,
    18, 21, 62, 67, 69–72; U.S. withdrawals,
    80; Vann view, 150n17. See also Tet
    Offensive, 1968
village destruction, 75, 130–32
Voices from Iraq (Kukis), 89–90,
    145n1
Vo Nguyen Giap. See Giap

Walker, Michael M., 95–96
Wall Street Journal, 114
war, perpetual. See perpetual war
Westmoreland, William, 3, 13, 17, 36, 60,
    63, 66–68, 69; Casey compared to,
    102; initiation of CORDS, 115;
    "one-war strategy" of, 70–72; PROVN
    and, 162n18

Weyand, Frederick C., 83, 159n1
will, political. *See* political will
Wissing, Douglas A.: *Funding the Enemy*,
    6, 173n4, 176n25
Wheeler, Earl, 69
Woodward, Bob: *Obama's Wars*, 147n17,
    179n46

World War II, 3, 14, 37, 38, 116–17, 134
Wright, Donald, 92

Yale University, 4
Yemen, 137, 138

Zaidiyyah Shia, 137

# PUBLISHING IN
# THE PUBLIC INTEREST

Thank you for reading this book published by The New Press. The New Press is a nonprofit, public interest publisher. New Press books and authors play a crucial role in sparking conversations about the key political and social issues of our day.

We hope you enjoyed this book and that you will stay in touch with The New Press. Here are a few ways to stay up to date with our books, events, and the issues we cover:

- Sign up at www.thenewpress.com/subscribe to receive updates on New Press authors and issues and to be notified about local events.
- Like us on Facebook: www.facebook.com/newpressbooks
- Follow us on Twitter: www.twitter.com/thenewpress

Please consider buying New Press books for yourself; for friends and family; or to donate to schools, libraries, community centers, prison libraries, and other organizations involved with the issues our authors write about.

The New Press is a 501(c)(3) nonprofit organization. You can also support our work with a tax-deductible gift by visiting www .thenewpress.com/donate.